BRI
The Bidder's Game

by George Rosenkranz

**Published by
Devyn Press, Inc.,
Louisville, Kentucky**

Cover by Bonnie Baron Pollack

Printed in the United States of America.

Devyn Press, Inc.
151 Thierman Lane
Louisville, KY 40207

ISBN 0-910791-20-1

To Edith, Bobby, Jerry and Ricky
my favorite partners in life
and play.

Foreword

George Rosenkranz is a good friend. He is also an esteemed opponent at the bridge table — thanks in great measure to the effectiveness of his Romex bidding methods. Therefore, it gives me great pleasure to be asked to write a foreword for this book.

In my opinion, Romex is the most intelligent of the three-level bidding systems, where the opener's partner is immediately aware which of the three types of hands he faces: limited strength, good hand, or powerhouse force to game. Intelligent and, in this book, intelligibly presented.

Any player, from less experienced to expert, will get many useful ideas which can be adopted piecemeal to the reader's present methods or embraced as a whole. To make this achievement easier, the book is divided into three major parts, first presented the basic ideas; second, the logical developments; and, finally, what may be called the sophisticated touches — bridge as the Romexpert plays it.

It's all here, presented by a man who is perhaps the most fertile innovator of good ideas in bridge today.

— Edgar Kaplan

In addition to being one of the world's greatest players and most enjoyable and knowledgeable commentators at important championships, Edgar Kaplan is editor of the world's most prestigious bridge magazine, *The Bridge World*.

— George Rosenkranz

Acknowledgement

Many ideas in this book represent the distillation and refinement of expert thinking over the last two decades. The majority are the result of an analytical approach, continuous tournament experience and a lot of hard work put in with my regular ROMEX partners and teammates, in particular Eddie Wold and Eric Rodwell.

Many people helped in the development of ROMEX and in the preparation of this book. I would particularly like to thank:

Eric Rodwell for his stimulating input of bridge theory and invaluable help in the preparation of the manuscript; George and Roni Abrahamsohn for substantial analytical contributions, new ideas, continuous discussions and encouragement; Alan Truscott for contributions in the development of novel Romex concepts, particularly in the area of relays; Tannah Hirsch for constructive discussions and criticism; Ron Andersen for his suggestions in preparation of the manuscript; Jeff Rubens for help in the development of the earlier Romex concepts.

All my Romex partners, especially Edith Rosenkranz and Eddie Wold, Roger Bates, the late Fernando Diez Barroso, Sol Dubson, Odon Duran, Constant Fua, Robert Lipsitz, John Mohan, Dan Morse, Robert Nail, Miguel Reygadas and Mauricio Smid.

My fond memories go to the late Mrs. Ma. Rosario Arrieta and to Mrs. Beatrice Plech, Mrs. Teresa Cortes and Miss Lyn Balfour for unfailing assistance, hard work and long hours in the technical preparation of the manuscript.

A Personal Note to You
from the Author

ROMEX has developed from a few novel, sound ideas, into a complete integrated bidding system which has proven its merits in the hardest-fought battles of top level competition.

This book is aimed at three different audiences, with several purposes in mind. The organization of this book into three parts reflects this objective.

Part 1 aims at the average interested duplicate player. My principal goal is to provide him with a few simple tools which will improve his bidding accuracy substantially. At the same time, I hope to dispel the false notion that Romex is a complicated, artificial and difficult bidding system and prove how this blend of natural methods and a few novel ideas can produce vastly improved scores.

Part 2 has a dual purpose: it is directed to both Romex and non-Romex players. The first group, who have already embraced our methods, will find an up-to-date version — and a handy reference book — of the system as it is played today by the large majority of successful Romex pairs.

The second group, serious competitors interested in improving their bidding methods, will find an attractive collection of modern gadgets, tools and treatments, which collectively or individually can easily be incorporated into most of the "scientific" systems using five-card majors.

Part 3 introduces the relay concept and its partial application to selective bidding situations. It is guaranteed to improve the accuracy of your slam bidding.

My main goal is to reach the advanced player — Romex or non-Romex — and provide him with a delicate, sophisticated but superbly effective precision tool. My intention is not to propose a relay version of Romex.

Examples used in this book are overwhelmingly "real life" hands played in important tournaments.

Some of the novel ideas — hitherto unpublished — which you will find in this book are:

A new approach to Romex Key Card Blackwood. A new way of using Roman Key Card Blackwood with a suit lacking controls: Key Card Lackwood. An innovative treatment for inverted minor raises. A complete and super-effective structure after 2 NT and related strong balanced openings using a novel Puppet Stayman approach. The Spiral Cue-Bid, a new method to identify special key features in slam oriented trump bidding sequences. Novel void-showing bids after opening one-bids.

Further thoughts I want to convey are eloquently expressed in the Introduction by George Abrahamsohn. I urge you to read his presentation, not only for the contents of his message but also because of the type of experience he represents.

George and Roni Abrahamsohn from Toronto became enthusiastic Romex fans after reading *Win With Romex*. As a result, their game improved spectacularly. They have had impressive successes in their home country, Canada. Extensive correspondence between us led to many constructive discussions and original ideas. Eventually some of their contributions were incorporated into the System. (References will be found in appropriate sections of the text.)

It is my feeling that their background and first hand experience qualify them as eminent spokespersons for Romex.

Whatever the purpose of your reading this book may be, I hope you will have as much fun reading it as I had writing it.

Bon Voyage!

Introduction

Let's be honest! How often, after a match or tournament, have you gone home only to realize that victory was well within your grasp had you only been able to bid a laydown game or slam, or stay out of an unmakeable one? If you are like the majority of bridge players, this scenario is very familiar indeed. Sure, you could also have won by just playing better or defeating beatable contracts. The frustrating point is that with all of your mistakes you could have emerged victorious if only you had bid better.

Do I hear you say, "Systems do not win matches, players do!" You are quite right of course, but bidding systems provide the framework and the tools to forge effective partnerships.

When David faced Goliath, he had the skill as well as the right tool to defeat his enemy. One without the other would not have done! David, as the story goes, had also received a little divine assistance. Such support we can't guarantee, but we can guarantee that your bidding will improve when you play Romex. That heretofore unexplored partnership cooperation will be yours to achieve.

You may choose to learn and play the whole Romex system or parts of it only. You may also choose to graft certain Romex tools and approaches to your present bidding methods. Whatever you choose your rewards will be gratifying.

WHY ROMEX?

First, Romex is a fully integrated, battle-hardened bidding system. Evolved over many years, it puts equal weight on low-level bidding, slam bidding and preemptive bidding by providing a comprehensive structure for each. Romex equips you not only with a basic outline but a very detailed follow-up structure.

Second, Romex is a flexible system. It helps the partnership to visualize the bidding mosaic by allowing either one or the other partner to take charge and fit the pieces into place.

Third, Romex is an accurate system with many checks and balances built in to allow a partnership to assess the combined hand potential.

Last but not least, Romex is a system that is well prepared for enemy interference. Romex's relative immunity to interference is due to its limited and graduated bidding structure as well as its very effective defenses against enemy butt-ins.

By and large, Romex is a natural system designed for maximum effectiveness. Programmed sequences allow the partnership to assess distributional fit, key card fit and specific honor card fit. The availability of a variety of bidding tools and sequences provides additional means for information exchange arising from the deliberate selection of one bidding tool or sequence as opposed to another. This inferential information exchange which makes for expert bidding, is clearly outlined in the text and allows partnerships using Romex to achieve high bidding proficiency in a relatively short time.

IS ROMEX FOR YOU?

If you are serious about your bidding, if you are dissatisfied with all or parts of your present methods, if you are looking for new and better bidding tools, if you are result-oriented, if you are simply curious about developments in bridge bidding, the answer is "Yes!" Romex will provide you with the tools and "easy to follow instructions" to help you become an accurate and effective bidder. The rest is up to you and your partner. GOOD LUCK!

— George Abrahamsohn

Table of Contents

PART 1

Chapter 1

BASIC TOOLS

Hand Evaluation

Hand evaluation means "point count" to the average player — High Card Points (HCP) plus possibly points for distribution. There is no doubt that point-count is a useful guide to bidding. However, the research by some of the greatest names in the game have produced some simple yet extremely useful supplemental approaches. The ones we particularly recommend are: Losers and Cover Cards.

The Losing Trick Count

This method of evaluation was first used by F. Dudley Courtenay in 1934. Largely ignored at the time, it was revived by the late great M. Harrison-Gray, and then adopted for the Roman System, used successfully by the Italians in World Championship play. Whereas point-count works well for balanced hands (and notrump bidding), the Losing Trick Count was designed for evaluation of unbalanced holdings.

The principles of the Losing Trick Count are as follows:

1. "Losers" are counted in each suit, then totalled for the hand. [1]
2. In each suit count one Loser for every top honor (ace, king or queen) that is missing, except that:
   1. There cannot be more Losers than the number of cards held in the suit.
   2. A doubleton is a two-Loser suit, unless it has the ace or king (one Loser) or both (no Loser).
   3. A singleton is a Loser, unless it is the singleton ace.

---

[1] Throughout this book the word "Loser" will be capitalized when referring to the Losing Trick Count.

Although this is somewhat difficult to put into words, you will find it simple in practice. For example:

No Losers = Void; A; AK; AKQ(x)
1 Loser = Singleton; Ax or Kx; AKx or AQx or KQx
2 Losers = Qx or xx; Axx or Kxx or Qxx
3 Losers = xxx, Jxxx, xxxx

Note that a suit never has more than three Losers.

The addition of the jack, and/or extra length (beyond three cards) does not affect the Losing Trick Count.

An example hand:

♠ A K x x x	1
♡ A K x x	1
◇ x x	2
♣ x x	2
	6

This hand has six Losers — one in each major and two in each minor.

In my previous book *Win with Romex* I described some "fine tuning" that can be applied to the Losing Trick Count. For most purposes, though, the simple method described above will serve you quite well. As you will see, most bids in Romex give a "Loser range" as part of the requirements for the bid.

Example: The intermediate opening of 1 NT (The Romex Dynamic 1 NT opening bid will be discussed in Chapter 3) shows a hand containing four or five Losers.

Cover Cards

The value of indicating the number of Losers is that your partner can use this information to determine how many Losers he can "cover" — i.e., prevent from being lost. Any value that is likely to match up with a loser in partner's hand is called a "Cover Card." All partner has to do to place the contract is a little arithmetic:

Of course, it's not quite that simple. Some things that need to be taken care of first include:

1. Finding the best trump suit or notrump. (Simple point count is adequate for notrump bidding.)
2. The Losing Trick Count for a particular bid is usually a range rather than a specific number of Losers. It may be necessary to let the bidding clarify whether he has a minimum or a maximum, in terms of Losers, before placing the contract.
3. If some of the advanced Romex slam bidding tools are used, it will usually be possible to discover whether all of the potential Cover Cards cover all of the Losers. For the time being, though, the simple approach to counting Cover Cards will suffice.

Some points about counting Cover Cards:

1. Any value that is likely to match up with a Loser in partner's hand counts as one Cover Card. Any value that will, on the average, match up about half the time with one of partner's Losers counts as a "half cover card." As the bidding progresses, half Cover Cards will either increase in value to a full Cover Card if we discover that it covers a Loser in partner's hand, or lose its half value when it represents duplication.
2. Initial Cover Card count:

    1 Cover Card   = Any ace or king; a queen in a suit where partner is known to have three or more cards.

    1/2 Cover Card = A queen in a suit where partner's length is unknown.

With a four-card trump fit:

    A doubleton = 1/2 Cover Card

    A singleton = 1 Cover Card

    A void   = 1 1/2 Cover Cards

With a three-card trump fit:

    A singleton = 1/2 Cover Card

    A void   = 1 Cover Card

    A doubleton is considered a plus value (useful in border line decisions)

3. Adjust the Cover Card count any time information from the bidding warrants such action. If you discover that a Cover Card (such as a king), or a 1/2 Cover Card (such as a queen, a doubleton, or a singleton) is facing shortage in partner's hand, you have discovered duplication and must adjust downward the originally assigned value of your Cover Cards.

This ''adjustment factor'' available to users of the Losing Trick Count/Cover Cards concept allows for more accurate bidding than Courtenay's original approach by point-count methods. Duplication of values cannot be easily reflected in these methods.

This interplay between Losers and Cover Cards is an integral part of hand evaluation in Romex. However, it is equally useful in any system. Once the Losing Trick Count range is established for each type of opening, great benefits are possible.

> ONCE A FIT HAS BEEN FOUND, DEDUCT THE NUMBER OF COVER CARDS YOU HOLD FROM THE LOSERS PARTNER HAS SHOWN BY HIS BIDDING. THE RESULT IS THE COMBINED NUMBER OF LOSERS THAT YOUR PARTNERSHIP SHOULD HAVE ON THE HAND.

In the following chapters you will find numerous examples of the successful application of this concept. Study them carefully — it will give you a new perspective in bidding!

Controls

Another important hand evaluation concept is that of controls. Unfortunately the word is used in several ways, each too deeply ingrained in the bridge world's conciousness to suggest entirely new terminology. We will, however, make the following distinction:

Control Count [1]

The "Control Count" is like a point count that values only aces and kings:

Each ace counts as two Controls
Each king counts as one Control

This concept is most useful for slam bidding because successful slam contracts require most of the aces and kings. There are 12 Controls in the deck — eight in aces and four in kings.

Examples: A hand containing five Controls would contain:

Two aces and one king or
One ace and three kings.

Many of the bids in Romex have requirements dealing with the Control Count. This allows partner to add up the combined number of Controls to see how many are missing. In this sense the concept of Control Count is similar to the Losing Trick Count/Cover Card concept.

Degree of Control (in a particular suit)

Degree of control in a suit refers to how well we can prevent the opponents from cashing fast tricks or "quick tricks" in the suit. Thus, we speak of first, second or third round control in a suit.

[1] Throughout this book the word "Control" will be capitalized when referring to the Control Count.

In a trump contract a player has:

First round control of a suit holding the ace or a void
Second round control of a suit holding the king or a singleton
Third round control of a suit holding the queen or a doubleton

Occasionally we will say a player has total control in a suit. This means he can assume no losers in the suit — quick losers or delayed losers. Holdings that constitute total control of a suit are:

Void or singleton ace (with adequate trumps)
AK doubleton or AKQ(x)

Ace Asking

Romex employs two variations of the Blackwood ace-asking convention:

Key Card Blackwood	*Blackwood*
There is an agreed suit.	There is no agreed suit.
The king of the trump suit counts as an ace, making five "aces" in all.	The four aces are all that count in the responses.
The four aces and the trump king are called Key Cards.	
The queen of the trump suit is shown in some cases. However, the trump queen is not a Key Card. It is shown as a separate feature.	

Key Card Blackwood is also known as Roman Key Card Blackwood among tournament players.

Blackwood uses the same response scheme as Key Card Blackwood except that there is no fourth step (which deals with the trump queen):

Responses to Key Card Blackwood	Responses to Blackwood
5♣ = 0 or 3 Key Cards	5♣ = 0 or 3 aces
5◊ = 1 or 4 Key Cards	5◊ = 1 or 4 aces
5♡ = 2 or 5 Key Cards; no trump queen	5♡ = 2 aces
5♠ = 2 or 5 Key Cards and the trump queen	

How does a player know if 4 NT is Key Card Blackwood or Blackwood? The rules to apply:

4 NT is Blackwood unless there is a clearly agreed fit OR it is a specially defined Key Card Blackwood sequence.
Blackwood never applies following a Dynamic 1 NT or Romex 2♣ opening bid.

Several special uses of Key Card Blackwood will be outlined in the advanced section. There are three "basic" situations that are Key Card Blackwood:

1. There is a clearly agreed fit.
   Examples:

   1♠ — 3♠
   4 NT = Key Card Blackwood with spades as trump

   1♠ — 2♣
   3♣ — 4 NT = Key Card Blackwood with clubs as trump

15

1 ♠ — 4 ♣ (Splinter bid)
4 NT = Key Card Blackwood with spades as trump

2. When 4 NT immediately follows a jump bid, the suit in which the jump occurred is considered the trump suit in the Key Card Blackwood sequence.
Examples:

1 ♠ — 2 ♣
3 ♠ — 4 NT = Key Card Blackwood with spades as trump

1 ♠ — 2 ♣
3 ♥ — 4 NT = Key Card Blackwood with hearts as trump

1 ♣ — 1 ♥
1 ♠ — 3 ♥
4 NT = Key Card Blackwood with hearts as trump

3. A jump to 4 NT directly over a one-level suit rebid.
Example:

1 ♣ — 1 ♥
1 ♠ — 4 NT = Key Card Blackwood with spades as trump

If responder does not want to use Key Card Blackwood he can bid 2 ◇, forcing, and bid a non-Key Card Blackwood 4 NT later.

4. A jump to 4 NT after

1 ♥ — 1 ♠
2 ♥

is Key Card Blackwood for hearts.

In all other cases, 4 NT is Blackwood, not Key Card Blackwood, even over an opening bid:

$$1 \spadesuit — 4 NT \qquad 2 \spadesuit — 4 NT \qquad 3 \spadesuit — 4 NT$$

In each sequence spades are not agreed; 4 NT is not Key Card
Blackwood.

$1 \clubsuit — 1 \spadesuit$	$1 \spadesuit — 2 \clubsuit$	$1 \spadesuit — 2 \diamondsuit$
$2 \clubsuit — 4 NT$	$2 \spadesuit — 4 NT$	$2 \heartsuit — 3 \diamondsuit$
		$4 NT$

In each case 4 NT is not Key Card Blackwood — there has
been no jump.

Responses to show a void

A player must be careful about employing a void-showing
response to 4 NT. He should be fairly confident that partner will
find the void useful and that he will know where the void is.
This is the scheme:

4 NT— 5 NT = Two Key Cards and a void
    Six of the trump suit = One Key Card and a
               void in a higher-
               ranking suit
    Six of a lower suit = One Key Card and a void
               in the bid suit

The natural "quantitative" meaning of 4 NT — a natural
notrump raise inviting 6 NT — is almost non-existent in Romex.

Asking for kings.

1. After Blackwood

5 NT by the Blackwood bidder asks for kings
  First step = 0 or 3 kings
  Second step = 1 or 4 kings
  Third step = 2 kings

Any other bid at the five-level is a signoff.

2. After Key Card Blackwood

The cheapest non-signoff bid after a first or second step response asks for the trump queen with two step responses:

First step = No trump queen
Second step = Trump queen

To ask for outside kings use your own methods but I strongly recommend the approach described in the sections on Key Card Ask and Spiral Scan.

A good illustration of the effective use of Key Card Blackwood took place in the 1982 Vanderbilt. After being down a few IMPs in the first quarter we recouped our losses on the first hand of the second quarter by reaching an excellent grand slam with only 23 HCP.

Vulnerable: None
Dealer: North

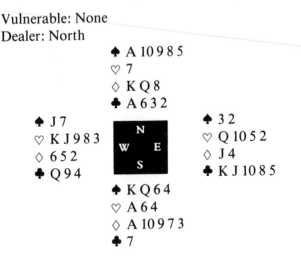

♠ A 10 9 8 5
♥ 7
♦ K Q 8
♣ A 6 3 2

♠ J 7
♥ K J 9 8 3
♦ 6 5 2
♣ Q 9 4

♠ 3 2
♥ Q 10 5 2
♦ J 4
♣ K J 10 8 5

♠ K Q 6 4
♥ A 6 4
♦ A 10 9 7 3
♣ 7

North	East	South	West
Eddie		George	
Wold		Rosenkranz	
1 ♠	Pass	4 ♣ (1)	Pass
4 NT (2)	Pass	5 ♣ (3)	Pass
5 ◇ (4)	Pass	5 ♠ (5)	Pass
7 ♠ !	Pass	Pass	Pass

(1) Splinter bid
(2) Key Card Blackwood
(3) 0 or 3 Key Cards
(4) Queen of trump?
(5) "I have it."

+ 1510 was worth 11 IMPs since our counterparts at the other table reached only 6 ♠. The keys to our success were the use of the splinter bid and Key Card Blackwood.

Simple Asking Bids

There are two basic Asking Bids used in the Romex system:

Trump Asking Bid (TAB)	*Control Asking Bid (CAB)*
Asks partner for step responses to describe his length and strength in the trump suit.	Asks partner for step responses to describe his control in a side suit (any non-trump suit).

Asking Bids are employed only by a strong hand, when it faces a much weaker hand. There are two cases:

After a preemptive opening: Responder can ask.
After a Dynamic 1 NT or 2 ♣ opening: Opener can ask.

CAB

There are six step responses to CAB, which asks for control in a specific suit (other than trump):

Normal Responses	First step	= No control
	Second step	= Second round control (king or singleton)
	Third step	= First round control (ace or void)
	Fourth step	= Second and third round control (KQ)
Special Responses	Fifth Step	= AKx
	Sixth step	= Total control (AKQ, AK, or, with numerous trump, singleton ace or a void)

If interested only in third round control, the Asking Bid must be repeated. The second CAB can be made in the same suit or a new suit. Responses to the second CAB are:

First step = No third round control
Second step = Doubleton
Third step = Queen

Example:

Opener	Responder
1 NT (1)	2 ♡
2 ♠	3 ♠
4 ♣ (2)	4 ♢ (3)
4 ♡ (4)	5 ♣ (5)

(1) The Dynamic 1 NT
(2) CAB
(3) No control
(4) Second CAB
(5) Third step = the queen

TAB applies only after a 2♣ or a Dynamic 1 NT opening. TAB can be employed by a raise below game or a notrump rebid, depending on the sequence. Refer to the chapter on the Dynamic 1 NT for a full explanation.

Example sequences:

1 NT — 2 ◇
2 ♠   — 3 ♠
3 NT = TAB in spades

1 NT — 2 ◇
2 ♡   — 2 ♠
3 ♠   = TAB in spades

2 ♣   — 2 ♡
2 ♠   — 3 ♣
4 ♣   = TAB in clubs

The responses to TAB are:

First step	=	Worst possible holding (for previous bidding)
Second step	=	Minimum trump length plus one of the top three trump honors
Third step	=	One or more extra trumps; no top trump honor
Fourth step	=	One or more extra trumps; one top honor
Fifth step	=	Two top trump honors; minimum trump length
Sixth step	=	Two top trump honors; extra length

The Principle of Fast Arrival

The advantage of a "game-forcing" auction is simple: The players can make as many bids as necessary to describe their hand. No jumping is necessary — bidding space is used as effectively as possible.

What, then, does it mean if a player does make an unnecessary jump to game in a game-forcing auction? The implication is that the jumper is trying to place the contract and discourage partner from moving toward slam. Otherwise, he would avoid jumping and use the available bidding space to explore slam prospects.

We can now state the Principle of Fast Arrival:

The Principle of Fast Arrival

1. An unnecessary jump to game — unnecessary in the sense that a force to game already existed — is a relatively weak bid, showing minimum values for the previous bidding and/or lack of interest in slam.
2. As a corollary: Failure to jump to game, when a game force has been established, in the agreed suit implies a maximum for the previous bidding and/or slam suitable values. Partner is encouraged to make a slam-exploratory move.

Examples:

    1. 1♠ — 2♣   2. 1♠ — 2♣
       2♠ — 3♠ (1)   2♠ — 4♠ (2)

(1) Strong, forcing and unlimited (assuming that a two-over-one creates a game force).

(2) Limited and no slam interest.

The hand described in Sequence 2 is weaker than the one in the first example.

Chapter 2

LIFE WITHOUT THE STRONG NOTRUMP — OR ANY NATURAL NOTRUMP OPENING

One of the first things that most players learn about bridge is that a 1 NT opening shows a balanced hand with 16-18 HCP. My suggestion that this use of the bid be abandoned altogether may therefore appear heretical. I am not suggesting switching to "weak" notrump openings wherein the strong notrump hand is shown by rebidding 1 NT on the second round. The Romex idea is to use no "notrump" opening at all — at least not in the traditional sense of showing a balanced hand.

This idea may seem revolutionary, but it is not entirely new. Two important systems in the history of the game have used a 1 NT opening as a strong forcing opening, not necessarily balanced. The first was the Austrian System which won the 1937 World Team championship in Budapest. The second was the Little Roman (Arno) System which, in the hands of Massimo D'Alelio and Camillo Pabis-Ticci, helped Italy win six World Team titles.

The cornerstone of a good system is limiting the range of the opening bid of one of a suit. This is achieved by "strong club" systems, but the valuable natural meaning of the 1 ♣ opening must be abandoned to do so. Romex achieves the same result by using a 1 NT opening for many hands, balanced and unbalanced, in the 19-21 point range.

How do we show the hands which would usually be opened with a strong notrump? The basic idea:

> With 16 HCP rebid a major at the one-level; otherwise rebid 1 NT.
> With 17-18 rebid a major at the one-level; otherwise rebid 2 NT.

We will now consider the development of the bidding in two sections:

Opener has 16 HCP
Opener has 17-18 HCP

The 16 Point Hand

A balanced hand of 16 HCP is "squeezed in" with the hands which rebid 1 NT. The range becomes a very strong 12 to 16 HCP instead of the customary 13-15 HCP.

A wide-range 1 NT rebid is relatively easy to handle if you have an efficient method of conducting subsequent developments. We use a 2♣ "checkback" procedure closely resembling the method devised by the English theorist, Eric Crowhurst and known as Crowhurst in the United Kingdom. This is how it works:

Checkback After a 1 NT Rebid

Responder bids 2♣ over a 1 NT rebid to:

1. Force opener to describe his hand, and
2. Show at least game invitational values

Examples:

Opener	Responder
1 of a suit	1 of a suit
1 NT	2♣ (Checkback)

Note that 2♣ is artificial even if the opening bid is 1♣.

Opener gives an accurate description of his hand with his rebid. He tells, in order of priority:

1. Whether he has three-card support for responder's major.
2. Whether he has a minimum (13-14 HCP) or a maximum (15-16 HCP).
3. What holding he has in the other major, when relevant:
   A four-card heart suit after a 1♠ response
   A good five-card heart suit after a 1♡ opening bid.

That is the basic idea. After a bit we will look at some very useful adjuncts that allow for precise game and slam bidding.

Opener rebids in a natural way to define his strength:

> With a minimum — Bid at or below two of responder's suit.

> With a maximum — Bid above two of responder's suit.

Examples:

```
1 ♣  — 1 ♠
1 NT — 2 ♣
2 ◇ , 2 ♡ or 2 ♠  = minimum rebids
2 NT and beyond = maximum rebids
```

The precise meaning of opener's rebid depends on the auction. Each case will be considered in turn.

AUCTION 1: 1 ♣ or 1 ◇ — 1 ♠
                1 NT   — 2 ♣

When the response is 1 ♠, a four-card heart suit can be important, especially if opener lacks three-card spade support.

This is the schedule:

$$1 \clubsuit \text{ or } 1 \diamond - 1 \spadesuit$$
$$1 \text{ NT} \qquad - 2 \clubsuit$$

Minimum Rebids	2 ♠	=	Three spades; 13-14 HCP; not-forcing
	2 ♡	=	Fewer than three spades; four hearts; 13-14 HCP; not forcing
	2 ◇	=	Fewer than three spades; fewer than four hearts; 13-14 HCP; artificial but not forcing

Maximum Rebids	3 ♠	=	Three spades; 15-16 HCP; game forcing
	2 NT	=	Fewer than three spades; 15-16 HCP; game forcing

With a maximum that lacks three spades, opener bids 2 NT. If responder is interested in a 4-4 heart fit he can rebid 3 ♡.

You may have noticed that bids of 3 ♣, 3 ◇ and 3 ♡ are "idle" . . . It is a Romex philosophy to make good use of idle bids. These bids will be examined after looking at the basic sequences.

How does responder continue? These rules guide his actions:

1. If opener showed a maximum, the bidding is forced to game.
2. If opener showed a minimum, these bids can lead to under-game contracts:
   Two of responder's major
   2 NT
   2 ♡ after a 1 ♠ response
   3 ♡ or 3 ♠ if responder raises opener's 2 ♡ or 2 ♠ rebid to the three-level.

Any jump or bid of three of a minor suit is game forcing.

Examples:

Opener	Responder
♠ K x	♠ Q J 9 x x
♡ A J x x	♡ K x
◇ Q x x	◇ J x
♣ A 9 x x	♣ K 10 x x

1 ♣	1 ♠
1 NT (1)	2 ♣ (2)
2 ♡ (3)	2 ♠ (4)
Pass	

(1) 13-16 HCP; balanced
(2) Checkback
(3) 13-14 HCP; four hearts; fewer than three spades
(4) Sign-off attempt

Opener	Responder
♠ x x	♠ A 10 x x x
♡ A Q x x	♡ J 10 9 x
◇ A K 10 x	◇ Q x
♣ Q J x	♣ K x

1 ◇	1 ♠
1 NT	2 ♣
2 NT (1)	3 ♡ (2)
4 ◇ (3)	4 ♡ (4)
Pass	

(1) 15-16 HCP; fewer than three spades; game force
(2) Natural
(3) Cue-bid, showing the ace of diamonds and a good hand for
    hearts
(4) No slam interest

AUCTION 2: 1 ♣ or 1 ◇ — 1 ♡
            1 NT   — 2 ♣

This sequence is the same as Auction 1, except that there is no possible fit in the unbid major (spades).

The auction develops the same as Auction 1.

The sequence: 1 ♣ or 1 ♢ — 1 ♡
                1 NT   — 2 ♣
                2 ♢ or 2 ♡ — 2 ♠ = Natural, game forcing reverse

AUCTION 3: 1 ♡   — 1 ♠
                1 NT — 2 ♣

Opener's rebids are identical to Auction 1 except that a 2 ♡ rebid shows a minimum with good hearts (QJ10xx or better) and denies three-card spade support.

AUCTION 4: 1 ♣   — 1 ♢
                1 NT — 2 ♣

This sequence is rare. Responder has denied a major — he would either bid it over 1 ♣ or reversed on the second round over 1 NT. Thus opener merely shows his strength:

    1 ♣   — 1 ♢
    1 NT — 2 ♣
    2 ♢   = 13-14 HCP
    2 NT = 15-16 HCP; game forcing

Making Use of Idle Bids

Let us begin by considering a pair of hands:

Opener	Responder
♠ A Q x	♠ K J 10 x
♡ x x	♡ x x
◇ K Q x	◇ J x x
♣ A J x x x	♣ K Q x x

1♣	1♠
1 NT	2♣
3♠	???

Responder can't be sure what to do. If opener has good hearts, 3 NT is best. If, however, opener has good diamonds and weak hearts, 4♣ is right. What's the solution?

The answer is for opener to show concentration in a side suit. It works like this:

1. Opener shows concentration in one side suit to draw attention, by inference, to weakness in the other side suit. For example:

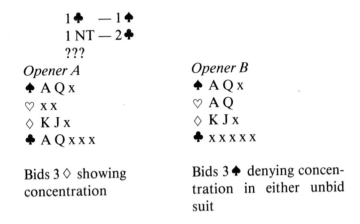

$$
\begin{array}{l}
1♣ \ —1♠ \\
1\,NT —2♣ \\
???
\end{array}
$$

Opener A	Opener B
♠ A Q x	♠ A Q x
♡ x x	♡ A Q
◇ K J x	◇ K J x
♣ A Q x x x	♣ x x x x x
Bids 3◇ showing concentration	Bids 3♠ denying concentration in either unbid suit

Concentration is shown at the three-level only. Thus it also shows a maximum.

A special sequence:

1♣ or 1◊ — 1♠

1 NT — 2♣

3♡ = Three spades AND four hearts. Responder may prefer a 4-4 heart fit

3♠ = Three spades and denies four hearts

2. Opener shows a three-card fit and concentration in his suit by rebidding it at the three-level:

1♡ — 1♠

1 NT — 2♣

3♡ = Three spades AND five good hearts

3. "Impossible" bids at the two-level show a maximum with concentration but deny a fit for responder's major.

There are two sequences:

1♣ or 1◊ — 1♡

1 NT — 2♣

2♠ = 15-16 HCP; fewer than three hearts; spade concentration

2 NT = 15-16 HCP; fewer than three hearts; denies spade concentration

1♣ — 1◊

1 NT — 2♣

2♡ or 2♠ = 15-16 HCP; concentration in the bid suit

2 NT = 15-16 HCP; no concentration

Returning to our example hand, we see that it is easy to bid using these refinements:

Opener	Responder
♠ A Q x	♠ K J 10 x
♡ x x	♡ x x
◊ K Q x	◊ J x x
♣ A J x x x	♣ K Q x x
1 ♣	1 ♠
1 NT	2 ♣
3 ◊ (1)	4 ♠ (2)
Pass	

(1) Diamond concentration; 15-16 HCP; three spades; fewer than four hearts; heart weakness by implication
(2) The 4-3 fit looks best

Responder's Other Calls After a 1 NT Rebid

Responder should not use checkback if he has a suitable natural call available. His choices include:

1. Bidding a lower-ranking new suit at the two-level after a 1 ♣ or 1 ♡ opening bid (except 2 ♣) is natural and non-forcing. A 2 ◊ rebid promises five diamonds because opener can't have four diamonds. Thus if responder rebids 2 ◊ after an initial response in a major, opener should not show preference for responder's major unless he has two diamonds and three cards in responder's major.
2. Rebidding his suit or raising opener's suit at the two-level. This is "to play" (except a 2 ♣ rebid).
3. Reverses and jump shifts, which are natural and game forcing.
4. A jump rebid of responder's suit, which shows a six card or longer suit and is invitational to game.
5. A response of 2 ♣ followed by 3 ♣ by responder is game-forcing with clubs.

6. A jump to the three-level in opener's suit which is game invitational.

EXCEPTION: 1 ♣ — 1 ◇ , 1 ♡ or 1 ♠

                        1 NT — 3 ♣ = Sign-off, due to the use of 2 ♣ as checkback

17-18 HCP Hands

A balanced 17-18 HCP hand should rebid a major at the one-level when possible. Otherwise the rebid is 2 NT. The 2 NT rebid is not needed to show 19-20 HCP as "Standard" players do — Romex has another way to show these hands.

English players have been using the 2 NT jump rebid to show 17-18 HCP for nearly half a century (with no ill effect). With 19-20 HCP they rebid 3 NT, and so should the reader of this book — until he learns our approach in the next chapter.

Developments After a 2 NT Rebid

The approach is largely natural and straightforward. A special convention — the Wolff Signoff or Wolff Adjunct — is suggested. It works like this:

1 ♣ , 1 ◇ or 1 ♡ — 1 ◇ , 1 ♡ or 1 ♠
2 NT   — 3 ♣ = A demand for opener to bid three of responder's major with a three-card fit; otherwise bid 3 ◇ .

Responder's intention is to pass 3 ◇ or to make another weak bid at the three-level.

Example:

Opener	*Responder*
♠ K x	♠ Q 10 x x x
♡ A x x	♡ J 9 x x x
◇ K Q J x	◇ 10 x
♣ A x x x	♣ x

```
1 ♣               1 ♠
2 NT              3 ♣ (1)
3 ◇ (2)           3 ♡ (3)
Pass (4)
```

(1) Wolff Signoff
(2) Lacking three spades
(3) Weak hand with the majors
(4) No reason to bid on

The object of the Wolff Signoff is to allow responder to "have his cake and eat it, too." If responder makes any bid other than 3 ♣ the bidding is forced to game.

Developments After Other Responses

1. 1 NT
A 1 NT response shows:

6-9 HCP after a 1 ♣ opening bid
6-10 HCP after a 1 ◇ opening bid

A two-level response promises at least 11 points, so 1 NT is forced with a balanced 10 points after a 1 ◇ opening, especially with club length.
After 1 ♣ — 1 NT opener raises to 2 NT with 17-18 HCP and passes with less.
After 1 ◇ — 1 NT, a 2 ♣ rebid is "Checkback":

```
1 ◇ — 1 NT
2 ♣ — 2 ◇ = 6-8 HCP
        2 ♡ or 2 ♠ = Concentration in suit bid; 9-10 HCP
        2 NT = No concentration in either major; 9-10
                HCP
```

This bars playing 2 ♣ on some hands. In practice though, the opponents would usually be able to compete in a major.

2. 1 ♦ — 2 ♣

This procedure works nicely:

1 ♦   — 2 ♣
2 NT = 13-14 HCP or 17-18 HCP
3 NT = 15-16 HCP
          The 2 NT rebid is forcing

With the stronger 2 NT rebid (17-18 HCP), opener follows a raise to 3 NT with 4 NT.

Weighing the Evidence: Pros and Cons

The main purpose of these methods is to free the 1 NT opening bid for other purposes. Let's compare the advantages and disadvantages in a table:

The Pros and Cons of an Artificial 1 NT Opening

Advantages

Disadvantages

1. There is more room to explore for the best contract. It is often possible to find a useful suit fit while Standard bidders languish in 1 NT or 3 NT.

1. Sometimes 2 NT is reached with 17-18 HCP opposite 6 or 7 points, while Standard bidders open 1 NT and play it there. However, the combined hands will have at least 23 HCP.

2. The opponents have less information about the hand to guide them in their dummy play, should we become the defenders.

2. A suit opening gives the opponents room to enter the auction at a lower level.

3. There is more room to probe for minor suit slams.

3. Standard bidders can respond on weaker hands as they do not fear a 2 NT rebid with 17-18 HCP. This may or may not work well for them.

4. By opening 1 NT with 19-21 points opening bids of one of a suit are limited. This is accomplished without losing the natural suit openings — very effectively, as you will see.

4. There is no answer to this advantage — the biggest one of all!

In the 1966 World Championships there were 22 hands qualifying for a strong 1 NT opening. One team opened these hands with 1 NT. The other opened them with one of a suit. The net score for the 1 NT openings was +350, but the net score for the-one-of-a-suit openings was +3590.

In the 1965 World Championships eight strong 1 NT openings produced a net score of +1510, while one-of-a-suit openings on these same hands produced a net score of +4490. (These statistics were compiled by H. C. Horn and mentioned in his book *Contract Bridge: Limited Opening Bids.*)

Even allowing for improved methods in notrump bidding in the last 17 years these statistics seem impressive.

Let's look at a few more examples that illustrate the simple and natural effectiveness of the method.

Opener	Responder
1.	
♠ A Q	♠ K x x
♡ K J x x	♡ A Q x x x x
◇ Q x x	◇ x
♣ A Q x x	♣ K x x
1 ♣	1 ♡
3 ♡	4 NT
5 ♣	6 ♡
Pass	

The jump raise shows four hearts and a hand worth about 17 points. It is then easy for the responder to use Key Card Blackwood.

2. Challenge the Champs, 1976.

Opener	Responder
♠ 8 5	♠ 10 9
♡ K 8 3	♡ A Q 9 4
♢ A K 10 7 2	♢ Q J 6 4
♣ A Q J	♣ 8 6 3

1 ♢	1 ♡
2 ♣ (1)	2 ♢
2 ♡	3 ♡
4 ♡	Pass

(1) Awkward. 2 NT cannot be rebid with a weak doubleton spade, so a temporizing bid of 2 ♣ is made. The subsequent 2 ♡ bid shows three card heart support and considerable extra values. 3 ♡ instead of 2 ♡ would not be wrong and would have made life easier for responder. Standard bidders would always open 1 NT, test for hearts, and play 3 NT.

3. Bermuda Bowl, 1957. U.S. vs. Italy.

Opener	Responder
♠ Q 6 2	♠ A K 10 5 3
♡ K 4 2	♡ A 5
♢ A 8 7	♢ 10 6 4
♣ A K J 2	♣ Q 7 6

1 ♣	1 ♠
2 NT	3 ♠ (forcing)
4 ♣ (1)	4 ♡ (2)
5 ♢ (3)	6 ♠
Pass	

(1) Spade fit; club ace; slam interest.
(2) Cue-bid.
(3) Cue-bid.
Both teams missed this laydown slam.

Here are some more examples to illustrate some "bread and butter" sequences:

4.

Opener
♠ AJxx
♡ KJx
◇ Jxx
♣ Kxx

Responder A
♠ 10xx
♡ Qxxx
◇ A10x
♣ Q10x

1♣ (1) — 1♡ (2)
1♠ (3) — 1 NT (4)
Pass (9)

Responder B
♠ Qx
♡ Q10xxx
◇ xx
♣ Q98x

1♣ (1) — 1♡ (2)
1♠ (3) — 2♣ (5)
2♡ (10) — Pass (9)

Responder C
♠ K10xx
♡ Axxx
◇ xx
♣ xxx

1♣ (1) — 1♡ (2)
1♠ (3) — 2♠ (6)
Pass (9)

Responder D	*Responder E*
♠ Kxx	♠ K10xx
♡ A98x	♡ Axxx
◇ A108	◇ xx
♣ xxx	♣ QJx

1♣ (1) — 1♡ (2)	1♣ (1) — 1♡ (2)
1♠ (3) — 2 NT (7)	1♠ (3) — 3♠ (8)
Pass (9)	Pass (9)

(1) Minimum opening hand
(2) Natural response; usually six or more points
(3) Don't bypass a four-card spade suit
(4) Natural; up to 10 HCP.
(5) Natural; four or more clubs; not suited to notrump
(6) About 8-10 points in support of spades
(7) Invitational; about 11-12 HCP
(8) Invitational; about 11-12 points in support of spades
(9) No reason to bid on
(10) The preference is in order, especially with only three clubs

5.

Opener	*Responder*
♠ K Q x x	♠ J x x x
♡ Q x	♡ J x x x
◇ A x x	◇ J x
♣ A Q J x	♣ K x x

1♣	1♡
1♠	Pass (1)

(1) Opener's hand is limited to 18 HCP, so game is very unlikely. If responder bids 2♠ opener would bid game, which
would probably go down one.

6.

Opener A	Opener B	Responder
♠ K Q 10 x	♠ A 10 x x	♠ J x x
♡ x x	♡ x	♡ A x x x
◇ A x x	◇ A x	◇ Q x x
♣ A K J x	♣ A K x x x x	♣ 10 x x

Sequence A	Sequence B
1♣ — 1♡	1♣ — 1♡
1♠ — 1 NT	1♠ — 1 NT
2 NT (1)—Pass (2)	3 NT (3) — Pass

(1) 17-18 HCP.
(2) Refusing the try with a "flat" 7 HCP.
(3) The strong club suit and side aces make it worth a shot at 3 NT.

Chapter 3

THE DYNAMIC 1 NT OPENING

The Dynamic 1 NT Opening is used to show those trouble-some hands in the 19-21 point range. Getting these in between hands "out of the way" dramatically improves the accuracy of our opening one bids and stronger opening (2♣, 2♢ and 2 NT).

There are two basic hand types that open 1 NT:

1. <u>Balanced.</u> Balanced with 19-20 HCP; usually six or more Controls.

2. <u>Unbalanced.</u> Unbalanced with four or five Losers; five or more Controls; and 19-21 HCP (can be shaded slightly under certain circumstances which will be explained). There are four subcategories:
   1. One-suited hands. (ACOL Two-Bids in a major should be opened 2♢ if using the advanced methods to be described later.)
   2. Two-suited hands.
   3. Three-suited hands.
   4. Freakish game or quasi-game hands.

One note — neither opener nor responder can ever bid Black-wood in any form after a Dynamic 1 NT opening bid.

Balanced Hands

Balanced patterns include 4-3-3-3, 4-4-3-2 and 5-3-3-2 (a five-card major is no bar to opening 1 NT if the other requirements are met).

The range is, in principle, 19-20 HCP. However, opener should re-evaluate his point-count up or down if warranted. Some factors to consider:

1. Add one point for a reasonable five-card suit (something like KJ9xx or better). 4-3-3-3 distribution is a negative

feature, but don't deduct a point unless other evaluation factors are also negative.

2. The table on page 330 listing the expected number of Controls in balanced hands, says six Controls are expected when the strength is 19-20 HCP. This is not strictly observed per se, though opener should tend to demote a poorish 19 point hand with five Controls to the 17-18 range. Similarly he can promote a good hand with seven Controls to the 21-22 range.

3. In close cases opener can consider other factors: "body" (tens and nines); whether honors are in long suits or short suits; etc.

See the Chapter "Strong Balanced Hands" for a discussion of many sequences that follow when opener has a balanced hand.

Unbalanced Hands

There is ample room for judgment and evaluation in deciding whether to open 1 NT with an unbalanced hand. Each subtype will be discussed separately. First, though, a warning:

Do not be tempted to overuse the Dynamic 1 NT — its usefulness comes from the carefully defined limits that the bid conveys.

The One-Suiter

Possible distributions: 6-3-3-1; 6-3-2-2; 7-3-2-1; 7-3-3-0. The hand should contain four or five Losers and at least five Controls.

Below are two sample hands that qualify:

1.

Opener	Losers	HCP	Controls
♠ A J x	2	5	2
♡ A K x x x x	1	7	3
◇ A K x	1	7	3
♣ x	1	0	0
	5	19	8

2.

Opener	Losers	HCP	Controls
♠ K J	1	4	1
♡ A K J	1	8	3
◇ K Q J x x x x	1	6	1
♣ x	1	0	0
	4	18	5

With compensating features — good body in the long suit (tens and nines or extra length) and four or five Losers — opener may shade the point-count requirements to as low as 17 HCP. Example:

3.

Opener	Losers	HCP	Controls
♠ A 10 x	2	4	2
♡ A K 10	1	7	3
◇ K Q J 10 9 x	1	6	1
♣ x	1	0	0
	5	17	6

Don't open the hand below with 1 NT — your long suit lacks the texture for you to shade the requirements:

4.

Opener	Losers	HCP	Controls
♠ Q x x	2	2	0
♡ K J x x x x	2	4	1
◇ A K	0	7	3
♣ K J	1	4	1
	5	17	5

The Two-Suiter

A hand with at least 5-4 in two suits: 5-4-3-1; 5-5-2-1; 5-4-2-2; 5-5-3-0; 6-5-1-1; 6-5-2-0; 6-4-2-1; and 6-4-3-0.

These hands are very flexible, offering game prospects in notrump or in one of opener's suits. Occasionally game will be available in opener's three-card fragment when responder has length there.

Once again, the point-count requirement can be lowered to 17-18 HCP as long as the hand is otherwise suitable.

Examples:

1.

Opener	Losers	HCP	Controls
♠ A K J 10 x x	1	8	3
♡ A Q x x	1	6	2
◇ K 10	1	3	1
♣ x	1	0	0
	4	17	6

2.

Opener	Losers	HCP	Controls
♠ K Q J x	1	6	1
♡ x	1	0	0
◇ A Q J 10 x x	1	7	2
♣ A Q	1	6	2
	4	19	5

Opener should be much more cautious about opening 1 NT with a minor two-suiter because minor suit games are tougher to make. If the hand is not truly powerful he is better off opening the longer minor, planning to reverse or to jump shift (not forcing in Romex). If responder can't bid over an opening one-bid, game is unlikely.

Four types of minor two-suiters should be opened 1 NT:

1. 2-2-5-4 or 2-2-4-5 with stoppers in both majors: opener plans a 2 NT rebid.
2. 5-4-3-1 types containing a three-card major suit that are sufficiently strong: Four Losers; at least 20 HCP.
3. 6-4 types can open 1 NT with 19 HCP because of the brighter prospects for 3 NT.
4. With a "normal" minor-suiter, opener should expect a modest fit to produce game. The requirements are: at least 19 HCP with no more than two quick losers.

Examples:

Opener	Losers	HCP	Controls
1.			
♠ A Q	1	6	2
♡ A K	0	7	3
♢ K J x x	2	4	1
♣ Q J 10 x	2	3	0
	5	20	6
2.			
♠ A Q	1	6	2
♡ x	1	0	0
♢ K Q J x x	1	6	1
♣ A K J x	1	8	3
	4	20	6
3.			
♠ x	1	0	0
♡ K J	1	4	1
♢ A K J 10 x x	1	8	3
♣ A K x x	1	7	3
	4	19	7

Opener	Losers	HCP	Controls
4.			
♠ A Q J	1	7	2
♡ 2	1	0	0
◊ K Q J 10 8	1	6	1
♣ A K 10 9	1	7	3
	4	20	6
5.			
♣ Q J 10	2	3	0
♡ x	1	0	0
◊ A K J x	1	8	3
♣ A Q J 10 x	1	7	2
	5	18	5
6.			
♠ x	1	0	0
♡ K Q x	1	5	1
◊ A K J 10 x	1	8	3
♣ K Q J x	1	6	1
	4	19	5
7.			
♠ A K	0	7	3
♡ x x	2	0	0
◊ A Q J x x	1	7	2
♣ K Q J 10	1	6	1
	4	20	6
8.			
♠ 10	1	0	0
♡ Q J	2	3	0
◊ A K Q J x	0	10	3
♣ A Q 10 x x	1	6	2
	4	19	5

Hands 1, 2, 3 and 4 qualify for a 1 NT opening, while hands 5, 6, 7 and 8 should be opened in the longer minor. These last four hands need not fear missing game if responder lacks the six points necessary for a response.

The Three-Suiter

At least four cards in three suits: 4-4-4-1 or 5-4-4-0. Three-suiters are very flexible and offer multiple choices for the final contract. The requirements are as usual: 19 or more HCP; four or five Losers. With good intermediates, the point count can be shaded to 18.

Examples:

Opener	Losers	HCP	Controls
1.			
♠ A K J 9	1	8	3
♡ x	1	0	0
◇ Q J 10 x	2	3	0
♣ A K J 9	1	8	3
	5	19	6
2.			
♠ K J x x x	2	4	1
♡ A K Q J	0	10	3
◇ —	0	0	0
♣ K J x x	2	4	1
	4	18	5

The "Freakish-Game" or "Quasi-Game" Hand

Freak distributions: 7-4-1-1; 7-4-2-0; 6-5-1-1; 8-4-1-0; etc. This category includes hands which, by virtue of their distribution, can make game opposite a fit and/or the right king or queen. The high-card requirements can be relaxed considerably — but not the requirements for Controls, Losers and defensive tricks (three or more).

Examples:

Opener	Losers	HCP	Controls
1.			
♠ A J x x x x x	2	5	2
♡ A Q x x	1	6	2
◊ —	0	0	0
♣ K Q	1	5	1
	4	16	5
2.			
♠ A Q J	1	7	2
♡ A 10 x x x x x x	2	4	2
◊ A	0	4	2
♣ J	1	1	0
	4	16	6

Hand 1 needs no more than a fit in either major to have a good shot at game. Hand 2 is cold for 4♡ opposite a 4-3-3-3 yarborough if hearts break.

Now that you know when to open 1 NT, let's consider how to respond when partner opens with a Dynamic 1 NT.

Responses to the Dynamic 1 NT

The responses are designed to tell opener about the potential that responder's hand contains. Responses attempt to identify:

1. Whether there are sufficient values for game, 2♣ is the negative response; all others are forcing to game.
2. The slam potential of the hand expressed in terms of Controls and potential Cover Cards. A 2◊ response denies three Cover Cards in combination with two or more Controls and thus slam will be unlikely. Higher responses promise at least three Cover Cards and show Controls by steps (starting with two Controls).

This is the response schedule:

Responses to the Dynamic 1 NT Opening

2♣ = 0-5 HCP

2◊ = At least 6 HCP; game force; zero to four Controls. If the hand has two, three or four controls, it has fewer than three potential Cover Cards in high cards.

2♡ = Two Controls with at least three potential Cover Cards in high cards: ace-queen-queen or king-king-queen.

2♠ = Three Controls with at least three potential Cover Cards in high cards: ace-king-queen or king-king-king.

2 NT = Four Controls with at least three potential Cover Cards in high cards: ace-ace-queen, ace-king-king or king-king-king-king.

3♣ = Five Controls

3◊ = Six Controls

4 NT = Seven Controls (you should be so lucky!)

Responses of 3♡ to 4♠ are specialized "pattern" bids and are relatively rare. They will be described later.

The responses give an excellent picture of the trick-taking potential of responder's hand. As the bidding develops responder can show additional features — queens, jacks and distributional features (short suits) by specialized Romex sequences. Cue-bidding sequences are never used after a Dynamic 1 NT or Romex 2♣ opening.

Examples of responses to 1 NT:

1. ♠ xxx
   ♡ Qxxxx
   ◊ Jxxx
   ♣ x
   Bid 2♣

2. ♠ Axx
   ♡ Jxxx
   ◊ xxx
   ♣ xxx
   Bid 2♣

3. ♠ QJ10xxx
   ♡ KJxx
   ◊ —
   ♣ QJx
   Bid 2◊

4. ♠ Kxxx
   ♡ Kxx
   ◊ Qxxx
   ♣ Qx
   Bid 2♡

5. ♠ Axxx
   ♡ Kxx
   ◊ x
   ♣ xxxxx
   Bid 2◊

6. ♠ Axx
   ♡ xxx
   ◊ Ax
   ♣ 10xxxx
   Bid 2◊

7. ♠ AJx
   ♡ KQxxx
   ◊ x
   ♣ xxxx
   Bid 2♣

8. ♠ ᵀx
   ♡ xx
   ◊ Kx
   ♣ xxx
   Bid 2 NT

9. ♠ Kx
   ♡ Kxx
   ◊ Kxxx
   ♣ Kxxx
   Bid 2 NT

10. ♠ Kxxx
    ♡ AJx
    ◊ Kx
    ♣ Kxxx
    Bid 3♣

11. ♠ Ax
    ♡ xxxx
    ◊ Axx
    ♣ Axxx
    Bid 3◊

Example 2 has only five HCP, so a 2♣ response is indicated in spite of having two Controls.

Example 4 meets the requirements for a 2♡ response: two Controls; four Cover Cards; 10 HCP.

Example 5 has only two Cover Cards so must respond 2◊. The singleton diamond cannot be counted at this stage — it will be useless unless a fit is found.

The Development of the Auction

1. Developments After 1 NT — 2♣

Finding a safe resting place is of major importance after a 2♣ response. Game is not particularly likely unless opener has a freak or responder has a suitable maximum. Let's start by looking at opener's options over 2♣:

1. Pass = Long clubs and no four-card major
2. 2◇ = Stayman, probing for a 4-4 major fit
3. 2♡ or 2♠ = Natural, showing five or more cards in the suit bid
4. 2 NT = Balanced 19-20 HCP with no four-card major
5. 3♣ = Minor two-suiter
6. 3◇ = Natural, with at least six diamonds and no four-card major
7. 3♡, 3♠, 4♣ and 4◇ = At least 5-5 in the majors with four Losers
8. 3 NT = Gambling — solid minor with nine playing tricks

Some explanations:

A.   Pass

Opener must pass with a one-suiter in clubs and not enough for game. The 3♣ rebid is reserved for minor two-suiters with game potential. Example:

♠ x	1 NT — 2♣
♡ A x	Pass
◇ A Q J	
♣ K Q J 10 x x x	

B. 2 ◇

This is the most common rebid — used on any hand with a four-card major[1] with the possible exception of some hands with a five card or longer major and four cards in the other major. The bid operates like Stayman — responder bids a four-card major if he has one. The schedule of responder's bid are:

2♡ or 2♠	= Four-card or longer suit
2 NT	= No four-card major or six-card minor
3♣ or 3◇	= Six-card minor; no four-card major
3♡ or 3♠	= Good five-card or longer suit (usually six or more): maximum
3 NT	= Five HCP with 4-4 in the majors

[1] The use of the 2◇ rebid instead of 2 NT with balanced hands containing a four-card major follows a suggestion of George and Roni Abrahamsohn. Tournament experience and computer analysis of several hundred deals has confirmed the superiority of this approach which, in many cases, allows the partnership to stop in 2♡ or 2♠. The field (after a 2 NT opening) is at least one level higher.

After rebids by responder of 2 NT or higher, the bidding is natural. A few points about developments after a 2♡ or 2♠ rebid.

1. These responses are non-forcing. With a balanced hand and five Losers, opener may pass.
2. Virtually any unbalanced hand with a fit justifies a raise. If opener has an "almost game" raise he can bid the other major to give responder a chance to get out below game with a hopeless hand. (This bid can't be needed in a natural sense — if opener had a one-suiter with a five-card or longer major, he would have bid it over 2♣). Examples:

$$1\,NT - 2♣$$
$$2♢ \quad - 2♠$$
$$???$$

1. ♠ A K x x
   ♡ A x
   ♢ A J x x x
   ♣ A x
   Raise to 3♠
   (with five Losers)

2. ♠ A K x x
   ♡ A x
   ♢ A Q x x x
   ♣ A x
   Rebid 3♡ (strong raise) (with four Losers)

3. If opener doesn't fit responder's major, he bids naturally — 2 NT or three of a long minor.
4. With 5-4 in the majors, opener should usually bid 2♢. An exception would be a 5-4-2-2 hand with five Losers because the risk of getting too high exceeds the possible benefit from finding a 4-4 fit.

Example:

Opener	Responder
♠ A x x x	♠ J x x x
♡ K Q x	♡ x x
◇ K Q J x	◇ x x x
♣ A J	♣ x x x x
1 NT	2 ♣
2 ◇	2 ♠
Pass (1)	

(1) With only six Controls and a balanced hand, opener happily passes in the spade partial

C. 2♡ or 2♠

A rebid of 2 ♡ or 2 ♠ is natural and non-forcing, promising at least a five-card suit. The suit is usually fairly strong so it will represent a fair final contract if responder lacks game ambitions.

Opener's hand may be one-suited or two-suited.

Examples:

1.		2.	
♠	K J 10 9 x	♠	Q
♡	A Q x	♡	K Q 10 x x x
◇	A K J x	◇	A K x
♣	x	♣	K Q x

D. 2 NT

Opener's rebid of 2 NT shows a balanced hand of 19-20 HCP denies a four-card major (bid 2 ◇ instead). With 5-3-3-2 and a five-card major, opener should bid the major, not 2 NT.

Further development after 1 NT — 2♣
                                                2 NT
     is as follows:

There is no need for a 3♣ Stayman bid because opener cannot have a four-card major. Therefore:

3♣ = "Flint" transfer to 3◇ allowing a sign-off in diamonds, hearts or spades. As an option you may use the "impossible" sequence of

1 NT	— 2♣
2 NT	— 3♣
3◇	— 3 NT

to show a minor two suiter with heart shortage. Opener can pass, bid a minor suit game or sign off at 4♣ or 4◇.

3◇ = Transfer to hearts. Invitational, opener bids 4♡ with a fit.

3♡ = Transfer to spades. Invitational, opener bids 4♠ with a fit.

3♠ = Minor two-suiter with spade shortage.

3 NT = To play.

Examples:

1.

Opener	Responder
♠ K J x	♠ x x x
♡ Q x x	♡ x x
◇ A K x	◇ Q J x x x
♣ A Q J x	♣ x x x

1 NT	2♣
2 NT (1)	3♣ (2)
3◇ (3)	Pass (4)

(1) No four-card major; balanced; 19-20 HCP
(2) Flint
(3) Yes sir!
(4) Should be a good result

2.

Opener	Responder
♠ A x x	♠ J 10 x x x
♡ A x x	♡ x x
◇ A Q x	◇ x x x
♣ K Q x x	♣ J x x

1 NT	2 ♣
2 NT (1)	3 ♣ (2)
3 ◇ (3)	3 ♠ (4)
Pass	

(1) No four-card major; balanced 19-20 HCP.
(2) Flint
(3) Yes sir!
(4) Sign-off

3. Mixed Pairs. Mexico, 1982.

Opener	Responder
Edith	George
Rosenkranz	Rosenkranz

♠ K J	♠ Q 10 9 6 4
♡ A Q 4	♡ J 10 8 5 2
◇ A K 6 2	◇ J 3
♣ Q J 6 3	♣ 4

1 NT	2 ♣
2 NT	3 ♡ (1)
3 ♠ (2)	4 ♡ (3)
Pass (4)	

(1) Invitational transfer
(2) Rejecting the game invitation
(3) Maybe you like this suit better
(4) Yes

E. **3♣**

3♣ is a specialized rebid used to show a powerful minor two-suiter. The hand has at most two quick losers and is too good to open at the one-level. Possible games are in a minor, notrump, or rarely in a major when opener has a three-card fragment.

Examples:

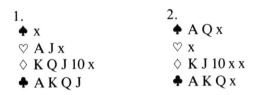

1.
♠ x
♡ A J x
♢ K Q J 10 x
♣ A K Q J

2.
♠ A Q x
♡ x
♢ K J 10 x x
♣ A K Q x

F. **3♢**

A 3♢ rebid shows a six-card or longer diamond suit; either one-suited or with four clubs. If opener has a four-card major, he must bid 2♢.

Examples:

1.
♠ K Q
♡ x
♢ K Q J 10 x x
♣ A K x x

2.
♠ x
♡ A Q 10
♢ A K J 10 x x
♣ A Q x

G. 3 NT

This rebid shows a nine-trick hand with a long solid minor.
Here is an example from the 1980 Blue Ribbon Pairs:

Opener	*Responder*
George	Eddie
Rosenkranz	Wold

♠ A 7	♠ 9 6 5 4
♡ A 4	♡ 10 7 3 2
◊ A K Q J 10 9 7	◊ 6
♣ J 6	♣ 9 7 5 4

1 NT	2 ♣
3 NT	Pass

H. 4 ♡ or 4 ♠

Opener's rebid of 4 ♡ or 4 ♠ is to play. He usually has a
freak, though he can have a good one-suited hand with a seven
or eight-card suit. The negative response rules out the
possibility of slam so responder will pass. An exception could
occur with an ace and a side suit void: ♠ xxxx ♡ xxxx ◊ —
♣ Axxxx. Show the void by bidding 5 ◊ .
  Example:

  ♠ A K J
  ♡ K Q 10 x x x x
  ◊ K Q
  ♣ x

I. 3 ♡

This rebid shows 5-5 in the majors, four Losers, and at most
three quick losers. The suits are usually broken, meaning opener
is willing to stop at the three-level if responder's hand is
worthless.

Example:

♠ K J 10 x x
♥ K Q J x x
♦ A K
♣ Q

J.   3♠

This rebid also shows 5-5 in the majors, but with excellent suits. Opener expects to make game opposite a minimal fit.
Example:

♠ A K J 10 x
♥ K Q J 10 x
♦ A
♣ x x

K.   4♣ or 4♦

Rebids of four of a minor show 5-5-3-0 distribution with three cards in the bid minor. Opener has a four Loser hand with excellent suits. The purpose of these bids is to bring the three-card minor into focus as a possible trump suit.
Example:

♠ A K J 10 x
♥ K Q J 10 x
♦ A x x
♣ —

Following are a lot of examples from tournaments and bidding contests. For maximum benefit, cover the suggested auction and bid the hand yourself first (or with your partner).

Examples:

1. Challenge the Champs, 1982.

Opener	Responder
♠ A K 9 2	♠ 8 3
♡ A K 8 2	♡ 9 6
◇ 4	◇ K J 8 6 3 2
♣ A 8 6 3	♣ 9 7 2

1 NT	2 ♣ (1)
2 ◇ (2)	3 ◇ (3)
Pass	

(1) 0-6 HCP
(2) Stayman
(3) Six card diamond suit and game interest, otherwise he would pass 2 ◇

2. Reisinger, 1974.

Opener	Responder
Sol	George
Dubson	Rosenkranz

♠ K 10 5 2	♠ Q J 8 6
♡ J	♡ 10 5 4
◇ A 3	◇ 10 7 6 4
♣ A K Q 10 6 5	♣ 3 2

1 NT	2 ♣
2 ◇	2 ♠
3 ♡ (1)	4 ♠ (2)

(1) Strong spade raise (four Losers)
(2) One sure Cover Card for spades

The opposing team opened 1 ♣ and played there.

3. Challenge the Champs, August, 1973.

Responder	*Opener*
♠ Q 8 5 2	♠ —
♡ K 8 3 2	♡ A J 9 4
◊ 6 5 4	◊ A K J 10 9 7
♣ 9 3	♣ K Q 10
Pass	1 NT
2 ♣	2 ◊
3 NT (1)	4 ♡
Pass	

(1) Maximum with 4-4 in the majors

The Romex pair (Miguel Reygadas and George Rosenkranz) reached 4♡. However, their opponents had no convenient method available and reached a partscore after:

Pass   — 1 ♣ (a)
1 ◊ (b) — 2 ◊ (c)
Pass
(a) Big club: 16 or more HCP
(b) Negative: 0-7 HCP
(c) Natural

4. Life Masters Men's Pairs, 1971.

Opener	*Responder*
♠ A 10 3 2	♠ Q
♡ A	♡ 10 4 3
◊ K Q 6 5	◊ 8 7 2
♣ A K 9 8	♣ 7 6 5 4 3 2
1 NT	2 ♣
2 ◊	3 ♣ (1)
5 ♣ (2)	Pass

(1) Six or more clubs, but not promising any values
(2) Opener bids the game knowing all he needs is three hearts

in responder's hand. Failing that, the diamond jack or the spade jack may be enough.

5. U. S. Trials, 1965.

Opener	Responder
♠ Q J 10	♠ 6 5 4
♡ A K 10 9 7	♡ Q 8
◇ Q 10 4	◇ J 9 6 2
♣ A K	♣ Q 9 8 3

1 NT	2 ♣
2 ♡ (1)	3 ♡ (2)
3 NT (3)	Pass (4)

(1) Originally planning to rebid 2 NT. The 2 ♣ response warns opener to look for a safer contract.
(2) With five HCP and two possible Cover Cards responder's hand is worth a game try. Doubleton queen is an adequate trump holding for a raise.
(3) Trying for the nine trick game. If 3 NT fails, 3 ♡ may also fail.
(4) "Fine with me."

6. Challenge the Champs, 1973.

Responder	Opener
♠ 10 6	♠ A K Q J 3
♡ 5 4 2	♡ Q 8
◇ J 8 7 6 3	◇ A 4
♣ 9 5 4	♣ A K 7 2

Pass	1 NT (1)
2 ♣	2 ♠
Pass (2)	

(1) 1 NT is correct in spite of 23 HCP — the hand has four Losers.
(2) No reason to disturb 2 ♠. In the bidding contest both pairs got too high.

7. Mexican Nationals, 1978.

Opener Edith Rosenkranz	*Responder* George Rosenkranz
♠ K Q J 5 4	♠ 9 8 7 2
♡ A J 8 7 2	♡ Q 6
♢ A K	♢ 10 7 5
♣ 2	♣ J 6 4 3
1 NT	2 ♣
3 ♡ (1)	4 ♠ (2)
Pass	

(1) Major two-suiter with four Losers and broken suits.
(2) One sure Cover Card and a spade fit easily justify a 4 ♠ bid.

We were the only pair to bid this excellent game.

8. Acapulco Regional, 1981.

Opener Edith Rosenkranz	*Responder* Eddie Wold
♠ K 4	♠ Q 6 5 2
♡ A K J 9 6 5 4 2	♡ 10
♢ A 10	♢ J 3 2
♣ 2	♣ J 8 7 6 5
1 NT (1)	2 ♣
4 ♡ (2)	Pass

(1) With six Controls and four Losers (3-1/2 Losers — the heart queen is not as likely a Loser with the eight-card suit), this hand is too strong to open 4 ♡.
(2) Slam is out of the question after a 2 ♣ response. Needing next to nothing for game, opener leaps to 4 ♡.

These preceding examples illustrate the simple and natural effectiveness of the Dynamic 1 NT.

2. Developments After 1 NT — 2 ◇

The most common response to 1 NT is 2 ◇. A game force is established, but responder denies much slam interest. His hand lacks sufficient Controls or three potential Cover Cards for opener's four or five Losers. Therefore there is no slam unless responder has an extra Cover Card from distribution.

Since opener has the equivalent of 19 points and responder at least 6, game at 3 NT should have an excellent chance even without a suit fit.

The bidding proceeds along natural lines. Some rules:

Opener's Second Bid:

1) Opener bids 2 NT with 19-20 HCP and balanced distribution (See the chapter Strong Balanced Hands for a full discussion.)
2) A minor suit bid at the three-level shows a six-card or longer suit
3) A 2 ♡ or 2 ♠ bid can be made with a four-card suit in two instances:
    a) With 4-4-4-1 opener bids his lower major
    b) With a four-card major and exactly a five-card minor, opener bids his major at the two-level

Examples:

♠ AKxx ♡ x ◇ AKx ♣ K10xxx. Rebid 2 ♠
♠ AKxx ♡ x ◇ Ax   ♣ AK10xxx. Rebid 3 ♣

Responder's Second Bid:

1) Raising a major directly promises four or more trumps. A jump by responder in a new suit is a splinter raise.
2) The length promised by a new suit depends on whether 2 NT is available as a "waiting" or "tem-

porizing'' bid:
   a) If 2 NT is available: 2♠ over 2♡ shows four or more spades. New suits at the three-level promise five or more cards.
   b) If 2 NT is not available: Responder bids as naturally as he can.

Later bidding:
A new suit at the three-level shows a five-card or longer suit if a 2 NT bid is available.

   Example sequences:

1 NT — 2♢	1 NT — 2♢
2♡ — 2♠	2♡ — 2♠
3♣ or 3♢ = Five-card suit	2 NT — 3♣ or 3♢ = Four-card or longer suit

Bids beyond 3 NT, in the absence of a major suit fit, show extra values — the safest game might be bypassed otherwise.

Slam methods have only moderate importance after a 2♢ response. Opener does have simple Asking Bids (TAB and CAB) at his disposal if a fit is found.

Let's try some examples:

1.

Opener	*Responder*
♠ A Q 10 x	♠ x x x
♡ A x	♡ K 10 x x
♢ x x	♢ K 10 x x
♣ A K Q x x	♣ J x
1 NT	2♢
2♠ (1)	2 NT (2)
3♣	3♠ (3)
3 NT (4)	Pass

(1) Correct bid with a four-card major and a five-card minor
(2) Cannot raise . . . yet.

(3) Delayed raise showing three spades
(4) Denying a fifth spade

2.

Opener	Responder
♠ x	♠ J x x x x
♡ A K J x x	♡ x x
◇ A Q J x	◇ K 10 9 x
♣ A Q x	♣ K J

1 NT	2 ◇
2 ♡	2 ♠
2 NT (1)	3 ◇
4 ◇ (2)	4 ♠ (3)
5 ♣ (4)	5 ♡ (5)
6 ◇	Pass

(1) A 3 ◇ bid promises five diamonds
(2) TAB
(3) Minimum length headed by a top honor (ace, king or queen)
(4) CAB
(5) Second round control

3. Challenge the Champs, 1973.

Opener	Responder
♠ A K 9 7 3	♠ J 10 8 6
♡ K 8	♡ 6
◇ 8 5	◇ A Q 10 9 2
♣ A K Q J	♣ 10 9 3

1 NT	2 ◇ (1)
2 ♠	4 ♡ (2)
4 ♠	Pass

(1) Another queen would qualify this hand for a 2 ♡ response
(2) Splinter; heart shortage
(3) Too much duplication, partner probably lacks two Controls
   (See Advanced 1 NT Sequences)

One pair, using a club system, got to the dangerously high contract of 5♠.

4. Mexican Trials, 1980.

Opener	*Responder*
Sol	George
Dubson	Rosenkranz

♠ A K J 7 5	♠ Q 9
♡ A 5 3	♡ J 8 4
◇ A	◇ 7 5 3
♣ A Q 5 4	♣ K J 10 8 6

1 NT	2 ◇
2 ♠	3 ♣ (1)
4 ♣ (2)	4 ♡ (3)
4 ♠ (4)	4 NT (5)
5 ♠ (6)	6 ◇ (7)
7 ♣ (8)	Pass

(1) Five or more clubs — 2 NT is available
(2) TAB
(3) Minimum length with one high honor
(4) CAB. The raise committed the contract to clubs
(5) No control (as expected)
(6) Repeat CAB — asking for third round control
(7) Third step = the queen
(8) This cold grand slam was missed at the other table

5. European Championships. France vs. Italy, 1981.

Opener	Responder
♠ Q J 9 5	♠ 10
♡ A	♡ Q 8 7 2
◇ A K 10 2	◇ J 9 8 7 6
♣ A K 8 2	♣ Q J 5

1 NT	2 ◇
2 ♠	3 ◇ (1)
4 ♠ (2)	5 ♣ (3)
6 ◇	Pass

(1) Five or more diamonds
(2) CAB in spades. If he wants to play 4 ♠, he bids 3 ♠ followed by 4 ♠.
(3) Second round control

6. Challenge the Champs, 1977.

Opener	Responder
♠ A 3	♠ K Q J 5 4
♡ A	♡ Q 7 6 3
◇ A K 7 5 4 2	◇ Q J
♣ A 8 7 5	♣ J 2

1 NT	2 ◇
3 ◇ (1)	3 ♠
4 ♣ (2)	4 ◇ (3)
4 NT (4)	5 ◇ (5)
5 ♠ (6)	6 ♡ (7)
7 ♣ (8)	7 ♠ (9)
Pass	

(1) Six or more diamonds
(2) Natural. Opener has an excellent hand (nine Controls, four Losers) which he shows by going beyond 3 NT.
(3) Preference
(4) TAB
(5) Minimum length with one top honor

(6) CAB
(7) Fourth step = KQ
(8) "Pick the grand slam."
(9) Excellent spades

The challengers failed to bid even a small slam!

7. Mexico, 1982.

Opener	*Responder*
George	Sol
Rosenkranz	Dubson

♠ J 7 4 2	♠ K 8 5 3
♡ A K J 10 4	♡ 9 8
◇ A K 3	◇ Q 10 9 6
♣ A	♣ Q J 10

1 NT	2 ◇
2 ♡	2 ♠
3 ♠ (1)	4 ♣ (2)
4 ♠ (3)	Pass

(1) TAB
(2) Minimum length with one high honor
(3) Too many trump losers. Opener hoped for ♠ KQxxx.

8. Mexican Team Trials, 1980.

Opener	*Responder*
Sol	George
Dubson	Rosenkranz

♠ 9	♠ Q J 6
♡ K J 7 5 3	♡ A 2
◇ A K 5 2	◇ Q J 10 9 7 4
♣ A K J	♣ Q 3

1 NT	2 ♡
3 ♡ (1)	4 ◇ (2)
6 ◇ (3)	Pass

(1) Five or more hearts.
(2) Five or more diamonds. Responder shows extra values when he bypasses 3 NT.
(3) A major suit ace is missing

9. Bermuda Bowl. U. S. vs. Sweden, 1953.

Opener	*Responder*
♠ A 3	♠ Q 10 9
♡ A 3	♡ K 10 8
◇ A K J 6 3 2	◇ 10 7 5
♣ Q 9 4	♣ A 10 7 6

1 NT	2 ♠
3 ◇	3 NT (1)
Pass (2)	

(1) No good fit; no four-card major. With a minimum (three Cover Cards and nothing extra), caution is indicated.
(2) Five Losers opposite three Cover Cards implies no slam

Sweden lost an important swing by going one down in 6 ◇. The U. S. pair played 3 NT.

10. Challenge the Champs, 1981.

Opener	Responder
♠ K J 6	♠ Q 5
♡ A Q J 9 6 2	♡ K 10 8 3
◇ A K 7 3	◇ J 8 5 4
♣ —	♣ A 9 2

1 NT	2 ♠
3 ♡	4 ♡ (1)
4 ♠ (2)	4 NT (3)
5 ♡ (4)	Pass

(1) Balanced minimum raise: only three Cover Cards — the ace, king and queen
(2) CAB — Slam is possible opposite the right cards
(3) No spade control
(4) "Too bad. Your club ace is wasted."

Both pairs reached the inferior slam contract.

11. International Popular Bridge Monthly Bidding Contest, 1980.

Opener	Responder
♠ A J	♠ K Q 8 4
♡ 9	♡ K 4 3
◇ Q J 9 6	◇ K 10 7 4 3
♣ A K Q J 9 8	♣ 7

1 NT	2 ♠
3 ♣ (1)	3 ◇ (2)
4 ♡ (3)	4 NT (4)
5 ◇ (5)	Pass

(1) Five or more clubs
(2) Four or more diamonds
(3) CAB in hearts; agreeing diamonds
(4) Second step = second round control
(5) "We are off two Key Cards. I was hoping you did not have the king of hearts."

12. Challenge the Champs, 1973.

Responder	Opener
♠ K 5	♠ A Q J 10 9
♡ A 3	♡ K Q J 8 4
◊ Q 10 7 5 3	◊ A 8 4
♣ J 9 4 2	♣ —
Pass	1 NT
2 ♠	4 ◊ (1)
4 ♠ (2)	Pass

(1) 5-5-3-0; (diamond fragment); four Losers
(2) Sign-off. It is tempting to bid on but the lack of good fit and fillers indicate caution.

George Rosenkranz partnered with Miguel Reygadas, as well as opponents Alan Sontag and Peter Weichsel, stopped at 4 ♠.

13. Bermuda Bowl. U. S. vs. Italy, 1966.

Opener	Responder
♠ A Q J 10 7	♠ K 4
♡ A Q 10 4 3	♡ K J 9 6
◊ A J 8	◊ K Q 10 9 3
♣ —	♣ 8 2
1 NT	2 ♠
4 ◊ (1)	7 ♡ (2)
Pass	

(1) 5-5-3-0; four Losers
(2) Four Cover Cards

The North American pair reached 6 ♠ after a 2 ♣ opening. Hearts were never mentioned. The Roman bidders reached 7 ♡ after an auction that included three asking bids and five rounds of bidding.

14. Mexican Knockout Teams.

Opener	Responder
Fernando	George
Diez Barroso	Rosenkranz
♠ A Q 10 3 2	♠ K 6 5 4
♡ A 8	♡ K 3 2
◊ K 10	◊ A 9 6 5 3
♣ A K 6 4	♣ 7
1 NT	2 NT (1)
3 ♠ (2)	5 ♣ (3)
7 ♠ (4)	Pass

(1) Four Controls
(2) Five or more spades
(3) Splinter with four or more trumps
(4) "I can count 13 tricks!"

The other table arrived at 6 ♠ .

15. Bermuda Bowl. U. S. vs. Sweden, 1953.

Opener	Responder
♠ K Q J 10 3	♠ A 9 7 2
♡ J 5	♡ A 8
◊ A Q 8 4	◊ K 9 2
♣ A K	♣ 10 8 7 3
1 NT	3 ♣ (1)
3 ♠	4 ♠ (2)
5 ◊ (3)	5 ♠ (4)
6 ♠ (5)	Pass

(1) Five Controls
(2) Balanced minimum raise. With extra values responder could use the "Romex Raise."
(3) CAB
(4) Second round control. Not a singleton — responder didn't

splinter

(5) There is probably a heart loser

The absence of a Romex Raise helped in the evaluation to avoid the bad grand slam. The Swedish pair at the other table stopped in 4♠.

16. Mexican Team Trials, 1978.

Opener George Rosenkranz	Responder Sol Dubson
♠ Q J 4 2	♠ A K 5
♡ A K Q	♡ J 5 2
◇ A Q 10 9 8	◇ 2
♣ 10	♣ A K Q J 9 8

1 NT	3 ◇ (1)
3 ♠ (2)	4 ♣ (3)
4 ◇ (4)	5 ♣ (5)
5 ◇ (6)	7 ♣
Pass	

(1) The rare response showing six Controls. It creates a slam force.
(2) More economical to show the spades first
(3) Five card or longer suit. With only four-card suits responder would "temporize" with 3 NT.
(4) Natural, at least four cards
(5) Good suit, at least six cards in length
(6) Confirming a fifth diamond

By now you should be well equipped to handle the overwhelming majority of hands after a Dynamic 1 NT opening. Occasionally you will encounter some situations that require inventiveness, imagination, or at worst a guess. However, many of these problems can be solved with some of the tools described in the advanced section.

Bidding to the optimum spot without interference is nowadays a rare pleasure. However, after a strong Dynamic 1 NT opening (or a 2♣ opening) the opponents have to come in at the more dangerous two-level.

For the moment, here is my suggestion:

IF OPPONENTS INTERFERE AFTER THE 1 NT OPENING, USE THE SAME FAMILIAR METHODS YOU ARE ALREADY EMPLOYING TO COUNTER INTERFERENCE AFTER THE GAME FORCING 2♣ OPENING BID.

In the forthcoming chapters we will offer two approaches:

A simple method and a more advanced treatment to satisfy all tastes.

Chapter 4

THE REST OF THE STRUCTURE

Some of the hallmarks of Romex are that the system is adaptable, natural and easy to learn. To play Romex all you really need to use is:

> The Dynamic 1 NT opening on hands of approximately 18-21 HCP
> A 2♣ opening as a game force OR as a strong balanced hand

The other strong openings of 2♢ and 2 NT fill in the structure very nicely. (See Chapter 21 Strong Balanced Opening in Part 3).

The approach to other openings — one of a suit and pre-empts — can be anything the reader chooses. Of course, I don't leave it at th t; I will present my preferred methods. These recommendations have been developed over many years and have stood the test of time, so I urge the reader to give them a try.

Following is a very brief outline of the other openings in the system. All these openings are covered in detail in the following chapters.

Opening Bids

Opening	Meaning
1♣ or 1♢	Three-card or longer suit; usually 12-18 HCP
1♡ or 1♠	Five-card or longer suit; usually 12-18 HCP
2♡ or 2♠	"Sound" weak two-bids: a good six-card suit with 7-12 HCP
3♣ or 3♢	"Solid suit": a seven-card suit headed by the AKQ or AKJ, with at most a queen outside
3♡ or 3♠	Standard preempt according to the Rule of 500 (Two and Three): seven losers if not vulnerable; six losers if vulnerable
3 NT	A hand worth a four-level preempt in either minor
4♣ or 4♢	A very sound opening of four of a major (4♣ = hearts; 4♢ = spades). Known as "NAMYATS " (Stayman spelled backwards.)
4♡ or 4♠	Normal preemptive opening
4 NT	Ultra-sound opening of five of either minor: Two or three losers
5♣ or 5♢	Normal preemptive opening

PART 2

Chapter 5

ADVANCED TOOLS

Distributional Descriptions

One of the cornerstones of modern scientific bidding is showing important distributional features. This is often done by conventional means when a fit is found. An example is the "splinter" raise where a player shows a fit and shortness in a particular side suit. The object of all such conventional sequences is to judge the quality of the fit (or to put it negatively, the extent of "duplication of values.")

Romex uses the standard splinter bid as well as more specialized tools: Asking Bids, other types of shortness-showing bids and relays that can determine partner's exact distribution.

The technique of distributional description used in relay methods is well illustrated in the chapter on the "Maxi-Raise" of an opening bid. The "Inquirer" initiates the Maxi-Raise to establish the trump suit and set up a game forcing (slam probe) situation. From there he asks his partner ("Scanner") to scan his hand and tell about his features — distribution and useful cards.

The relay process is described in detail in Chapter 18 "Relays." For now, we are concerned only with the method "Scanner" uses to describe his distribution. It follows this pattern:

1. Scanner shows his long suit(s). This is almost always done with natural bids.
2. Scanner clarifies his exact pattern. In some cases only a close approximation of the pattern can be given. Two features are clarified:
   a) The nature of the length in the long suit(s):
   The length of the long suit in a one-suiter
   The length of both suits in a two-suiter

b) The length of the "remainders." The remainders are the suits other than the long suit(s).

Artificial step responses are used to clarify Scanner's distribution. The scheme used to clarify the long suit(s) distribution is usually simple, though it varies depending on the context.

Remainders are always shown numerically. This is a "code" that allows Scanner and Inquirer to know what's going on in any relay auction. It works like this:

The Numerical Principle

Make a number out of the length of the "remainders." Higher ranking suits always come first.

Examples:

Remainders		*Remainders*		*Remainders*	
♠ Axxxx		♠ Axxxx		♠ Axxxx	
♡ Axx	3	♡ Ax	2	♡ Axx	3
◇ Kxx	3	◇ Kxx	3	◇ Kx	2
♣ Kx	2	♣ Kxx	3	♣ Kxx	3
= 332		= 233		= 323	

The remainders are shown in ascending numerical order. In the case of five spades with 3-3-2 in the side suits:

First step   = 233 (5-2-3-3)
Second step = 323 (5-3-2-3)
Third step   = 332 (5-3-3-2)

Note that shortness in a higher ranking suit is shown with a lower step response than shortness in a lower ranking suit. This makes for easier memorization — encoding and decoding the distributional message that Scanner transmits.

One more example:

Scanner has shown five spades, four hearts and has denied

holding a 5-4-4-0 or a 5-4-0-4 pattern. The remainder is shown as follows:

	♢	♣	Corresponding number
First step	= 1	— 3	13
Second step	= 2	— 2	22
Third step	= 3	— 1	31

Some step(s) may be eliminated if the preceding bidding makes a particular shape impossible. If in the above example Scanner had promised a short suit somewhere, the steps would be:

	♢	♣	Corresponding number
First step	= 1	— 3	13
Second step	= 3	— 1	31

One fact remains constant: the "Numeric Principle" — lower numbered remainders are shown by lower steps — is always applied to whatever shapes are still possible for the bidding to date.

Special Raises after a 1 NT or 2♣ Opening

1. The Romex Raise of 4 NT

The "Romex Raise" of 4 NT is designed to handle a difficult problem that arises after a 1 NT or 2♣ opening. The situation is as follows:

The bidding is forced to game; slam is possible

There is no agreed trump suit

A player has an unusually good hand in support of partner's last bid suit, but cannot raise below the game level

Example:

1 NT — 2♠
3♡ — ???

♠ K x x x   ♡ Q x x x   ◇ A Q x x   ♣ x x

4♡ would be non-forcing
A new suit would be natural
5♡ or 6♡ would be a "shot in the dark"

The Romex solution to this problem is to use a jump to 4 NT to show:

1. A fit for the last bid suit
2. Extra values (more potential Cover Cards than promised.)
3. No singleton in an unbid suit — with a singleton or void, make a splinter bid

The example hand above is perfect for the Romex Raise. It has an excellent fit, and two extra potential Cover Cards — the queen of diamonds and the doubleton club.

Another sequence:

2♣ — 2♡
2♠ — 3♣
3♠ — 4 NT = Romex raise: spade fit

Opener can employ the Romex Raise also:

1 NT — 2♡
3◇ — 3♠
4 NT = Romex Raise: spade fit.

Bidding after a Romex 4 NT Raise follows the pattern of the auction that preceded it:

1. If the weak hand made the Romex Raise, a new suit by opener is CAB. The auction continues with CAB and

TAB.

2. If opener bid 4 NT, it is TAB. Subsequent new suit bids are CAB.

2. The Impossible Fourth Suit Raise

The essence of this extremely valuable adjunct, which occurs frequently after Romex 1 NT and 2♣ openings, was suggested by George and Roni Abrahamsohn of Toronto.

If opener and responder have bid three suits, the bid of the fourth suit is artificial, agreeing the third suit. This convention applies only after a 1 NT or 2♣ opening bid.

The purpose of the bid is the same as the Romex 4 NT Raise, and it is handled in much the same way:

1. By responder, the Fourth Suit Raise promises four or more Cover Cards. Opener can employ CAB by bidding a new suit or TAB by bidding notrump at the cheapest level.
2. By opener, the Fourth Suit Raise is TAB. New suit follow-ups are CAB.

Example:

♠ xx	1 NT — 2♡	
♡ KQxx	2♣ — 3♣	
◇ xx	3♡ — 4◇	= The Fourth Suit Raise:
♣ KJ10xx		balanced heart raise with an extra potential Cover Card (the spade doubleton)

With length in the fourth suit, a player must make another bid.

The Grand Slam Force

The Grand Slam Force, once a valuable bidding tool, is rarely needed in Romex: Key Card Blackwood and TAB serve the same purpose, more effectively and at a lower level. However the Grand Slam Force is useful when:

1. TAB is not available
2. The "Inquirer" has a void, rendering Key Card Blackwood ineffective.

5 NT is available as a Grand Slam Force if:
1. It is bid with a jump, and
2. No other conventional slam sequence is in effect — Cue-bidding or CAB

When spades are trump the Romex responses to 5 NT describe the trump holding exactly:

5 NT—	First step	= 6♣	= The ace or king of trump
	Second step	= 6♢	= Queen of trump
	Third step	= 6♡	= No top honor; minimum length
	Fourth step	= 6♠	= No top honor; extra length
	Fifth step	= 6 NT	= Two top honors; minimum length
	Sixth step	= 7♣	= Two top honors; extra length

Over a first or second step response, Inquirer can relay to ask for extra trump:

— 5 NT (1)	(1) Grand Slam Force
6♣ (2) — 6♢ (3)	(2) Ace or king of trump
6♡ (4)	(3) Extra length?
6♠ (5)	(4) No extra length
	(5) Extra length

Problem: What if spades aren't trumps? How does "Replier" give the desired information at a safe level?

Romex offers the following solution, adopting a method suggested by Tommy Sanders and Lou Bluhm:

The Romex Grand Slam Force

Romex replaces the standard treatments of the Grand Slam Force where only 5 NT is used as the Grand Slam Force with the use of the jump to the five-level in the suit that is "one above" the trump suit — this becomes the Grand Slam Force. This allows all the steps to be used with full effectiveness.

Example:

    1 ♡ — 2 ◇
    2 ♡ — 5 ♠ = Romex Grand Slam Force for hearts

Some examples:

1.

Opener	Responder
♠ Q	♠ A K x
♡ K Q J x x x	♡ —
◇ 10	◇ A K Q x
♣ A x x x x	♣ K 10 x x x x

1 ♡	2 ♣
3 ♣	5 ◇ (1)
5 ♡ (2)	5 ♠ (3)
6 ♣ (4)	7 ♣ (5)
Pass	

(1) Romex Grand Slam Force (Key Card Blackwood with a void is useless and 5 NT does not solve your problem!)
(2) First step = One top honor
(3) Extra length?
(4) Second step = Yes
(5) Great!

2.

Opener	Responder
♠ J 10 x x x	♠ A K Q
♡ x x	♡ A x x
♢ A Q x	♢ K 10 9 x x x x
♣ A Q x	♣ —

1♠	2♢
3♢	5♡ (1)
6♡ (2)	7♢
Pass	

(1) Romex Grand Slam Force
(2) Fifth step = Two of the top three honors; no extra length

CONFIT

CONFIT is a specialized Romex slam tool. It is used to determine slam prospects in a number of sequences where two balanced hands face each other.

A successful slam contract with two balanced hands normally requires approximately 33 combined HCP. However, this is only a rough guide as these two example hands illustrate:

1.

Opener	Responder
♠ A Q x	♠ K J x
♡ K x x x	♡ A Q J x
♢ Q J x	♢ A x x
♣ K x x	♣ Q J 10

2.

Opener	Responder
♠ K J x x	♠ Q x x
♡ A x x	♡ K x
♢ K x	♢ A x x x
♣ K J 10 x	♣ A Q 9 x

In Example 1 there is virtually no play for any slam in spite of the 33 HCP. There are only 30 HCP in Example 2, yet 6♣ is, for all practical purposes, a laydown (not 6 NT, however).

What is the lesson of these hands? They illustrate that there are three basic ingredients of a successful slam with two balanced hands:

1. <u>Enough power (HCP).</u> 30 HCP will be the absolute minimum requirement. In most cases 31 HCP or more will be needed, unless the fit is ideal as in Example 2.
2. <u>Adequate Controls.</u> The minimum requirements:
   At least 10 Controls for a small slam
   All 12 Controls for a grand slam
3. <u>A good fit.</u> If the power isn't overwhelming a good trump fit will be required. A good trump fit would be:
   At least eight combined trumps with no more than one loser.

Counting the "power" — the combined HCP — is simply a matter of addition.

Checking the adequacy of CONtrols and FIT is what CONFIT (CONtrols-FIT) is all about.

Initiating CONFIT

CONFIT is used when opener shows a strong balanced hand. It can be used after a 1 NT, 2♣, 2◇ or 2 NT opening bid or after the opener jumps to 2 NT when opener has bid one of a suit and responder has bid one of a suit. The CONFIT convention is initiated by responder's 4♣ bid, in certain sequences.

The 4♣ bid:

Announces	*Requests Information About*
Slam interest and	Opener's number of controls
A balanced hand	and
	Opener's long suit(s)

In this way responder hopes to discover, simultaneously, whether opener's hand is suitable in fit and controls.

Responses to CONFIT

Opener's responses to CONFIT are tailor-made to fit the specific situation at hand:

> Controls are always shown relative to expected number of controls (See Appendix A). Opener always gives new information about his distribution. The 4♣ CONFIT bid is often made after responder has used "Romex Stayman" — a bid of 3♣ on the previous round. In such a case opener adds to the information he has already supplied.

Example sequences:

Sequence A

1 NT (1) — 2♠ (2)
2 NT (3) — 3♣ (4)
3 NT (5) — 4♣ (6)

4 ◊   = 4-4-2-3 with six Controls — the expected number
4 ♡   = 4-4-3-2 with six Controls — the expected number
4 ♠   = 4-4-2-3 with seven Controls — one more than expected
4 NT = 4-4-3-2 with seven Controls — one more than expected
5 ♣   = 4-4-2-3 with eight Controls — two more than expected
5 ◊   = 4-4-3-2 with eight Controls — two more than expected

Sequence B

1 NT (1) — 2♠ (2)
2 NT (3) — 3♣ (4)
3 ◊ (7)   — 4♣ (6)

4 ◊   = A four or five-card diamond suit with six Controls — the expected number
4 ♡   = A four or five-card club suit with six Controls — the expected number
4 ♠   = No minor; 4-3-3-3 with six Controls — the expected number

4 NT = Both minors; 2-3-4-4 or 3-2-4-4 with six Controls — the expected number

5♣ = A four or five-card diamond suit with seven Controls — one more than expected

5◇ = A four or five-card club suit with seven Controls — one more than expected

5♡ = No minor; 4-3-3-3 with seven Controls — one more than expected

5♠ = Both minors; 2-3-4-4 or 3-2-4-4 with seven Controls — one more than expected

5 NT = A four or five-card diamond suit with eight Controls — two more than expected

6♣ = A four or five-card club suit with eight Controls — two more than expected

6◇ = No minor; 4-3-3-3 with eight Controls — two more than expected

6♡ = Both minors; 2-3-4-4 or 3-2-4-4 with eight Controls — two more than expected

(1) Dynamic 1 NT Opening
(2) Three Controls with at least three potential Cover Cards
(3) 19-20 HCP; balanced
(4) Romex Stayman (a Stayman-like relay that will be explained later)
(5) 4-4 in the majors
(6) CONFIT
(7) Fewer than four hearts; fewer than five spades

In both sequences opener gives his response artificially. There are more steps in Sequence B because opener has not defined his hand as precisely as in Sequence A. The artificial steps follow these principles:

1. There is one step for each basic type that opener can have on the auction. When opener's shape is quite limited, as in A, he can show his exact pattern over CONFIT.

2. The steps are based on "The Numeric Principle" (Sequence A) or "as natural as possible" (Sequence B).
3. The steps are arranged in "tiers":
    1. The lowest tier shows the expected number of Controls (or rarely, one less)
    2. Each additional tier shows one additional control

It is not important for the reader to fully understand these sequences at this point, just the principles involved. They will be covered again in great detail in the Chapter "Strong Balanced Hands."

Subsequent Bidding

Responder will have very precise information at this point:

1. Opener's HCP within one HCP
2. Opener's exact number of Controls
3. Opener's exact shape, or very nearly

He will often be able to place the contract at this point:
    A jump to slam is a signoff
    4 NT is a signoff attempt (opener may overrule in rare cases with a maximum and good Controls)

If responder desires to cooperate further, he has several choices:

1. Bid a new suit that could logically be natural, i.e., a possible five-card suit or a suit in which opener may have four cards. New suit bids are always forcing, and opener replies in the most appropriate and natural way.
2. Bid 5 NT or raise opener's suit to the five-level. This is a strong invitation to slam, asking opener to look at intermediates, etc., to decide whether to bid on.
3. Bid a new suit at the six-level without jumping. Assuming responder could have five cards in that suit, it is natural and asking for a choice of that suit or 6 NT.

If responder makes an "impossible" bid in a new suit — one that can't be natural — it has a conventional meaning, such as asking for a Spiral Cue Bid starting with the queen of the agreed suit. This will be explained and illustrated in the Chapter on "Strong Balanced Hands."

Here's an example that offers a taste of things to come.

Opener	Responder
♠ A K Q J	♠ x x x x
♡ A K 10 x	♡ Q x x x
◊ A K Q	◊ x x
♣ x x	♣ A x x
2 NT (1)	3 ♣ (2)
3 NT (3)	4 ♣ (4)
4 ♡ (5)	5 ♡ (6)
6 ♡ (7)	Pass

(1) 25-26 HCP; balanced (rarely 29-30 HCP)
(2) Romex Stayman
(3) 4-4 in the majors
(4) CONFIT
(5) Second step = exactly 4-4-3-2 with the expected nine Controls
(6) It is nice that opener has three diamonds and two clubs rather than vice-versa. However, there are still some holes to fill. Opener could have ♠ AKxx ♡ AKJx ◊ AKQ ♣ Jx in which case slam would be hopeless.
(7) With a maximum, good trumps, and honors in his long suits, opener has an easy acceptance.

Chapter 6

THE DYNAMIC NOTRUMP: ADVANCED SEQUENCES AND HIGHER RESPONSES

Picture Bids

In the first part of this book we have seen the responses up to 3 ♢ and the follow-up after a Romex 1 NT opening bid.

Higher responses, starting with 3 ♡ to 4 ♠ are "picture bids." They occur relatively seldom, show precise distributions and controls — but are forcing to game.

Picture Bids		
Minor Two-Suiter Pattern Bids	3♡ = 2-2-4-5; six or more HCP; 0-2 Controls; a maximum of Qx in a major; at least one top honor in a minor	
	3♠ = 2-2-5-4; six or more HCP; 0-2 Controls; a maximum of Qx in a major; at least one top honor in a minor	
One-Suiter Pattern Bids	3NT = AKQxxxx or longer in a minor	No side
	4♣ = AKQxxxx in hearts	ace
	4♢ = AKQxxxx in spades	or
	4♡ or 4♠ = Seven or eight-card major — KQxxxxx(x)	king

The 3♡ and 3♠ Responses

Limited minor two-suiters of 6-10 HCP opposite strong hands with concentration of values in the minors are notoriously difficult to describe. After showing the longer minor the weak hand is generally faced with the dilemma of whether to go past 3 NT to show the shorter minor.

Romex has put the relatively idle responses of 3♡ and 3♠ to work to describe minor two-suiters with 2-2-4-5 distributions, no ace, no control card in the majors and at most two Controls in the minors. Jx or Qx in the majors is admissible.

In most cases opener can immediately place the final contract or he can investigate responder's minor suit holdings by using CAB. Responses to this specialized CAB are in four steps:

First step   = the jack
Second step = the queen
Third step   = the king
Fourth step = the KQ

Some examples:

1.

Opener	Responder
♠ A K Q x x	♠ x x
♡ A K Q x	♡ x x
◇ 10 x	◇ Q J x x
♣ x x	♣ K Q x x x

1 NT	3♡ (1)
3 NT (2)	Pass

(1) The picture bid to show 2-2-4-5 with concentration in the minors

(2) Probably the same number of tricks at spades or notrump. Two aces are missing. 4♠ will go down on a 4-2 trump break.

2. Mexican Nationals, 1982.

Opener	Responder
George	Eddie
Rosenkranz	Wold

♠ 10 4	♠ J 2
♡ A K J 6 4	♡ 8 7
◇ A 9	◇ K J 8 7 6
♣ A K 6 4	♣ Q J 9 2

1 NT	3 ♣ (1)	(Double)
5 ♣ (2)	Pass	

(1) 2-2-5-4

(2) A great contract. 4♡ is also sound and could be bid by opener.

The 3 NT Response

The opener generally closes the bidding. Once in a blue moon opener won't be able to tell which solid minor responder holds, or he is interested in responder's exact distribution. When this happens, opener bids 4♣ and the follow-up proceeds:

First step	= Long diamonds. Opener can now relay by bidding 4♡ to get the same four-step response listed below.
Second step	= Long clubs. I am balanced.
Third step	= Long clubs; singleton in the highest side suit (spades)
Fourth step	= Long clubs; singleton in the middle side suit (hearts)
Fifth step	= Long clubs; singleton in the lowest side suit (diamonds)

Opener may relay for responder's distribution and extra length.

The next relay asks responder for extra length:

1 NT	— 3 NT	(1)	Long clubs; singleton or void in
4♣	— 4♠ (1)		spades
5◇ (2)	— 5♡ (3)	(2)	How many clubs?
	— 5♠ (4)	(3)	Seven clubs
	— Etc. (5)	(4)	Eight clubs
		(5)	Etc.

Examples:

1. Challenge the Champs, 1977.

Opener	*Responder*
♠ A K 3	♠ 5
♡ A K 8 7 6 4	♡ 5 2
◇ 8	◇ A K Q 10 7 5 3
♣ K 10 9	♣ Q J 5

1 NT	3 NT (1)
6◇ (2)	Pass

(1) Solid seven-card or longer minor
(2) At matchpoints I would ask for extra length to explore the possibility of playing 6 NT.

The defending champions missed the slam.

2.

Opener	*Responder*
♠ A K Q J x	♠ x x
♡ x x x x	♡ x
◇ A K Q	◇ x x x
♣ x	♣ A K Q x x x x

1 NT	3 NT
4♣ (1)	4 NT (2)
6♣ (3)	Pass

(1) Tell me more

(2) Fourth step = Long clubs; middle shortage (hearts)

(3) If you had bid anything else we would have stopped at 5♣.

3.

Opener	Responder
♠ Q J x x x	♠ x
♡ x	♡ A K Q x x x x
◇ A K J	◇ x x x
♣ A K Q x	♣ x x

1 NT	4♣ (1)
4◇ (2)	4♠ (3)
6♡	Pass

(1) Seven-card or longer solid major

(2) Distribution?

(3) Second step = high singleton (spades)

Following is a discussion of a number of useful refinements and extensions of the concepts already described in the first part of this book.[1]

1 NT — 2♣ Sequences

In the auction

1 NT — 2♣	or	1 NT — 2♣
2◇ — 2♡		2◇ — 2♠
2♠		3♡

opener's last bid describes a strong raise of responder's major with four Losers and not more than three quick losers. Responder can give a good description of his hand with the following responses:

1. Three of responder's original major is a signoff
2. Four of responder's original major shows one Cover Card

---

[1] Your author is indebted to George and Roni Abrahamsohn who have contributed many useful ideas to Romex auctions that start with a Dynamic 1 NT opening.

3. Step Responses
    1. The first step shows a shortage in the high side suit and one Cover Card
    2. The second step shows a shortage in the middle side suit and one Cover Card
    3. The third step shows a shortage in the low side suit and one Cover Card
4. The cheapest notrump bid always shows a balanced hand including two Cover Cards.

Examples:

1. Texas Bridge Bidding Contest, 1960.

Opener	*Responder*
♠ A K Q 4	♠ J 10 6 5
♡ A J 8 7 6	♡ 3
◇ A K 2	◇ 10 5 4 3
♣ 4	♣ 10 9 8 2

1 NT	2 ♣ (1)
2 ◇ (2)	2 ♠ (3)
3 ♡ (4)	4 ♠ (5)
Pass (6)	

(1) Less than 6 HCP.
(2) Do you have a four-card or longer major?
(3) Yes, spades.
(4) The other major is used for the strong raise with four Losers (but not four quick losers)
(5) The singleton heart should be a working Cover Card, but no other Cover Card
(6) In 1960 both competing pairs, which included George Rosenkranz and Dr. L. N. Leishman, missed the game and played in a heart partial. Today Romex would reach 4 ♠ easily.

2. Vanderbilt, 1978.

Responder	*Opener*
George	Eddie
Rosenkranz	Wold

♠ 10 9 7 6 2	♠ A K 8 3
♡ 3	♡ A J 7 4 2
◇ K 10 7 4	◇ A Q 9 6
♣ J 6 2	♣ —

Pass	1 NT
2 ♣	2 ◇
2 ♠	3 ♡ (1)
4 ♣ (2)	4 ◇ (3)
4 ♠ (4)	4 NT (5)
5 ♡ (6)	6 ♠ (7)
Pass	

(1) Strong spade raise with four Losers
(2) First step (3 ♠ and 3 NT are not steps) = one Cover Card and shortage in the highest side suit
(3) CAB. (Responder may have useless club values.)
(4) Second step = second round control. Here the king, as responder has already shown heart shortage.
(5) TAB
(6) Third step = one extra trump; no top honor
(7) An excellent slam. One World Championship pair lingered in 1 ♡ ! Romex makes it easy!

The next two examples show how the bids of 4 ♣ , 4 ◇ and 4 ♡ can be put to use to describe major two-suiters of 4-5, 5-4 or 5-5 distribution after 1 NT — 2 ♣ /2 ◇ .

3. Mexican Team Trials, 1975.

Responder Sol Dubson	*Opener* George Rosenkranz
♠ Q 10 9 7 3	♠ K J 8 4
♡ J 10 3 2	♡ —
◇ 8 4	◇ A K J
♣ 7 6	♣ A K J 10 8 2
Pass	1 NT (1)
2 ♣	2 ◇ (2)
4 ◇ (3)	5 ♠ (4)
6 ♠ (5)	Pass

(1) Nearly a 2 ♣ opening
(2) Asking for a four-card major
(3) Five spades and four hearts. 4 ♣ would show five hearts and four spades.
(4) Do you have good spades?
(5) Yes!

4. Mexican Nationals. Mixed Pairs, 1978.

Opener Edith Rosenkranz	*Responder* George Rosenkranz
♠ A Q 7 4 3	♠ K J 10 8 6
♡ Q	♡ J 9 6 5 4
◇ A K 6 2	◇ 3
♣ A Q 8	♣ 10 9
1 NT	2 ♣
2 ◇	4 ♡ (1)
5 ♠ (2)	6 ♠ (3)
Pass	

(1) 5-5 in the majors; two Cover Cards
(2) I need good trumps

101

(3) You won't be disappointed. In spite of a trump lead, 6♠ was made for a top as hearts divided 4-3.

1 NT — 2 ◊ Sequences

As the 2 ◊ response includes a very large number of hands which do not qualify for a control-showing response some further differentiation is necessary. Thus a splinter bid after an original 2 ◊ response shows a good trump fit with at least four-card support and two, three or four Controls, but denies three Cover Cards in aces, kings and queens.

Opener will generally know where responder's Key Cards are located as he has so few of them. If opener does need further definition of responder's Controls he has CAB and TAB available.

Examples:

1. Challenge, the Champs, 1975.

Opener	Responder
♠ K J	♠ A Q 9 6 5 2
♡ A K Q 10 7 3	♡ J 8 4 2
◊ J 10 6 4	◊ —
♣ A	♣ 10 4 2
1 NT	2 ◊
2 ♡	4 ◊ (1)
4 ♠ (2)	5 ◊ (3)
6 ◊ (4)	6 ♠ (5)
7 ♡	Pass

(1) Splinter bid with four-card support, one or two Controls and two Cover Cards (in high cards)
(2) CAB
(3) Third step = the ace
(4) For his positive response responder must have a black queen and the ace already shown. How short are you in diamonds?
(5) Second step = a void

The challengers stopped at 6♡. Notice that opener did not show an ACOL Two-Bid because of his four-card diamond side suit.

2.

Opener	Responder
♠ x	♠ A J x x x
♡ K Q J x x	♡ A x x x
◇ A K Q J	◇ x x x
♣ A J x	♣ x

1 NT	2 ◇ (1)
2 ♡	4 ♣ (2)
4 ♠ (3)	5 ◇ (4)
5 NT (5)	6 ♣ (6)
7 ♡	Pass

(1) In spite of four Controls the hand lacks a third Cover Card
(2) Splinter bid showing at least four hearts, a singleton or void in clubs
(3) CAB
(4) Third step = the ace
(5) Grand Slam Force
(6) First step = ♡A or ♡K
   Responder could have held

   ♠ A Q x x x
   ♡ x x x x x
   ◇ x x x
   ♣ —

With fewer than two Controls responder is not allowed to splinter. With fewer than two Controls but enough extra values to hope for slam — one Control, several queens and usually a short suit — he gives a single raise. This is in line with the Principle of Fast Arrival and shows slam interest. Compare this with the double raise which denies slam interest.

Example:

Opener	Responder
♠ A 7 5 2	♠ J
♡ A K Q 8 4	♡ 10 9 7 6 5 2
◇ A J	◇ K Q 10 6
♣ A 8	♣ Q 4

1 NT	2 ◇
2 ♡	3 ♡ (1)
3 ♠ (2)	4 ♣ (3)
4 ◇ (4)	5 ◇ (5)
6 ◇ (6)	7 ♡ (7)
Pass	

(1) Excellent raise with lots of extra values
(2) CAB
(3) Second step = second round control: the king or a singleton
(4) Second CAB
(5) Fifth step = king and queen in this situation as responder cannot have an ace. The modified responses are:
   First step   = no control
   Second step = third round control: a doubleton
   Third step   = third round control: the queen
   Fourth step = second round control
   Fifth step   = king and queen
(6) Opener cannot use the 5 NT bid which would be the Grand Slam Force so he bids the suit below the agreed trump suit as a Baron Grand Slam try asking for extra length
(7) Yes, I have an extra trump.

Responding to 1 NT with minor two-suiters of 5-5-2-1 distribution and fewer than two Controls is facilitated by the following treatment:
The sequence

    1 NT   — 2 ◇
    2 ♡ or 2 ♠ — 3 NT

pictures this hand. A bid of four of a minor at this point sets the trump suit and asks for an exact description of responder's distribution. He shows his residue as follows:

First step   = higher singleton, i.e., 1-2-5-5
Second step = lower singleton, i.e., 2-1-5-5

Example:

Opener	Responder
♠ A x x x	♠ x
♡ A x	♡ x x
♢ A J x x x	♢ K Q x x x
♣ A K	♣ Q 10 x x x

1 NT	2 ♢
2 ♠	3 NT (1)
4 ♢ (2)	4 ♡ (3)
5 NT (4)	6 NT (5)
7 ♢ (6)	Pass

(1) Picture bid showing 5-5 in the minors and 2-1 in the majors
(2) Asking for an exact description
(3) First step = higher singleton
(4) Grand Slam Force in diamonds
(5) Fifth step = king and queen; no extra length
(6) I don't even need the queen of clubs because the fifth club should set up for a heart discard.

Balanced hands with four Controls after a 2 ♢ response pose a different problem. The following hands present a solution.

1. Olympiad. Australia vs. The Netherlands, 1968.

Opener	Responder
♠ A 10 7	♠ J 9 6 3 2
♡ K 10 4	♡ A 6 5
◇ A K Q J 10 2	◇ 9 8
♣ 4	♣ A 6 2

1 NT	2 ◇
3 ◇ (1)	3 ♠ (2)
4 ♠ (3)	5 ♣ (4)
6 ◇ (5)	Pass (6)

(1) Long diamonds — probably six cards
(2) Natural
(3) Spade support
(4) AN EXCEPTION: When responder has four Controls he bids again. With an ace outside of the trump suit, he cue bids. With the ace or king of trump, he bids 4 NT.
(5) Stressing the solid diamonds but offering a choice of contracts
(6) OK with me.

Australia missed this excellent slam.

2. Detroit, 1981.

Opener	Responder
H.	George
Jacobs	Abrahamsohn

♠ A 9 7 5 2	♠ K Q J 10 6 4
♡ A J 10 3	♡ 8 7
◇ A K J 10	◇ 6 5
♣ —	♣ 8 4 2

1 NT	2 ◇
2 ♠	3 ♠ (1)
3 NT (2)	5 ◇ (3)
6 ◇ (4)	6 ♠ (5)
Pass	

(1) Encouraging raise — Principle of Fast Arrival
(2) TAB
(3) Seventh step. Since the scale ends with the sixth step which shows two top honors with extra length you can imagine how good my suit is!
(4) CAB in diamonds. Responder has denied two Controls by his 2 ◇ bid and has shown a balanced hand with the king and queen of spades. Therefore this bid must ask about third round diamond control.
(5) Doubleton diamond, but not the queen

The important use of strong raises by responder and opener respectively can be seen in action in the next two examples.

Examples:

1. Mexican Nationals. Open Pairs, 1981.

Opener	*Responder*
Eddie	George
Wold	Rosenkranz

♠ A 8 6 4	♠ K Q J 2
♡ 3	♡ 9 7 4
◊ A K	◊ Q J 10 6
♣ A K 9 8 6 5	♣ Q J

1 NT	2 ◊ (1)
3 ♣ (2)	3 ◊ (3)
3 ♠ (4)	4 ♡ (5)
4 NT (6)	5 NT (7)
6 ♠	Pass

(1) Game force
(2) Natural, almost always six or more clubs
(3) Natural
(4) Showing six clubs and four spades
(5) The Impossible Fourth Suit Raise = strong spade raise with four potential Cover Cards
(6) TAB in spades
(7) Fifth step = two top honors; no extra length

2. Mexican Nationals. Swiss Teams, 1980.

Opener	*Responder*
George	Eddie
Rosenkranz	Wold

♠ A K J 8 7	♠ 9 3
♡ A J 6 4	♡ 2
◇ —	◇ Q J 8 6
♣ A Q 9 6	♣ K J 10 5 4 3

1 NT	2 ◇ (1)
2 ♠ (2)	3 ♣ (2)
3 ♡ (2)	4 ♣ (3)
4 ◇ (4)	4 ♠ (5)
5 ♡ (6)	5 NT (7)
7 ♣ (8)	Pass

(1) Game force
(2) Natural
(3) Six or more clubs
(4) The Impossible Fourth Suit Response. Opener cannot have four diamonds as he would have bid 3 ◇, not 3 ♡, over 3 ♣ if he had had four diamonds. Ergo, it is treated as TAB, accepting responder's suit (clubs).
(5) Second step = no extra length plus either the ace or the king. Thus responder shows either the Axxxxx or the Kxxxxx as he has already promised a six card suit by his third rebid.
(6) CAB in hearts
(7) Second round control — must be a singleton in view of the 2 ◇ response and the previous bidding.
(8) On a club lead we hope to establish a fifth spade. Otherwise a crossruff is available for 13 tricks.

1 NT — 2 ♡ and 1 NT — 2 ♠ Sequences

After a 2 ♡ or 2 ♠ response the bidding rapidly reaches high levels. To counteract the loss of bidding space after these responses, opener can profitably describe major two-suiters as follows:

1 NT — 2 ♡
3 ♠ = four spades and five hearts
3 NT = four spades and six hearts

1 NT — 2 ♠
3 NT = five or six spades and four hearts

These bids can save responder a guess about whether to bid beyond 3 NT.

Notice that 1 NT — 2 ♡
            3 ♡
denies four spades, therefore 1 NT — 2 ♡
                               3 ♡ — 3 ♠

promises five spades.

After 3 ♠ :
3 NT = to play
4 ♣ = transfer to 4 ♦
4 ♦ = transfer to 4 ♡
4 ♡ or 4 ♠ = to play; no extra values

1.

Opener	Responder
♠ K J x x	♠ Q 10 x x
♡ A K J x x	♡ x x
♦ A x	♦ Q J x x
♣ K x	♣ A Q x
1 NT	2 ♡
3 ♠ (1)	4 ♣ (2)
4 ♦ (3)	4 ♠ (4)
4 NT (5)	5 ♦ (6)
6 ♠	Pass

(1) 4-5 in the majors
(2) Transfer

110

(3) Forced
(4) Spade raise; slam invitation. The choice of 4♣ as a transfer (instead of 4♢) shows good clubs.
(5) TAB
(6) Second step = four to an honor

Notice that responder could have bid 4♢ instead of 4♣ and followed up the same way. This option sometimes permits responder to show honor concentration when spades is the agreed trump suit.

2.

Opener	Responder
♠ A J x x	♠ K Q x
♡ K Q J x x x	♡ x x x
♢ A x	♢ K Q x x
♣ A	♣ Q J x

1 NT	2 ♡
3 NT (1)	4 ♣ (2)
4 ♢ (3)	4 ♡ (4)
4 ♠ (5)	5 ♡ (6)
6 ♡	Pass

(1) Four spades and six hearts
(2) Transfer to 4 ♢
(3) Forced
(4) Heart fit with at least four probable Cover Cards. With only three Cover Cards responder should bid 4 ♡ instead of 4 ♣.
(5) CAB in spades
(6) Fourth step = king and queen

3.

Opener	Responder
♠ A K J x x	♠ Q x x x
♡ A Q x x	♡ K x
◇ x	◇ A Q x x
♣ K Q x	♣ x x x

1 NT	2 ♠
3 NT (1)	4 ◇ (2)
4 ♡ (3)	4 ♠ (4)
5 ♡ (5)	5 NT (6)
6 ♠ (7)	Pass

(1) Five spades and four hearts
(2) Transfer to 4 ♡
(3) Forced
(4) Spade raise with extra values
(5) CAB in hearts
(6) Second round control
(7) Responder is very likely to hold the spade queen for his strong bidding.

4.

Opener	Responder
♠ A Q x x x	♠ J x x
♡ K Q x x	♡ x x
◇ A x	◇ K Q x
♣ K x	♣ A Q J x x

1 NT	2 ♠
3 NT (1)	4 ♣ (2)
4 ◇ (3)	4 NT (4)
Pass (5)	

(1) Five spades and four hearts
(2) Transfer to diamonds
(3) Forced
(4) Balanced hand with the bid minor at least five cards long
(5) Slam seems unlikely

But with:

5.

Opener	Responder
♠ A Q x x x	♠ x x
♡ K Q x x	♡ x
◇ A x	◇ K Q J x x x
♣ K x	♣ A Q J x

The slam is reached from the right side.

1 NT	2 ♠
3 NT	4 ♣
4 ◇	5 ◇ (1)
6 ◇ (2)	

(1) Unbalanced slam try with six or more good diamonds
(2) Should be a reasonable slam.

6. Challenge the Champs, 1976.

Opener	Responder
♠ K 10 4	♠ A Q 7 6 3
♡ A K 8 6 3	♡ Q 7 4
◇ A	◇ 9 6 3
♣ A 8 4 2	♣ 6 5

1 NT	2 ♡
3 ♡ (1)	3 ♠ (2)
4 ♠ (3)	5 ♡ (4)
6 ♠ (5)	Pass

(1) At least five hearts but not four spades as he did not bid 3 ♠
(2) At least five spades
(3) With five Losers, opener makes a nonforcing natural bid showing three-card trump support
(4) Responder's 2 ♡ bid has promised a minimum of three Cover Cards in high honors in addition to his two Controls. With the doubleton club in addition, he makes a further slam try by showing his heart support.
(5) Opener now can easly bid the slam

7. Olympiad U. S. vs. Italy, 1964.

Opener	Responder
♠ A 7 2	♠ 10 8 6 5
♡ A J 9 8 7 5	♡ K Q 3
◇ A 2	◇ K
♣ A K	♣ Q 10 9 6 5

1 NT	2 ♡
3 ♡ (1)	4 ♣ (2)
4 ♡ (3)	4 ♠ (4)
4 NT (5)	5 NT (6)
7 ♡ (7)	Pass

(1) Five or more hearts; fewer than four spades
(2) Good five-card or longer club suit, better than a minimum hand. A singleton king should not be shown as a splinter since opener will expect the control card to be elsewhere. (But a singleton ace is all right since it does not represent wasted values.)
(3) Six-card heart suit confirmed. Opener is not afraid of a pass at this stage. Responder has a good hand — he bypassed 3 NT — and will make another bid.
(4) A very unusual bid. Responder has denied five spades and a 4-4 fit is impossible. The bid should show a good heart fit and an abundance of extra values equivalent to a Romex Raise of 5 NT, saving bidding space.
(5) TAB
(6) Two top honors; no extra length
(7) The U. S. pair missed the grand slam, losing 13 IMPs.

8. British Bridge Magazine, 1965.

Opener	*Responder*
Fernando	George
Diez Barroso	Rosenkranz

♠ A Q J 4	♠ K 8 7 5
♡ J 8 7 6 5	♡ Q 10 3 2
◊ A 4	◊ K Q J 2
♣ A K	♣ 8

1 NT	2 ♡
3 ♠ (1)	5 ♣ (2)
5 ♡ (3)	Pass

(1) Five hearts and four spades
(2) Fit in at least one of the majors; splinter with at least four-card support
(3) Sign-off in the lower ranking suit in view of the strong duplication.

Three Controls are missing in the three highest ranking suits.

In the bidding contest every pair reached the unmakeable heart slam.

The most difficult problem in slam bidding is illustrated in the following example. After a 5-3 or 5-4 fit is established most systems have no machinery to find the productive 4-4 fit which yields the additional trick required. The Search for the 4-4 fit Convention (to be discussed later) is the ideal tool!

9.

Opener	Responder
♠ A K 10 8 3	♠ Q J 9 4
♡ A K	♡ J 5 4
◇ 7 6	◇ A 9
♣ A K J 5	♣ Q 10 6 4

1 NT	2 ♡
2 ♠	3 ♠
3 NT (1)	4 ◇ (2)
4 ♡ (3)	4 ♠ (4)
5 ♣ (5)	5 ♠ (6)
5 NT (7)	6 ♣ (8)
6 ♡ (9)	6 ♠ (10)
7 ♣ (11)	Pass (12)

(1) TAB

(2) Four spades to an honor

(3) CAB in the cheapest suit to prepare for a second CAB

(4) No control . . . as expected

(5) Responder has the ace of diamonds and at least one more queen. Second CAB.

(6) Third step = club queen

(7) The Search for the 4-4 Fit Convention. Show me a four-card suit!

(8) Clubs

(9) Second CAB in hearts. If you have the queen of hearts we are cold for 7 NT. If you have two small hearts we can make 6 NT.

(10) No third round heart control

(11) Then you have a doubleton diamond and the grand slam must be cold if we play clubs.

(12) Wow!

10.

Opener	Responder A	Responder B
♠ K Q x x	♠ A x x	♠ A x x
♡ A J 9 x x	♡ K Q x x	♡ K Q x x
◇ A J	◇ Q x x x	◇ x x x x
♣ A J	♣ x x	♣ x x
	1 NT — 2♠	1 NT — 2♠
	3♡ — 4 NT (1)	3♡ — 4♡ (3)
	6♡ (2) — Pass	Pass (4)

(1) Romex raise: hearts agreed as trumps; at least four possible Cover cards; no short suit
(2) Even if responder has the "wrong" cards there will be a play for the slam
(3) Weak raise: only three Cover Cards
(4) No slam interest with five Losers

11. Challenge the Champs, 1972.

Opener	Responder
♠ A K Q 7 4 2	♠ 10 9 8
♡ A	♡ 10 9
◇ A 10 8 5	◇ K Q J 4
♣ 7 4	♣ A J 6 2
1 NT	2♠
3♠	4♣ (1)
4◇ (2)	4♡ (3)
4 NT (4)	5 NT (5)
7◇ (6)	Pass

(1) Responder, with extra values (a doubleton and two jacks) and spade support, shows his suit beyond the 3 NT level
(2) Opener elects to show his four-card side suit
(3) The Impossible Fourth Suit Bid showing a strong raise in opener's last bid suit
(4) TAB
(5) Fifth step = two top honors; no extra length
(6) Barring a 4-0 spade break or a 5-0 diamond break the grand slam is cold.

12. Masters Pairs. England, 1950.

Opener	Responder
♠ A Q	♠ 3
♡ A Q 10 7 5	♡ K J 4 2
◊ A K 6 4 2	◊ Q 9 8
♣ 10	♣ A J 8 6 4
1 NT	2 ♠
3 ♡	4 ♠ (1)
5 ♣ (2)	5 ♠ (3)
6 ◊ (4)	6 NT (5)
7 ♡ (6)	Pass

(1) Splinter raise with four-card support and three Cover Cards
(2) Opener now knows responder has four hearts and either the king of clubs or the king of hearts but not both. He knows he will bid at least 6♡ but to bid seven with confidence he has to discover which king responder has and whether he has third-round control in diamonds. This takes some planning. If responder has ace and king of clubs six is the limit. Hence CAB in clubs.
(3) Third step = first round control but no king
(4) Good news. Second CAB in diamonds.
(5) Third step = the queen
(6) The confident final bid

In a star-filled field only one pair, Ian Mac Leod and Maurice Harrison-Gray, reached the top contract.

13. Olympiad. U. S. vs. Italy, 1964.

Opener	Responder
♠ 7 5	♠ A Q J 9 6
♡ A K 9 8 7 6	♡ Q 5 4
◇ A	◇ K 7 5 3
♣ A K 8 3	♣ J

Opener	Responder
1 NT	2♠
3♡	3♠
4♣ (1)	5♡ (2)
6♣ (3)	6♡ (4)
7♡	Pass

(1) Having a second suit, excellent controls, unbalanced distribution and only four Losers entitle opener to bid beyond 3 NT.
(2) Trump support, thus a better than minimum hand with good spades. Responder cannot splinter in opener's first bid suit.
(3) CAB
(4) Second round control of clubs. Opener knows it is a singleton.

The U. S. pair reached 7♡ for a gain of 10 IMPs.

It is always helpful to use imaginative bidding as shown in the next example from the 1981 Reisinger.

14.

Opener	Responder
Eddie	George
Wold	Rosenkranz

♠ Q J	♠ A K 9
♡ A 5	♡ 8 2
◇ A K Q	◇ 9 5 2
♣ A J 9 6 4 2	♣ K 10 8 7 5

1 NT	2 NT (1)
3 ♣	4 ♣ (2)
4 ♡ (3)	4 ♠ (4)
5 ♠ (5)	5 NT (6)
7 NT (7)	Pass

(1) Four Controls; three or more Cover Cards
(2) Balanced raise with at least four-card trump support
(3) CAB in the suit where Eddie wants his partner not to have a control
(4) No control
(5) Second CAB
(6) No third round control
(7) Then you have at least three spades and I can count 13 tricks.

15. Challenge the Champs, 1971.

Opener	Responder
♠ 10	♠ A Q 5 4
♡ A K 6 5 2	♡ 9
◇ K Q J 7	◇ A 9 6 4
♣ A K J	♣ Q 10 4 2

1 NT	2 NT
3 ♡ (1)	3 ♠ (2)
4 ◇ (3)	5 ♣ (4)
7 ◇ (5)	Pass

(1) Five-card heart suit; may have four spades
(2) Checking for a 4-4 spade fit
(3) Four or five diamonds; denying four spades or four clubs
(4) The fourth suit showing a strong raise of opener's last bid suit. Cannot be natural as opener has already denied holding four clubs. As 2 NT promised at least three Cover Cards, a strong raise must have at least four Cover Cards.
(5) The four Cover Cards must consist of the two missing aces plus two out of three of the missing queens. Either the heart or club queen will give us an adequate play for the grand slam.

Chapter 7

THE 2 ♣ OPENING BID

The 2 ♣ opening in Romex is similar to the 2 ♣ opening used by most "standard" systems. The major difference is that our 2 ♣ is stronger — 1 NT or 2 ◇ are available on intermediate-type strong hands. This allows us to play the 2 ♣ opening as game-forcing, except

2 ♣ — 2 ◇
2 NT = 21-22 HCP.

The game-forcing aspect of this opening allows opener to develop his hand slowly, providing maximum room for game and slam exploration.

Requirements for the 2 ♣ Opening

There are two hand types that open 2 ♣ :

1. BALANCED. 21-22 HCP. Usually such a hand will have seven or more Controls. Developments after opener shows this hand (via a 2 NT rebid) are discussed in the Chapter "Strong Balanced Hands."
2. UNBALANCED, three or fewer Losers. The hand must have at least five Controls (very rare exception) and normally at least 22 HCP. The HCP requirement may be shaded if opener has powerful playing strength.

Examples:

A. ♠ A K 10 x x x x
   ♡ A K
   ◇ A K J
   ♣ x
   Bid 2 ♣ — three Losers; 22 HCP; nine Controls

B. ♠ x x
   ♡ A K Q J x
   ◇ A
   ♣ A K J x x
   Bid 2♣ — three Losers; 22 HCP; eight Controls

C. ♠ A K 10 5
   ♡ A K 7 6 4 2
   ◇ A Q 6
   ♣ —
   Bid 2♣ — three Losers; 20 HCP; eight Controls

The HCP requirement may be relaxed considerably with freak hands that include powerful suits.

D. ♠ A K
   ♡ Q J 10 9 x x x x
   ◇ A K x
   ♣ —
   Bid 2♣ — three Losers;
           17 HCP;
           six Controls

E. ♠ —
   ♡ K Q J x x x
   ◇ A
   ♣ K Q J 10 x x
   Bid 2♣ — two Losers;
           16 HCP;
           four Controls

Responses to 2♣

The responses to 2♣, and subsequent development of the auction, are very similar to those used after a Dynamic 1 NT opening. The responses are based on responder's Control count, with responses of 3♡ and higher being used as "Pattern Bids." These Pattern Bids, devised to handle troublesome responding hands, are exactly the same as those after the 1 NT opening. (See Chapter "Advanced Sequences After The Dynamic 1 NT Opening.")

There are two minor differences between responses to 2♣ and 1 NT:

   1. There is no Cover Card requirement attached to the responses.

2. There are two steps to show four Controls: 2 NT, which shows four Controls in at least three suits; and 3♣ which shows four Controls in only two suits.

This is the scheme of responses:

	2♦	= No more than one Control
	2♡	= Two Controls
	2♠	= Three Controls
Control	2 NT	= Four Controls in three or four suits (four kings or two kings and an ace in a third suit)
Responses		
	3♣	= Four Controls in two suits (two aces or ace-king in one suit and king in another suit)
	3♦	= Five or more Controls

	3♡	= 2-2-4-5; six or more HCP; no more than one Control; at least one top honor in a minor; majors tend to be weak (Qx at best)
Pattern		
Bids		
Minor		
Two-Suiter	3♠	= 2-2-5-4; six or more HCP; no more than one Control; at least one top honor in a minor; majors tend to be weak (Qx at best)

	3 NT	= AKQxxxx in a minor; no side ace or king
Pattern	4♣	= AKQxxx(x) in hearts; no side ace or king
Bids	4♦	= AKQxxx(x) in spades; no side ace or king
One-Suiter	4♡ or 4♠	= seven or eight-card major; KJ10xxxx or better (but not solid)

Examples of responses to a 2♣ opening:

1.
♠ x x x
♡ x x x x
♢ J x x
♣ x x x

Bid 2♢

2.
♠ K Q J 10 x x
♡ x x x
♢ x x x
♣ x

Bid 2♢

3.
♠ K Q x
♡ Q J x
♢ Q J x
♣ Q J x x

Bid 2♢

4.
♠ A x x x
♡ x x x x
♢ x x x x
♣ x

Bid 2♡

5.
♠ J x x x
♡ K x x
♢ K x x
♣ K x x

Bid 2♠

6.
♠ A x x
♡ K x x x
♢ K x x
♣ x x x

Bid 2 NT

7.
♠ A K
♡ K x x x
♢ Q x x x
♣ x x x

Bid 3♣

8.
♠ K x x x
♡ A x x x
♢ A x x
♣ x x

Bid 3♢

9.
♠ J x
♡ x x
♢ K Q x x
♣ Q x x x x

Bid 3♡

10.
♠ Q x
♡ J x
♢ Q x x x x
♣ K J x x

Bid 3♣

11.
♠ x x
♡ x
♢ x x x
♣ A K Q J 10 x x

Bid 3 NT

12.
♠ x
♡ A K Q x x x x
♢ x x x
♣ x x

Bid 4♣

13.
♠ A K Q J 10 9
♡ x x
♢ x x
♣ J x x

Bid 4♢

14.
♠ x
♡ K Q x x x x x
♢ J x x
♣ x

Bid 4♡

Subsequent Bidding

The development of the bidding after the Control-showing responses is largely natural. As after a Dynamic 1 NT opening, Blackwood in any form or cue-bidding sequences cannot be bid after a 2♣ opening. All the principles described in the chapter on the Dynamic 1 NT can be applied to 2♣ sequences, with a few minor adjustments.

Suits are shown according to length (longest first); the higher of two five-card suits is mentioned first. Opener's first suit is assumed to be at least five cards long. Responder can name a good five-card or longer suit of his own, but he should strain to raise opener's suit (especially a major) when the choice of bids is close.

When a fit is found, the same Romex slam tools are available: Asking Bids; Splinter Bids; and The Grand Slam Force. Some specialized sequences are discussed in other chapters: Specific Card Asking Bids (SCAB) and Romex Raises. Specific Controls Asking Bids (SCAB) are used only after a 2♣ opening and a Control showing response, when opener has a powerful freak and wants to know what specific control cards responder has. Romex Raises are also used after a 1 NT opening.

Following are some 2♣ sequences not used in the Dynamic 1 NT structure:

1. If opener rebids 2♡ or 2♠, a second negative is used to further clarify a 2◇ response:

    2♣   — 2◇
    2♡ or 2♠ — 3♣ = Artificial second negative; no more than 3 HCP; no king
                 — Any other bid = Natural; at least 3 good HCP

    This convention is used because the 2◇ response has a wide range (in HCP).

2. Opener does not use 4 NT as a Romex Raise. His use of the Asking-Bids depends on the response.

a) 2 $\diamond$ and 2 $\heartsuit$ Responses

These responses do not guarantee values worthy of going beyond game. Thus, opener's jump to 4 NT is TAB in responder's suit with a simple raise to game being non-forcing.

Example:

    2 $\clubsuit$ — 2 $\heartsuit$
    2 $\spadesuit$ — 3 $\heartsuit$
    4 $\heartsuit$ = Natural and nonforcing
    4 NT = TAB in hearts

Of course <u>responder</u> can still use the Romex Raise. This would be a jump to 4 NT, but only if no cheaper forcing raise is available.

2 $\clubsuit$ — 2 $\heartsuit$
2 $\spadesuit$ — 3 $\spadesuit$ = Natural and forcing. Better hand than a 4 $\spadesuit$ bid.
    — 4 $\spadesuit$ = Non-forcing; minimum (Principle of Fast Arrival)
    — 4 $\clubsuit$, 4 $\diamond$, or 4 $\heartsuit$ = Splinter raise

2 $\clubsuit$ — 2 $\heartsuit$
3 $\heartsuit$ — 4 $\heartsuit$ = Non-forcing; minimum
    — 4 NT = Romex Raise; heart fit; extra values; no short suit
    — 4 $\spadesuit$, 5 $\clubsuit$ or 5 $\diamond$ = Splinter raise

b) 2 $\spadesuit$, 2 NT, 3 $\clubsuit$ and 3 $\diamond$ Responses

These responses show excellent slam potential, so opener's raise to game is forcing and treated as TAB:

```
2♣ — 2♠ (1)        (1) Three Controls
3♣ — 3♡            (2) TAB in hearts
4♡ (2)
```

3. Specialized rebids are used to facilitate discovery of a 4-4
   fit. Two patterns are particularly difficult for opener to
   show:

   Long diamonds with a four-card major, and

   Long major with four cards in the other major. This
   is not a problem when the response is 2♢ as opener
   can bid 2♡ or 2♠ and discover a fit in the other
   major at a low level.

Thus the meaning of opener's jump rebids depends on the
responses:

   a) After a 2♢ response.

Jumps show a four-card major and five or more diamonds. This is the schedule:

```
2♣ — 2♢
3♡   = Four hearts; at least five diamonds, not
       4-4-5-0 or 0-4-5-4
3♠   = Four spades; at least five diamonds; three
       hearts
3 NT = Four spades; at least five diamonds; fewer
       than three hearts; not 4-0-5-4
4♣   = 4-0-5-4: void in the "corresponding suit"
4♢   = 0-4-5-4: void in the "corresponding suit"
4♡   = 4-4-5-0: void in the "corresponding suit"
```

Hearts and clubs are corresponding suits. Spades and diamonds are corresponding suits.

Some specialized follow-ups are used:

2♣ —2◇
3♠ —4♣ = Artificial with interest in a heart slam
    —4◇ = Natural diamond raise
    —4♡ or 4♠ = Natural and non-forcing
    —4 NT = Romex Raise in spades
    —5♡ = Splinter raise of spades or diamonds (or both)

2♣ —2◇
3♡ —3♠ = Natural; at least five spades
    —4♣ = Natural: opener has not denied holding three clubs
    —4◇ or 4♡ = Natural raise. 4♡ is non-forcing.
    —4♠ or 5♣ = Splinter raise of hearts or diamonds (or both)
    —4 NT = Romex Raise of hearts

When opener shows a 4-4-5-0, 4-0-5-4 or 0-4-5-4 pattern responder can bid naturally or he can bid opener's void to ask how many of the nine Controls outside of the void suit are missing. Thus:

2♣ — 2◇
4♣ — 4♡
4♠ = At least three Controls are missing (i.e., six Controls)
4 NT = Two Controls are missing (i.e., seven Controls)
5♣ = One Control is missing (i.e., eight Controls)
5◇ = No Controls are missing (i.e., nine Controls)

   b) After a 2♡ or 2♠ response.

Opener can no longer rebid 2♡, so jumps are used to show a long major with four cards in the other major, just as after a 1 NT opening:

2♣ —2♡
3♠ = Four spades and five hearts
3 NT = Four spades and six or more hearts (forcing)

2♣ —2♠
3 NT = Five spades and four hearts

After natural sequences, (including Romex and fourth suit raises), CAB, TAB and splinter raises are used, just as after a Dynamic 1 NT opening.

Let's look at some "real hands" to illustrate the Romex 2♣ opening:

1. Grand National Teams, 1982.

Opener	Responder
♠ A Q J 10 5	♠ 6 3 2
♡ A	♡ Q 5 4 2
◊ K Q J 3	◊ 9 6 2
♣ K Q J	♣ 10 9 8

2♣ (1)	2◊ (2)
2♠ (3)	3♣ (4)
3◊ (5)	4♠ (6)
Pass	

(1) 23 HCP; six Controls: three Losers. A sound 2♣ opening.
(2) 0-1 Control
(3) Five or more spades; game force
(4) Artificial second negative; no more than 3 HCP
(5) Natural
(6) The jump is discouraging (Principle of Fast Arrival). With any help in spades or diamonds, responder would have bid 3♠.

2. Challenge the Champs, 1982.

Opener	Responder
♠ 7 2	♠ K Q J 10 9 6
♡ A K Q J 10 8	♡ 4
◇ A K 5	◇ 9 7 4
♣ A K	♣ 6 4 3
2♣	2◇ (1)
2♡ (2)	2♠ (2)
3♡ (3)	4♠ (4)
6♠ (5)	

(1) 0-1 Controls
(2) Five-card or longer suit
(3) Six card or longer suit
(4) Semi-solid suit; exactly six cards. With a seven-card suit headed by the KQ, responder would have bid 4♠ instead of 2◇.
(5) Better than the heart slam

3. Challenge the Champs, 1981.

Opener	Responder
♠ A	♠ J 7 6 5 4 2
♡ A K Q 4	♡ J 7 3
◇ A 7 3	◇ 8
♣ A K J 10 3	♣ Q 6 5
2♣	2◇
3♣ (1)	3♠ (2)
3 NT (3)	4♣ (4)
4◇ (5)	4♠ (6)
4 NT (7)	5◇ (8)
7♣ (9)	Pass

(1) Five or more clubs
(2) Five or more spades
(3) Non-forcing
(4) Club fit with extra values (Principle of Fast Arrival)

(5) CAB. With an agreed fit, a bid in a new suit by opener is CAB.

(6) Second step = Second round control

(7) TAB

(8) One top honor with minimum length

(9) In 1957 a British bridge magazine declared that this was an unbiddable grand slam.

4. Mexican Nationals. Swiss Teams, 1981.

Opener	Responder
♠ A K Q 8 6	♠ J
♡ A K 2	♡ J 8 7
◇ A	◇ Q J 10 5 4
♣ K J 9 6	♣ Q 10 5 2
2 ♣	2 ◇ (1)
2 ♠ (2)	3 ◇ (3)
4 ♣ (4)	4 ♡ (5)
4 NT (6)	5 ◇ (7)
6 ♣ (8)	Pass

(1) 0 or 1 Control

(2) Five or more spades

(3) Five or more diamonds; at least one king or 4 HCP (no second negative)

(4) Four or more clubs. A slight risk in bypassing 3 NT, but so little is needed for slam.

(5) The Fourth Suit Bid = Romex Raise: club fit; extra values. With xxxx in clubs instead of the Qxxx, responder would raise quietly to 5 ♣.

(6) TAB

(7) Minimum length (four cards) with one top honor

(8) Perfect!

5. Bermuda Bowl, 1962.

Opener	Responder
♠ A K Q 3	♠ 9
♡ A K 9	♡ Q J 7 4 3
◇ A K 9 6 2	◇ J 5
♣ 6	♣ K Q 7 5 4
2♣	2◇
3♠ (1)	4♣ (2)
6♡ (3)	Pass

(1) 4-3-5-1; possibly 4-3-6-0
(2) Artificial; heart fit and extra values. As opener is known to be short in clubs, 4♣ is actually a Romex Raise.
(3) Accepting with good controls. Responder must have the heart queen, though opener could bid 4 NT as TAB to make certain.

6. U. S. Team Trials, 1983.

Opener	Responder
George	Eddie
Rosenkranz	Wold
♠ A K 9 2	♠ J 10 8 7 3
♡ A Q	♡ 3 2
◇ A K J 10 8	◇ Q 7 3
♣ A 10	♣ Q 5 4
2♣	2◇
3 NT (1)	5♠ (2)
6♠ (3)	Pass

(1) Five or more diamonds; four spades; fewer than three hearts
(2) I have some extras for a spade slam. If you feel likewise, please bid a slam.
(3) An easy acceptance.

7.

Opener	Responder
♠ K Q J x	♠ x x x x
♡ —	♡ x x x x x
◊ A K J x x x	◊ Q x x
♣ K Q x	♣ x

2 ♣	2 ◊
3 NT (1)	5 ♣ (2)
5 ◊ (3)	Pass (4)

(1) Five or more diamonds, four spades; fewer than three hearts
(2) Fit in one or both suits; splinter
(3) Danger! Duplication. Opener bids the cheapest suit to sign-off, knowing responder can correct with a spade fit.
(4) Heart forces jeopardize a spade contract, so play in diamonds

With ♠ KQJx ♡ — ◊ AKJxxx ♣ AQx opener would bid 6 ◊ based on the same logic as above.

8. Challenge the Champs.

Opener	Responder
♠ A Q J 7	♠ 10 5
♡ —	♡ 10 8 6 3
◊ A Q 9 6 3	◊ 10 2
♣ A K 9 4	♣ Q J 10 7 2

2 ♣	2 ◊
4 ♣ (1)	4 ♡ (2)
4 NT (3)	6 ♣ (4)

(1) 4-0-5-4
(2) Asking for missing controls
(3) Second step = two controls missing, i.e. I have seven of the nine possible controls.
(4) Should be a good slam.

One world champion pair lingered at 1 ◊ .

9.

Opener	Responder
♠ A x	♠ Q J 10 9 x x
♡ A	♡ x x x x
◇ A K J x x x	◇ x x
♣ K Q x x	♣ x

2♣	2◇
3◇	3♠ (1)
4♣ (2)	4♠ (3)
Pass	

(1) Five or more spades
(2) Four or more clubs. Spades, clubs or diamonds should play better than notrump.
(3) The obvious bid

10. A terrible misfit from the 1977 Cavendish Invitational Pairs.

Opener	Responder
♠ A 9	♠ J 8 7 4 2
♡ A	♡ 10 8 5 3
◇ A K Q 6 2	◇ 9 5
♣ A K 7 5 2	♣ J 8

2♣	2◇
3◇	3♠ (1)
4♣ (2)	4◇ (3)
4♠ (4)	Pass

(1) Five or more spades
(2) Still with high hopes
(3) Preference
(4) Delayed raise. With a real diamond fit and extra values, responder will go on.

3 NT has the best chance, though no game makes on best defense (the diamonds were 5-1).

11. Challenge the Champs, 1972.

Opener	Responder
♠ A 2	♠ J 3
♡ K Q 8 4	♡ J 10
◇ A Q J 9 5	◇ K 10 4
♣ A K	♣ J 10 8 6 5 3

2♣	2◇
3♡ (1)	4◇ (2)
5◇ (3)	Pass

(1) Five or more diamonds and four hearts
(2) Natural. At least one Cover card; some extra values; no singleton. With no Cover Cards responder would sign-off at game (Principle of Fast Arrival).
(3) Too many controls are missing for slam.

The contenders got to 3 NT and 6♣ — both inferior contracts.

12. Mexican Nationals. Mixed Pairs, 1980.

Opener	Responder
Edith	George
Rosenkranz	Rosenkranz

♠ A	♠ Q J 6
♡ K 2	♡ 8 5 4 3
◇ A Q J 9 8 6	◇ K 10
♣ A Q 10 4	♣ K 9 3 2

2♣	2♡ (1)
3◇ (2)	4 NT (3)
5♣ (4)	6♣ (5)
Pass (6)	

(1) Two Controls
(2) Natural: six or more diamonds
(3) Natural: no five-card suit but extra values. Not a Romex Raise as a forcing 4 ◇ raise is available.
(4) Natural and forcing (opener passes 4 NT without interest).
(5) With two sure Cover Cards responder bids slam in the 4-4 fit. Note that 6 ◇ requires the ace of hearts to be onside, while 6 ♣ does not.

Finding a 4-4 Fit

One nagging problem in 2 ♣ systems is locating a 4-4 fit, particularly when opener shows a five-card suit and responder raises. The 4-4 fit frequently produces one or two extra tricks since opener's long suit may provide useful discards. Any available major suit fit will usually suffice at game level, but at the slam level, and especially at the grand slam level, the 4-4 fit is "magic."

Romex has found some solutions to this recurring problem. Two of these solutions have already been discussed:

1. After the auction
    2 ♣ — 2 ◇
   a 3 ♡ or 3 ♠ bid shows long diamonds and a four-card major.
2. After the auction
    2 ♣ — 2 ♡ or 2 ♠
   a 3 ♠ or 3 NT bid shows a long major and four cards in the other major.

Two further ideas to handle this problem:

1. When opener rebids 3 ♣, responder rebids as follows:

3 ♣ —3 ◇ = Interest in a four-card major OR a hand that wants to make a natural 3 NT bid

—3 ♡ or 3 ♠ = Natural: at least a five-card suit

—3 NT = Long diamonds

—4 ♣ = Good hand for clubs; usually no four-card major

—4 ◇, 4 ♡, or 4 ♠ = Splinter raise; no four-card major. A splinter raise can be given after bidding 3 ◇ if responder has a four-card major.

Example:

13.

Opener	Responder
♠ A Q x x	♠ K J x x
♡ K x x	♡ A x x x
◇ A	◇ x x
♣ A K Q J x	♣ x x x
2 ♣	2 ♠ (1)
3 ♣ (2)	3 ◇ (3)
3 ♠ (4)	4 ♠ (5)
4 NT (6)	5 ◇ (7)
5 ♡ (8)	6 ♣ (9)
6 ♡ (10)	6 ♠ (11)
7 ♠	Pass

(1) Three Controls
(2) Five or more clubs
(3) Artificial: asks opener to bid a four-card major if he has one
(4) Four spades
(5) Minimum raise
(6) TAB

(7) Minimum length, one top honor

(8) CAB

(9) Third step = the ace

(10) Second CAB to check for the queen

(11) First step = no third round control

2. The remaining problem hands are those with a long major suit and a lower-ranking four-card suit, and long diamonds with a four-card major after a response other than 2 ♢ .

The solution comes from an ingenious use of idle bids which we call The Search for the 4-4 Fit.

The Search for the 4-4 Fit

If opener, after finding a fit, makes an otherwise meaningless bid, he is asking responder to show a four-card suit. Hopefully a 4-4 fit will be discovered thereby.

Notes about The Search for the 4-4 Fit Convention:

1. "Meaningless" bids include:
> A jump in a new suit
> A second bid of 4 NT or 5 NT when the previous bid of 3 NT or 4 NT was TAB

2. Responder should not show a four-card suit unless it is headed by at least the ace, king or queen

---

More examples:

14. Mexican Nationals. Charity Pairs, 1981.

Opener	Responder
George	Edith
Rosenkranz	Rosenkranz

♠ A K J 8 4	♠ Q 7 2
♡ A K 9	♡ 10 6 5 4
◊ A	◊ 5 4
♣ A Q 9 7	♣ K J 3 2

2 ♣	2 ◊ (1)
2 ♠ (2)	3 ♠ (3)
3 NT (4)	4 ◊ (5)
5 ♣ (6)	5 ♡ (7)
5 NT (8)	6 ♣ (9)
6 ♡ (10)	6 ♠ (11)
7 ♣ (12)	Pass

(1) 0 or 1 Control
(2) Five or more spades
(3) Natural raise showing three or more spades and extra values (Principle of Fast Arrival)
(4) TAB
(5) Second step = minimum length and the ace, king or queen
(6) CAB
(7) Second step = second round control which must be the king as the 3 ♠ bid denied a singleton
(8) The search for the 4-4 Fit! A second bid in notrump.
(9) Four or more clubs headed by a top honor
(10) Second CAB in hearts
(11) No third round control
(12) The only grand that makes!

15.

Opener	Responder
♠ A Q J x x	♠ K x x x
♡ —	♡ x x
◊ A K x x	◊ x x x
♣ A Q J x	♣ K x x x

2 ♣	2 ♡ (1)
2 ♠	3 ♠ (2)
4 ♣ (3)	4 ♡ (4)
4 NT (5)	5 ♠ (6)
5 NT (7)	6 ♣ (8)
6 ◊ (9)	6 ♡ (10)
7 ♣ (11)	Pass

(1) Two Controls
(2) Balanced raise with extra values
(3) CAB
(4) Second step = the king
(5) TAB
(6) Fourth step = one top honor and extra length
(7) The Search for the 4-4 Fit — the second notrump bid.
(8) Four clubs including a top honor
(9) Second CAB in diamonds looking for third round control
(10) No third round control
(11) Had responder bid 6 ◊ instead of 6 ♣, 7 ◊ would have been the final contract.

16. International Popular Bridge Monthly Bidding Contest, 1981.

Opener	Responder
♠ A Q 8	♠ K J 10 7
♡ A J 5 4	♡ K 6
◊ —	◊ 10 8 7 3
♣ A K Q J 8 7	♣ 10 5 3
2 ♣	2 ♡
3 ♣	3 ◊ (1)
3 ♡ (2)	4 ♣ (3)
4 ◊ (4)	4 ♡ (5)
5 ♡ (6)	5 NT (7)
7 ♣ (8)	Pass

(1) Artificial: asking for a four-card major
(2) Four hearts
(3) Club fit; spade fit by inference. If he had no interest in either major he would have raised clubs directly rather than bid 3 ◊ .
(4) CAB. With a void it is often best to see if responder has wasted values in the suit.
(5) First step = No control
(6) Second CAB for third round heart control
(7) Second step = A doubleton
(8) Looks easy!

17. Mexican Trials, 1972.

Opener George Rosenkranz	*Responder* Miguel Reygadas
♠ A K J 4	♠ 2
♡ A Q J 10 2	♡ K 9 6 3
◊ A K Q J	◊ 8 5 4 2
♣ —	♣ K J 8 4

2♣	2♡
3♠ (1)	4♣ (2)
4◊ (3)	4♡ (4)
4♠ (5)	5♣ (6)
5 NT (7)	6♣ (8)
7♡ (9)	Pass

(1) Four spades and five hearts
(2) Transfer to 4◊, planning to show a good major suit raise. The fact that clubs are bid for the transfer indicates some club values.
(3) Forced
(4) Identifying the major
(5) CAB
(6) Second step = second round control
(7) Grand Slam Force
(8) First step = the ace or king
(9) Perfect! I don't even need to bid 6♠ to ask for extra trump length.

18. Mexican Nationals. Masters Pairs, 1975.

Opener	Responder
George	Sol
Rosenkranz	Dubson

♠ A Q 8 3 2	♠ K 5
♡ A 5	♡ 3 2
◇ A K J 7 5	◇ Q 10 6 4 3 2
♣ A	♣ K 8 3

2♣	2♡
2♠ (1)	3◇ (1)
4◇ (2)	5♣ (3)
5♠ (4)	6♣ (5)
7◇ (6)	Pass

(1) Natural: at least a five-card suit
(2) Raise = TAB
(3) Fourth step = one top honor with extra length
(4) CAB
(5) Second step = second round control
(6) If responder has a singleton spade he must have both the king of hearts and the king of clubs.

The Romex pair was the only pair in the field to bid 7 ◇ .

144

19. Mexican Trials, 1974.

Opener	Responder
George	Sol
Rosenkranz	Dubson

♠ A K 4 2	♠ J 9 6 3
♡ A	♡ K 8
◊ A Q 10 5 3 2	◊ K 9 4
♣ A 5	♣ K 8 4 2

2 ♣	2 ♠
3 ◊	4 ◊ (1)
4 ♠ (2)	4 NT (3)
5 ♣ (4)	5 ◊ (5)
5 ♡ (6)	5 NT (7)
6 ♠ (8)	6 NT (9)
Pass (10)	

(1) Raise without a singleton
(2) CAB. Opener knows responder has three kings. He needs third round spade control for the grand, so he arranges his CABS in the most economical manner.
(3) No spade control
(4) Second CAB
(5) No third round control
(6) Maybe here
(7) Second step = a doubleton
(8) Last chance for third round control in spades
(9) No!
(10) Oh well

20.

Opener	Responder
♠ K Q J x	♠ A x x x
♡ A K x	♡ x x x x
◇ K Q 10 9 x	◇ A J x
♣ A	♣ x x

2♣	3♣ (1)
3◇ (2)	4◇ (3)
5♠ (4)	6♠ (5)
7♠ (6)	Pass

(1) Four Controls in two suits
(2) Natural
(3) Balanced raise
(4) The unusual jump is The Search for The 4-4 Fit Convention showing four spades and asking responder to raise spades with four or to bid an outside four-card suit headed by an honor. If opener had had four hearts or four clubs he would have jumped to 5♡ or 6♣ instead of 5♠ to initiate the Search for the 4-4 Fit Convention.
(5) Four spades to an honor
(6) Heart discards on the diamonds must be available

21. Olympiad. U. S. vs. Australia, 1968.

Opener	Responder
♠ A K 10	♠ Q 5
♡ A K	♡ 6 5
◇ A K Q 9 8	◇ J 7 5 4 2
♣ K 7 4	♣ Q 10 3 2

2♣	3♠ (1)
6◇ (2)	Pass

(1) Pattern Bid = Exactly 2-2-5-4; 0 to 1 Control presumably; 6 or more HCP; and at least one king or queen in the minors
(2) Romex bidding is easy!

The U. S. stopped at 4 NT, making five. Australia reached the excellent diamond slam but went down following an inferior line of play.

22. European Championships. Hungary vs. Italy, 1981.

Opener	*Responder*
♠ A K Q J 6	♠ 7 2
♡ 4	♡ A K Q J 10 6
◇ K Q 10 9 8	◇ 4
♣ A 7	♣ J 5 3 2
2 ♣	4 ♣ (1)
6 ♡ (2)	Pass

(1) Six or more solid hearts; no side ace or king
(2) The ace of diamonds is missing, a small slam is the limit

A famous Italian pair lost 13 IMPs on this hand. They had a bidding misunderstanding and failed to bid the slam.

23. Challenge the Champs, 1976.

Opener	*Responder*
♠ A	♠ K J 10 9 7 6 3
♡ A Q 10 6	♡ 7 2
◇ A K J 8 4	◇ 6 3
♣ A K 10	♣ 6 5
2 ♣	4 ♠ (1)
4 NT (2)	5 ♣ (3)
5 ◇ (4)	5 ♡ (5)
6 ♠ (6)	Pass

(1) Seven-card spade suit; at least KJ10xxxx but not solid; no side ace or king
(2) Distribution ask
(3) First step = balanced
(4) Extended TAB in spades

147

(5) First step = minimum length; minimum honors

(6) Only one pair reached the spade slam

The same principles were used for these responses after a 1 NT opening. Refer to Chapter "Advanced 1 NT Sequences" for explanations and examples.

The Specific Control Asking Bids (SCAB)

The bidding of freak hands is always difficult. Following is a method to bid powerhouse freak hands that need only a few specific cards to make a small or grand slam.

The situation is as follows:

1. Opener has opened 2♣.
2. The response has been 2♡, 2♠ or 2 NT, i.e., a two level response showing two or more Controls.
3. Opener has a powerful freak with an independent suit. He must have no interest in playing in any suit other than his independent suit and he must be willing to forego natural bidding.
4. Opener is unconcerned with third round controls.

Opener employs The Specific Control Asking Bid (SCAB) by jumping to 4♣:

Opener	Responder
2♣	2♡, 2♠, or 2 NT
4♣	= SCAB asking responder to identify and locate his Controls.

Responder replies as follows:

    1. 4 ◇ = I have an ace
    2. With no ace:
        1. He bids his lower king with one or two kings
        2. He bids the suit where he lacks the king with three kings
        3. He bids 4 NT with all four kings

Recall that opener knows responder's exact number of controls so there will be no ambiguity when responder shows or denies a specific king. There are two situations where opener may want further clarification:

After a 4 ◇ bid by responder showing an ace, opener may bid 4 ♡ to ask responder to identify his ace. Responder bids the suit in which he has the ace. To show the ace of hearts, he bids 4 NT. for example:

Opener	Responder	Meaning
2 ♣	2 ♡	Two Controls
4 ♣	4 ◇	"I have an ace."
4 ♡		Where?
	4 ♠, 5 ♣ or 5 ◇	"I hold the ace of the bid suit."
	4 NT	"I hold the ace of hearts."

After responder has shown two kings, his bid indentifies the lower king. Opener bids the next step to ask responder to identify his other king. Responder bids the suit in which he has his other king or he bids 4 NT to show the king of the relay suit.

149

For example:

Opener	Responder	Meaning
2♣	2♡	Two Controls
4♣	4♠	Two kings; the spade king is the cheaper, i.e., no heart king
4 NT		Where is the other king?
	5♣ or 5♢	King of the bid suit

If the responder's first bid is at the three-level opener cannot use SCAB. If he wants to ask about specific controls, opener can use CAB. For example:

Opener	Responder
2♣	3♣
4♢, 4♡ or 4♠ = CAB	

Examples of SCAB in action:

1. Toronto, 1981.

Opener	Responder
George	Roni
Abrahamsohn	Abrahamsohn
♠ A K Q J 10 7 6 5	♠ 4 2
♡ K 4	♡ A 10 8 7
◇ A K Q	◇ 10 9 8
♣ —	♣ K 6 4 2
2♣	2♠ (1)
4♣ (2)	4◇ (3)
4♡ (4)	4 NT (5)
7♣ (6)	Pass

(1) Three Controls

(2) SCAB

(3) I do have an ace, i.e., my three controls consist of one ace and one king.

(4) Which ace do you have?

(5) The heart ace (the 4 NT bid shows the ace of the relay suit)

(6) Just what I need!

2. Toronto, 1981.

Opener	Responder
George	Roni
Abrahamsohn	Abrahamsohn

♠ A Q J 10 9 7 4	♠ K 8
♡ A Q	♡ K 10 6 4
◇ A Q 6	◇ K 7 4 2
♣ A	♣ 10 9 8

2 ♣	2 ♠ (1)
4 ♣ (2)	4 NT (3)
7 NT (4)	Pass

(1) Three Controls

(2) SCAB

(3) Denies an ace, i.e., responder's three controls consist of three kings. Cue-bidding the suit in which he lacks the king. As clubs was the relay suit, 4 NT shows that the club king is missing.

(4) I can count 13 tricks

3. Toronto, 1981.

Opener	Responder
Roni	George
Abrahamsohn	Abrahamsohn

♠ Q J 5	♠ K 10 9
♡ A K Q J 10 7 2	♡ 4 3
◇ A Q J	◇ K 8 5
♣ —	♣ Q 10 6 4 3

2 ♣	2 ♡ (1)
4 ♣ (2)	4 ♠ (3)
4 NT (4)	5 ◇ (5)
6 ♡ (6)	Pass

(1) Two Controls
(2) SCAB
(3) Denies an ace, i.e., responder's two controls are two kings. The king of spades is the cheaper king.
(4) Where is the other king?
(5) The king of diamonds
(6) We can make 6 ♡

4. Toronto, 1981.

Opener	Responder
George	Roni
Abrahamsohn	Abrahamsohn

♠ A Q J 10 8 7 6 3	♠ K 5
♡ A Q 7	♡ K 4
◇ 3	◇ K J 8 6 4
♣ A	♣ K 9 7 2

2 ♣	2 NT (1)
4 ♣ (2)	4 NT (3)
6 NT (4)	Pass

(1) Four Controls in three or four suits (four kings or one ace and two kings, each in different suits)
(2) SCAB
(3) Denies an ace. Therefore responder has four kings.
(4) I hope that the king of diamonds isn't a singleton!

5.

Opener	Responder
♠ A K Q J 8 7 5 4	♠ 2
♡ A Q J 2	♡ K 7 3
◊ —	◊ A 5 4
♣ 5	♣ A J 9 6 4 2

2 ♣	3 ◊ (1)
4 ♡ (2)	4 NT (3)
7 NT (4)	Pass

(1) Five or more Controls
(2) CAB in hearts. Remember that you can't use SCAB after a three-level response.
(3) Second round heart control. It must be the king as a singleton is not counted as a Control until a trump suit is agreed upon.
(4) Thanks!

Notice that in spite of the four-card side suit opener is not interested in a heart fit.

6. Life Master Men's Pairs. Dallas, 1971.

Opener	*Responder*
George	Dan
Rosenkranz	Morse

♠ 8	♠ A 6 5 2
♡ A K Q J 10 7 5 3 2	♡ 8
◊ —	◊ Q J 10
♣ A J 10	♣ Q 8 7 6 5

2♣		2♡	(1)
4♣	(2)	4◊	(3)
4♡	(4)	4♠	(5)
6♡	(6)	Pass	

(1) Two Controls
(2) SCAB
(3) One ace
(4) Which?
(5) The ace of spades
(6) There should be some play for 6 ♡

Chapter 8

HANDLING INTERFERENCE
OVER 1 NT and 2♣ OPENINGS

One of the major drawbacks to strong 1♣ systems is that they are vulnerable to preemptive bidding by the opponents. Romex, fortunately, is better able to handle opposition bidding because:

1. The openings are at a higher level, making competition more dangerous and, consequently, less frequent.
2. The variety of strong openings available to Romex players makes each such opening fairly well defined. Thus the opponents have less to gain by trying to confuse the issue with overcalls and preempts.
3. Romex players can further improve this skill in handling competitive sequences by using the simple but effective method outlined in this chapter.

The Opponents Overcall or Double the Strong Opening

The suggested responses are very simple:

**Responses After Competition Over a
1 NT or 2♣ Opening**

Pass = A weak hand
Any bid or a Double = An intermediate hand
A Cue-Bid or Redouble over a Double = A strong
    hand

You may choose your own definitions for a "weak," "intermediate" and "strong" responses if you wish. We have found these definitions useful:

Weak, Intermediate and Strong Hands by Responder		
Hand Quality	1 NT Opening	2♣ Opening
Weak	0-5 HCP	0-1 Control
Intermediate	6 or more HCP but not enough Controls or Cover Cards for a strong hand response	2 Controls
Strong	4 or more Controls AND 3 or more Cover Cards	3 or more Controls

With these definitions in mind, the following structure is recommended for further development after competition:

Responder Makes a Weak Response

Responder's weak responses are:

> Without competition — the first step, i.e., 2♣ after a 1 NT opening or 2◇ after a 2♣ opening.
> With competition — Pass. When responder passes, opener bids naturally.

After the auction

Opener	LHO	Responder	RHO
1 NT	Overcall	Pass	Pass
		or	
2♣	Overcall	Pass	Pass

A SUIT BID is natural and not forcing if the opening bid was 1 NT, or forcing to game if the opening bid was 2♣.

A NOTRUMP BID is natural showing the balanced hand type. A notrump rebid shows 19-20 HCP if the opening bid was 1 NT, or 21-22 HCP if the opening bid was 2♣.

A DOUBLE is for takeout. Responder may pass if he has a trump stack.

If the overcall comes after the negative response, opener's rebids show the same types of hands as if the overcall had been on his left and there had been two passes to him, i.e., double is for takeout, suit bids and notrump bids are natural.

For example, after the auction

Opener	LHO	Responder	RHO
1 NT	Pass	2♣	2♡

DOUBLE = Takeout
2 NT = 19-20 HCP
2♠, 3♣ or 3♢ = Natural and nonforcing

Examples:

1. Mexican Nationals, 1982.

Opener	Responder
George	Mauricio
Rosenkranz	Smid

♠ A K 7 6 4	♠ J 9 5
♡ A 10 9	♡ J 6 2
◇ A 7 2	◇ 10 9 8 4
♣ A 5	♣ K 6 3

1 NT (1)	2♣	Pass (2)	Pass
2♠ (3)	Pass	3♠ (4)	Pass
Pass (5)	Pass		

(1) Planning a 2 NT rebid
(2) 0-5 HCP
(3) Choosing the safe spade contract, in view of the overcall and weak response
(4) Raising with one probable Cover Card and some useful-looking intermediates

157

(5) Passing quickly with six Losers

2. U. S. Team Trials, 1969.
   Both Vulnerable

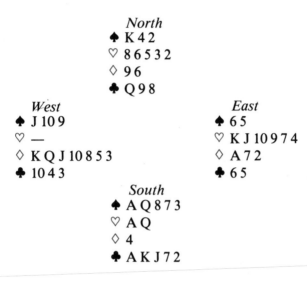

                        North
                        ♠ K 4 2
                        ♡ 8 6 5 3 2
                        ◊ 9 6
                        ♣ Q 9 8
        West   *East*
     ♠ J 10 9   ♠ 6 5
     ♡ —   ♡ K J 10 9 7 4
     ◊ K Q J 10 8 5 3   ◊ A 7 2
     ♣ 10 4 3   ♣ 6 5
                        South
                        ♠ A Q 8 7 3
                        ♡ A Q
                        ◊ 4
                        ♣ A K J 7 2

South	*West*	*North*	*East*
1 NT	3 ◊ (1)	Pass (2)	4 ◊ (3)
4 ♠ (4)	5 ◊ (5)	5 ♠ (6)	Pass
Pass (7)	Pass		

(1) A good bid at the vulnerability
(2) 0-5 HCP
(3) Furthering the preemption
(4) Opener takes a stab at the most likely game
(5) A risky bid, to be sure
(6) A tough choice. Perhaps a forcing pass is better here
(7) Too many possible losers to gamble on 6 ♠

Both teams reached the subpar slam and went down on a
diamond to the ace and a heart ruff.

3. Bermuda Bowl, 1953.

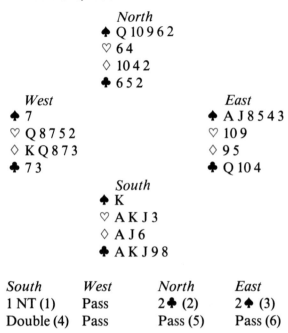

```
                        North
                        ♠ Q 10 9 6 2
                        ♡ 6 4
                        ◇ 10 4 2
                        ♣ 6 5 2
        West                            East
        ♠ 7                             ♠ A J 8 5 4 3
        ♡ Q 8 7 5 2                     ♡ 10 9
        ◇ K Q 8 7 3                     ◇ 9 5
        ♣ 7 3                           ♣ Q 10 4
                        South
                        ♠ K
                        ♡ A K J 3
                        ◇ A J 6
                        ♣ A K J 9 8
```

South	West	North	East
1 NT (1)	Pass	2♣ (2)	2♠ (3)
Double (4)	Pass	Pass (5)	Pass (6)

(1) In spite of 24 HCP there are five Losers
(2) 0-5 HCP
(3) A "naughty" bid
(4) Takeout
(5) I'm not taking this one out!
(6) Did I really enter this auction?

2♠ doubled was −700. At the other table 3 NT by North-South was set one trick.

Responder Makes an Intermediate Response

When the opponents intervene there is always the chance that the auction will quickly get to an uncomfortably high level. It is thus imperative for responder to tell about his strength/controls AND his distribution when he has an "intermediate" hand. Any intermediate strength-showing bid is forcing to

159

game.

Responder has three choices with an intermediate hand:

A. DOUBLE = a "card-showing" double, normally showing a balanced hand, although a 4-4-4-1 hand is also possible.

Responder should usually double rather than bid a five-card suit at the four or five-level.

The bidding follows the usual Romex path — natural bidding with CAB and TAB available to the opener.

Opener may pass the double with a suitable trump holding. Opener will tend to pass rather than bid his suit at the five or six-level unless his hand is strongly offense oriented.

Examples:

1. Canadian Nationals, 1980.

Opener		*Responder*	
♠ A K Q		♠ J 6 4 3	
♡ A Q 10 7 6 4		♡ 5 2	
◇ K 9		◇ A 10 6 5 4	
♣ 8 6		♣ K 2	
1 NT	5 ♣	Double (1)	Pass
Pass (2)	Pass		

(1) With only two Cover Cards, slam is out
(2) Not remotely tempted to bid 5 ♡

2.

Opener		Responder	
♠ A K Q x		♠ J 10 x x	
♡ A x x		♡ J x	
◇ A Q J x		◇ 10 9 x x	
♣ Q x		♣ A x x	

2 ♣	2 ♡	Double (1)	Pass
2 NT (2)	Pass	3 ♣ (3)	Pass
3 ♠ (4)	Pass	4 ♠ (5)	Pass
Pass	Pass		

(1) Intermediate hand: two Controls; no long suit
(2) 21-22 HCP; balanced
(3) Stayman. Use the same methods as you would without the overcall.
(4) Four spades
(5) Raising to the safest game

B. NEW SUIT = at least a five-card suit; forcing to game. Later bidding follows the usual Romex patterns — natural bidding with CAB and TAB sequences.
    Example:

Opener		Responder	
♠ x		♠ A x	
♡ A K x x		♡ J x x x x	
◇ A x		◇ K x x x	
♣ A K J x x x		♣ x x	

1 NT	2 ♣	3 ♡ (1)	Pass
4 ♠ (2)	Pass	5 ◇ (3)	Pass
5 NT (4)	Pass	6 ♣ (5)	Pass
6 ♡ (6)	Pass	Pass	Pass

(1) Five or more hearts; six or more HCP; but only three potential Cover Cards and three Controls
(2) CAB in spades. 3 ♠ would be a cue-bid, probably looking

for a spade stopper for 3 NT.
(3) Third step = First round spade control
(4) TAB
(5) First step = No top honor (ace, king or queen); minimum length.
(6) Too bad!

C. NOTRUMP = a balanced hand with a stopper in the opponent's suit. This response is not as useful as a double for two reasons:

1) Opener does not have the option to pass for penalties.
2) Opener, the strong hand, does not have the option to play notrump if he has a suitable hand.

Given these limitations, a notrump bid can be very descriptive on the proper hands. It is suggested that a club bid by opener over the notrump bid be used as Stayman, to explore for a 4-4 major suit fit.
    Example:

Opener		Responder	
♠ x x		♠ A Q	
♡ K J x x		♡ 10 9 x x	
◇ K Q x		◇ J x x	
♣ A K Q J		♣ 10 x x x	
1 NT	2 ♠	2 NT (1)	Pass
3 ♣ (1)	Pass	3 ♡ (3)	Pass
4 ♡ (4)	Pass	Pass	Pass

(1) With a double spade stopper and unfavorable vulnerability, responder chooses the descriptive 2 NT bid
(3) Stayman
(3) Four hearts
(4) Signoff

When the Overcall is Made After Responder's Intermediate or Strong Response

When an overcall comes after any intermediate or strong response, opener gets a "fielder's choice" — he can bid, double for penalties or pass it around to responder. ALL DOUBLES AFTER A POSITIVE RESPONSE ARE FOR PENALTIES.

Subsequent bidding follows the normal Romex path.

Example:

Mexican Nationals, 1981.

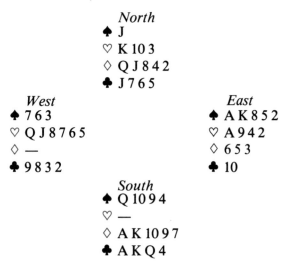

North
- ♠ J
- ♡ K 10 3
- ◇ Q J 8 4 2
- ♣ J 7 6 5

West
- ♠ 7 6 3
- ♡ Q J 8 7 6 5
- ◇ —
- ♣ 9 8 3 2

East
- ♠ A K 8 5 2
- ♡ A 9 4 2
- ◇ 6 5 3
- ♣ 10

South
- ♠ Q 10 9 4
- ♡ —
- ◇ A K 10 9 7
- ♣ A K Q 4

South	West	North	East
Mauricio		George	
Smid		Rosenkranz	
1 NT (1)	Pass	2 ◇ (2)	2 ♠
3 ◇ (3)	Pass	4 ♠ (4)	Pass
6 ◇ (5)	Pass	Pass	Pass

(1) Treating the three Loser hand as a 1 NT opening due to the lack of a spade control and only 18 HCP
(2) At least six HCP but fewer than three Cover Cards; forcing to game

(3) Natural. Opener expects a heart bid from partner over which he will bid 3 NT.

(4) Splinter raise = diamond fit; spade shortness

(5) Bidding what he thinks he can make

Responder Makes a Strong Response — The Direct Cue-Bid

Responder's cue-bid directly over an overcall confirms slam potential and defines the following values:

Responder's Cue-Bid		
Opening Bid	1 NT Four or more Controls AND at least three potential Cover Cards (ace, king, or queen)	2♣ Three or more Controls

Responder can use 2 NT as a "surrogate" cue-bid when the opening bid is doubled. If you prefer, you can ignore the double and bid as if RHO has passed. In fact we will recommend this treatment in Part 3. If you use 2 NT as a cue-bid, 3♣ is not Stayman — all bids would be natural.

Bidding is natural and follows the usual Romex path.

Examples:

1.

Opener		Responder	
♠ A		♠ 9 7 5	
♡ A Q J 10 8 6 4		♡ K	
◇ A K		◇ 9 6 5 4 2	
♣ K Q 6		♣ A 8 7 2	
2♣	3♠	4♠ (1)	Pass
5♠ (2)	Pass	6◇ (3)	Pass
6♡ (4)	Pass	7♡ (5)	Pass
7 NT (6)	Pass	Pass	Pass

(1) Three or more Controls. Slam is in view.
(2) Cue-bidding, presumably asking partner to pick a suit and showing some interest in a grand slam
(3) Showing my longest suit
(4) Cancel the last message. I have a self-sufficient heart suit and am interested in a grand slam.
(5) If you're interested in a grand slam I must have the right cards
(6) If we can make 7 ♡ , we can make 7 NT

We will look at this hand again in Part 3 when we discuss some additional refinements for competitive sequences.

2.

Opener		Responder	
♠ A K 4 3		♠ 8 7 5	
♡ A		♡ J	
◇ A Q J 9 8 6 5		◇ K 10 2	
♣ 9		♣ A K Q 10 4 2	
2 ♣	Pass	3 ♣ (1)	4 ♡
5 ◇ (2)	Pass	5 ♡ (3)	Pass
7 ◇ (4)	Pass	Pass (5)	Pass

(1) Four Controls in two suits
(2) Must show the long suit
(3) Cue-bid, showing more than a normally suitable hand
(4) Great!
(5) Responder might gamble 7 NT at matchpoints . . . but opener could be void in hearts!

165

3.

Opener		Responder	
♠ A K Q J 8 6 4 3		♠ 10 2	
♡ K 4		♡ A 10 6 3	
◊ A 3 2		◊ 7	
♣ —		♣ A Q J 10 6 5	

Opener		Responder	
2♣	2◊	3◊ (1)	Pass
3♠ (2)	Pass	4♣ (2)	Pass
4♠ (3)	Pass	5◊ (4)	Pass
5♡ (5)	Pass	6♣ (6)	Pass
7♠ (7)	Pass	Pass	Pass

(1) Three or more Controls
(2) Natural
(3) More spades
(4) Cue-bid: Suitable hand for spades, probably short in diamonds
(5) CAB
(6) First round control in hearts
(7) We should have 13 tricks

The tools suggested in this chapter are simple and effective and you will do well if you incorporate them. In Part 3 we will take another look at competitive sequences after strong openings.

Chapter 9

OPENING ONE-BIDS — WITHOUT COMPETITION

Romex is not only a simple and natural system, but a flexible one as well. To say you are playing Romex means:

1. Opening bids of 1 NT, 2♣ and 2♦ are strong and artificial. 1 NT is opened on those difficult "in-between" hands of 18-21 HCP; 2♣ on game-going hands.
2. Opening bids of one of a suit though limited, are all natural. The upper limit is 17 or 18 HCP.

How you play the rest of the structure is entirely up to you. You can play four-card majors, five-card majors and canapé (an approach in which the shorter suit is bid first with a two-suited hand) — all with increased effectiveness due to the Dynamic 1 NT opening. This chapter presents a structure that has been played by experienced players for a long time and has been found to be effective in even the toughest competition.

The Basic Approach to Romex Bids of One of a Suit

A detailed description of the Romex approach to opening bids of one of a suit is given in *Win With Romex*. These ideas are summarized in this book with additions and changes noted.

The Romex approach to opening bids of one of a suit is similar to "Eastern Scientific." Highlights of the method include:

1. Five-card majors. Five-card majors are strongly recommended for the following reasons:
   a. Opener can define his distribution more accurately.

    b. Knowing that opener has a five-card major makes life much easier for responder in competitive situations.

    c. A five-card major structure allows for many improvements in the responding structure, such as 1 NT forcing over an opening bid of 1 ♡ or 1 ♠, sound two-over-one responses, a system of "graded raises," etc.

2. Three-card minor openings. This is a necessity playing five-card majors. However, this is not usually a problem because:

    a. Minor suits are much less important than major suits and notrump, and

    b. Romex offers many bidding tools that allow responder to discover the nature of opener's hand. In other cases responder describes his holding and lets opener choose the final contract.

3. Responses promise a minimum of a good five or six HCP. Responses are kept "up to standard" in Romex because opener can rebid 2 NT with 17-18 HCP. Passing with weaker hands is not a problem, because opening bids of one of a suit are limited.

4. Many specialized sequences are available. These include graded raises, jump shifts, relays, Key Card Blackwood, fragment bids, splinter bids, void-showing sequences and more.

Requirements for an Opening Bid of One of a Suit

Any hand with 13 HCP is a mandatory opening. Weaker hands may be opened if they meet the following requirements:

Losers: Maximum of seven Losers
Quick Tricks: At least 1 1/2 Quick Tricks, usually more

Do not open hands with less than 10 or 11 HCP unless you have at least two Quick Tricks and the distribution and playing strength are exceptional.

The upper limit for a one-bid is 18 HCP (certain minor two-suiters with 19 or 20 HCP should be opened with one of a minor). Hands with more than 18 HCP and four or five Losers are generally opened with 1 NT (See The Dynamic 1 NT Opening).

Examples:

♠ Q x	♠ A K 10 9 x x
♡ x x x x	♡ K x x x x
◇ K Q J	◇ x
♣ A x x x	♣ x

Pass	Bid 1 ♠
(Only 12 HCP;	(10 HCP; five Losers
eight Losers)	2 1/2 Quick Tricks)

♠ x x	♠ K x
♡ K x x	♡ A x x x x
◇ A Q x x x	◇ K 10 x
♣ K x x	♣ Q 10 x

Bid 1 ◇	Bid 1 ♡
(12 HCP; seven Losers;	(12 HCP; seven Losers;
2 1/2 Quick Tricks)	2 Quick Tricks)

The Choice of the Suit for the Opening Bid

The rules for the choice of the suit should be familiar:
1. With a five-card or longer suit
    1. Open the longest suit
    2. Open the higher ranking suit with equal length
2. With no five-card or longer suit
    1. The opening must be in a minor suit
    2. Open the longer minor
    3. Open 1 ◇ with 4-4 in the minors
    4. Open 1 ♣ with 3-3 in the minors unless the diamonds are substantially stronger than the clubs

Responses to Opening Bids of One of a Suit

Responses are largely natural. The important point in this regard is that responder must pass the opening bid unless he has at least a good five or six HCP. Responder can answer with a little less with a long major suit or if he has a fit for opener's major and compensating distribution.

The correct response to an opening bid depends on which suit has been opened. Therefore responses to an opening bid of one of a major and one of a minor will be discussed separately.

1. RESPONSES TO MAJOR SUIT OPENING BIDS

The basic principles that guide responses to major openings are simple enough. These rules assume responder has sufficient values for a response.

1. With a fit for opener's major (three or more cards), responder must plan a raising sequence. This can be a direct raise, e.g., 1♠ — 2♠, or a delayed raise, e.g., 1♠ — 2♣/2♦ — 3♠.
2. With no fit for opener's major, responder has two basic options:
    1. A one-level response. A one-level response can be on a minimum responding hand. However, the choices are few — 1♠ or 1 NT. The 1 NT response is limited to 6-11 HCP.
    2. A two-over-one response. A new suit at the two-level is forcing to game, with one exception. When responder rebids his suit at the three-level and opener has not shown extra values opener may pass. The minimum point count for a two-over-one is 10 HCP if responder is planning to rebid his suit or 12 HCP otherwise.

Examples:

1♠ — 2♡	1♠ — 2♣ or 2♢	1♡ — 2♣
2♠ — 3♡	2♡ — 3♣ or 3♢	2♠ — 3♣
(nonforcing)	(nonforcing)	(forcing as
		opener has
		shown extra
		strength)

Raising Sequences

Romex uses a series of "graded raises" — a wide variety of raising sequences that allow responder to accurately describe the overall value of his hand. In many cases he can discriminate between three and four-card support. The stronger responding hands can show their holding more accurately as there is more bidding room available.

Following is a chart of the raising sequences. The chart lists responder's options depending on the quality of his hand, his trump support and his distribution. The "Cover Card" concept is used to evaluate the quality of the hand though approximate "Dummy point" ranges are included for convenience. In the chart "HCP" refers to high card points only while "points" refers to both high card points and distributional points.

Major Suit Raises

Sequence	Hand Quality	Trump Support	Side Suit Distribution	Sequence "Label"
1 ♡ or 1 ♠ — 1 NT 2X — 2♡ or 2♠	6-7 points 1 1/2 Cover Cards	Two or more trumps. Can be up to 9 HCP with only two trumps.	Lacks four spades after 1 ♡ opening, unless the heart fit is "real," i.e., three-card or longer support.	"Mini-Raise"
1 ♡ — 2♡ or 1 ♠ — 2♠	8-9 points 2 1/2 Cover Cards	Three or more trumps	Unspecified	"Constructive Raise"
1 ♡ — 1 ♠ or 1 NT 2X — 3♡ or 1 ♠ — 1 NT 2X — 3♠	10-11 points 3 1/2 Cover Cards	Exactly three trumps	Unspecified A 1 ♠ response to a 1 ♡ opening shows four or more spades.	"Three-card Limit Raise"
1♡ — 3♡ or 1 ♠ — 3 ♠	10-11 points 3 1/2 Cover Cards	Four or more trumps	Balanced or unbalanced	"Limit Raise"
1 ♡ — 4♡ or 1 ♠ — 4 ♠	12-15 points 0-2 Controls 4 1/2 Cover Cards	Four or more trumps, frequently five	Balanced or unbalanced	"Game Raise"
1 ♡ or 1 ♠ — 3 NT	12-15 points 3-4 Controls 4 1/2 Cover Cards	Four or five trumps	Balanced	"Balanced Forcing Raise"
1 ♡ — 2/1 X — heart raise or 1 ♠ — 2/1 X - spade raise	12 or more points 4 1/2 Cover Cards Can be stronger with only three trumps	Three trumps; or four trumps with a "real" side suit	Length in side suit	"Two-over-one Raise"

172

Bid	Requirements	Trumps	Distribution	Name
1♡ — 3♠, 4♣ or 4◇ or 1♠ — 4♣, 4◇ or 4♡	10 or more HCP Four or more Cover Cards	Four or more trumps	Singleton or void in the bid suit	"Splinter Raise"
1♡ - jump shift X - heart raise or 1♠ - jump shift X - spade raise	A good 13 or more HCP Five or more Cover Cards	Three or more trumps	Strong five-card or longer side suit	"Jump Shift Raise"
1♡ or 1♠ — 2 NT	13 or more HCP Five Losers Five or more Controls	Four or more trumps	No void Usually no good five-card or longer side suit	"Maxi Raise"

Cover Cards are evaluated as follows:

Cover Cards	
Holding in a Suit	*Number of Cover Cards*
Void with four or more trumps	1 1/2
Any ace or king	1
Queen of trump	1
Queen of opener's three-card or longer side suit	1
Void with three trumps	1
Side suit singleton with four trumps	1
Side suit singleton with three trumps	1/2
Side suit queen	1/2
Side suit doubleton with four or more trumps	1/2
Side suit doubleton with three trumps	Plus Value

Of course responder must be prepared to adjust the Cover Card count if new information obtained during the bidding so indicates. This usually means a downgrading: honors that aren't working because opener is known to be short in that suit, or duplication of short suits. However, a queen can improve in status to a full Cover Card if opener is known to have three or more cards in that suit.

Examples:

1.

Opener	Responder	Responder's Cover Cards
♠ Q J x	♠ x x x	0
♡ K Q 10 x x	♡ x x x x	0
◇ A x x	◇ Q x	1/2
♣ x x	♣ A x x x	1
		1 1/2

1 ♡	1 NT
2 ◇ (1)	2 ♡ (2)
Pass	

(1) Cheaper three-card minor — lacking a sound alternative
(2) 1 1/2 Cover Cards. The 2 ◇ bid improves the hand to two Cover Cards, though this has no effect on the bidding.

2.

Opener	Responder	Responder's Cover Cards
♠ K Q J x x	♠ A x x x	1
♡ K x x	♡ A x x x	1
◇ A K x x	◇ x x	1/2
♣ x	♣ x x x	0
		2 1/2

1 ♠	2 ♠ (1)
4 ♠ (2)	Pass

(1) 2 1/2 Cover Cards — a minimum constructive raise

(2) Five Losers minus 2 1/2 Losers = 2 1/2 losers. Game should be an excellent bet.

Readers who wish to see explanations and/or examples of "bread and butter" sequences — forcing 1 NT, raising sequences, and two-over-one sequences — are referred to *Win With Romex*.

Other Basic Sequences

Immediately following are suggestions for a "basic" structure. Later recommendations will be made for an "advanced" structure.

1. A two-over-one is forcing to game unless responder rebids his suit at the three-level at his next opportunity. Of course, any rebid by opener that promises extra strength creates an immediate game force.
2. Some particular two-over-one sequences worthy of discussion:
   a) Opener's notrump rebids show the following:

      2 NT = 13-14 HCP or 17-18 HCP
      3 NT = 15-16 HCP

   With 17-18 HCP opener follows up with a strong bid on the next round.

   Examples:
   1 ♠ — 2 ◇
   2 NT — 3 NT
   ????

   ♠ A K x x x   ♡ K x x   ◇ K x x   ♣ A x   Bid 4 ◇
   ♠ A Q 10 x x   ♡ K Q x   ◇ Q x   ♣ K Q 10   Bid 4 NT

b) If opener raises responder's suit directly he promises extra values. With a minimum he can "wait" by rebidding two of his major.

Examples:
1 ♠ — 2 ♣
????

♠ A K x x x ♡ A x ◇ x x x ♣ A x x   Bid 3 ♣
♠ A K x x x ♡ x x ◇ x x x ♣ A Q x   Bid 2 ♠

Both hands have seven Losers, but the first hand contains extra values: 15 HCP, seven Controls
The second hand is a minimum: 13 HCP; five Controls.

Responder must not assume that if opener rebids two of his original suit he shows a six-card or longer suit after a two-over-one response, though such a rebid would promise a six-card or longer suit if the original response had been at the one-level.

3. **Opener's reverses and jump shifts are limited due to the Dynamic 1 NT, and thus are nonforcing.** These bids show a maximum opening — four or five Losers. Distributional requirements:

Two-level reverse = at least 5-4
Three-level jump shift = at least 5-5
    Exception: 1 ♠ — 1 NT
              3 ♡   can be 5-4 with a four Loser hand.

Examples:

A.

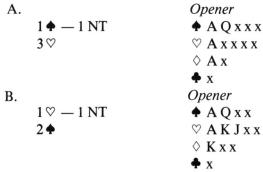

	Opener
1♠ — 1 NT	♠ A Q x x x
3♡	♡ A x x x x
	◇ A x
	♣ x

B.

	Opener
1♡ — 1 NT	♠ A Q x x
2♠	♡ A K J x x
	◇ K x x
	♣ x

4. Opener has a choice of rebids with 6-4. In general opener should rebid his major over a one-level response but show the side suit after a two-over-one. It is best to show the side suit after a two-over-one because opener can expect to be given the chance to show a sixth card in his suit on the third round of the auction.

Example:

1♠ — 1 NT	vs.	1♠ — 2♣	♠ A J x x x x
2♠		2◇ — 2 NT	♡ x
		3♠	◇ K Q x x
			♣ Q x

There are three exceptions when opener rebids the four-card suit after a one-level response:

a) The six-card suit is so weak that opener treats the hand as 5-4:

   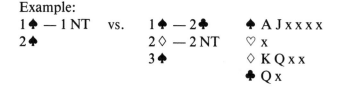
   ♠ 10 x x x x x ♡ K Q ◇ A K J x ♣ x

b) Always bid 2♡ with six spades and four hearts. Responder should give preference to spades with two spades and three hearts:

177

A.

	Opener	Responder
1♠ — 1 NT	♠ A J x x x x	♠ x
2♠ — Pass	♡ K Q x x	♡ A x x x x
vs.	◇ K x	◇ Q J x x
1♠ — 1 NT	♣ x	♣ x x x
2♡ — 3♡		
4♡ — Pass		

B.

	Opener	Responder
1♠ — 1 NT	♠ A J x x x x	♠ 10 x
2♡ — 2♠	♡ K Q x x	♡ J x x
Pass	◇ K x	◇ Q J x x x
	♣ x	♣ K J x

c) With 6-4 and a medium strength opening, opener can rebid his four-card suit in lieu of a jump rebid in his original major. Prefer this when the six-card suit is of indifferent quality.

Examples:
1♡ — 1 NT
????

♠ x	♡ A Q x x x x	◇ K x x x	♣ Q x	Bid 2♡
♠ x	♡ A K Q 10 x x	◇ A J 10 x	♣ x x	Bid 3♡
♠ x	♡ A Q x x x x	◇ A K x x	♣ x x	Bid 2◇

In the last example, follow with a heart rebid to show 6-4, a fair hand, but a weakish heart suit.

Advanced Sequences After Major Openings

This section lists some of the more advanced but still highly recommended treatments:

A direct jump to 4 NT over an opening one bid is regular Blackwood, i.e., not-Key Card Blackwood. This treatment is useful on hands of this type:

Opener	Responder	
♠ K Q x x x	♠ x	1♠ — 4 NT
♡ x	♡ A K Q J x x x x	5◊ — 6♡
◊ A J x	◊ K Q	(6 NT is
♣ K Q x x	♣ A x	reasonable
		at match-
		points)

If responder wants to use Key Card Blackwood he makes a forcing bid, raises the suit, and then bids 4 NT.

2. Special treatments to use after a single raise:

    A.   Three Way Game Tries: Opener may want to make any one of three different types of game tries:

        a) Short suit game try. Opener shows a side suit singleton or void and lets responder judge the quality of the fit.

        b) Power try. Opener just wants to make a quantative try for game without emphasizing any particular feature. Typically opener will have about 16 or 17 HCP and either 5-3-3-2 or 5-4-2-2 distribution. If he has a side four-card suit, it does not need "help."

        c) Long suit try. Opener shows a four or five-card side suit where he needs "help."

It works like this:

Three Way Game Tries

1 ♡ — 2 ♡ or 1 ♠ — 2 ♠

First step = Long suit try. Responder bids the cheapest step in reply, and opener bids his long suit:

1 ♠ — 2 ♠	1 ♡ — 2 ♡
2 NT — 3 ♣	2 ♠ — 2 NT
3 ◊ = Long suit try in diamonds	3 ♣ = Long suit try in clubs
3 ♡ = Long suit try in hearts	3 ◊ = Long suit try in diamonds
3 ♠ = Long suit try in the "missing" suit, i.e., clubs	3 ♡ = Long suit try in the "missing" suit, i.e., spades

Second, third or fourth step = Short suit try:

1 ♠ — 2 ♠	1 ♡ — 2 ♡
3 ♣ = Short suit try in clubs	2 NT = Short suit try in spades (the "missing" suit)
3 ◊ = Short suit try in diamonds	3 ♣ = Short suit try in clubs
3 ♡ = Short suit try in hearts	3 ◊ = Short suit try in diamonds

Where does the "power try" come in — all bids are taken. The solution: use the cheapest short suit try as a two-way bid:

1 ♠ — 2 ♠	1 ♡ — 2 ♡
3 ♣ = Short suit try in clubs OR power try	2 NT = Short suit try in spades OR power try

---

Over the two-way game try, responder bids as
follows:

1♠ — 2♠
3♣ — 3♠ or 4♠ = I don't care which game try
                      you have
        3♦ (first step) = I accept the short suit try
                            but not the power try
        3♡ (second step) = I accept the power try
                               but not the short suit try

In all cases responder uses the available information
to place the final contract. 3 NT is a possibility if
opener made a power try.

Examples:

1.

Opener	Responder	
♠ K Q x x	♠ x x x	1♡ — 2♡
♡ A Q x x x	♡ K x x	3♦ — 3♡
♦ x	♦ K Q x	
♣ K x x	♣ x x x x	

2.

Opener	Responder	
♠ A	♠ x x x	1♡ — 2♡
♡ A J x x x	♡ K Q x x	2♠ — 2 NT
♦ K J x x	♦ Q x x	3♦ — 4♡
♣ x x	♣ Q x x	

3.

Opener	Responder	
♠ x x	♠ x x x	1♡ — 2♡
♡ A K x x x	♡ J x x x	2 NT — 4♡
♦ K x x	♦ A Q x	
♣ A Q x	♣ K x x	

B. The meaning of opener's re-raise depends on the scoring:

> 1♠ — 2♠
> 3♠ = Preemptive at matchpoints
>   Asking for good trumps at IMPs

3. Some sequences after a two-over-one response:

A. 1♡ — Two-over-one or 1♠ — Two-over-one
    2♡ — 4♡ (1)   2♠ — 4♠ (1)

    (1) Sign-off (Principle of Fast Arrival)

Example:

> 1♠ — 2◇
> 2♠ — 4♠

> *Responder*
> ♠ Q x x x
> ♡ J x
> ◇ A Q J x x
> ♣ K x

B. 1♡ (or 1♠) — Two-over-one
    2♡ (or 2♠) — Four of responder's original
                        suit (1)

    (1) Rodwell slam try; all values in responder's suit and opener's major with no outside control

Example:

> 1♠ — 2♣
> 2♠ — 4♣

Responder
♠ K Q x x
♡ x x
♢ x x
♣ A K J x x

C. 1♡ (or 1♠) — Two-over-one
    Two of a new suit — 2♡ (or 2♠) (1)

    (1) Two or more cards in opener's original
        major: asks opener to continue describing
        hand pattern; game force

Example:
                1♠ — 2♢
                2♡ — 2♠

                Responder
                ♠ K x
                ♡ K x x
                ♢ A K x x x
                ♣ x x x

D. Jump raise in opener's major below game =
    strong hand; slam try; suggests cue-bidding

Example:
                1♠ — 2♢
                2♡ — 3♠

                Responder
                ♠ K J 10
                ♡ x x
                ♢ A K x x x
                ♣ K x x

        Void-showing sequences after a major suit open-
        ing and a two-over-one response will be de-
        scribed later.

                        183

4. After 1♡ (or 1♠) — 3♡ (or 3♠) both Short Suit Slam Tries and Long Suit Slam Tries are available. The structure is analogous to short and long suit game tries after the auction 1♡ (or 1♣) — 2♡ (or 2♠), but one level higher.

Examples:
1.

Opener	Responder
♠ x	♠ J x x
♡ A x x x x x	♡ K Q x x
◇ A J	◇ K x x
♣ A K x x	♣ Q x x

1♡	3♡
3 NT (1)	5♡ (2)
6♡ (3)	Pass

(1) Short Suit Slam Try in spades
(2) I accept the slam try but I have no ace to cue-bid.
(3) Happy to accept

2.

Opener	Responder
♠ A K x x x	♠ Q J x x
♡ K J x x x	♡ x x x
◇ K x	◇ x x
♣ x	♣ A K J x

1♠	3♠
3 NT (1)	4♣ (2)
4♡ (2)	4♠ (4)
Pass	

(1) Long Suit Slam Try in an unknown suit
(2) Forced
(3) My Long Suit Slam Try is in hearts
(4) No help in hearts; Cover Cards are duplicated

Over 1♡ or 1♠ — 3 NT only Short Suit Slam Tries can be used. Any new suit bid is a Short Suit Slam Try.

Example:

Opener	Responder
♠ K Q x x x x	♠ A x x x
♡ A J x x	♡ K x
◇ Q x x	◇ x x x
♣ —	♣ K Q x x
1 ♠	3 NT
4 ♣ (1)	4 ♠ (2)
Pass	

(1) Short in clubs
(2) A signoff is in order. Partner's try in clubs depreciates the working Cover Cards to two.

5. Forcing notrump adjuncts:

1 ♡   — 1 NT
2 ♣, 2 ◇ or 2 ♡ — 3 NT = Doubleton heart; 13-15 HCP; balanced

1 ♡   — 1 NT
2 ♣, 2 ◇ or 2 ♡ — 4 ♡ = My hand improved with your last bid

1 ♠   — 1 NT
2 ♣, 2 ◇, 2 ♡ or 2 ♠ — 4 ♠ = My hand improved with your last bid

1 ♡ or 1 ♠ — 1 NT
3 NT = I have a solid major

Examples:

1.

Opener	Responder
♠ Q 10 9 7 4 2	♠ K 3
♡ 6	♡ A J 4
◇ A J 8 5	◇ K 10 4 2
♣ A 4	♣ Q J 3 2
1 ♠	1 NT
2 ♠	3 NT
4 ♠	Pass

2.

Opener	Responder
♠ A x x x x	♠ K Q J
♡ K x x	♡ A x x
◇ A J x	◇ Q 10 x x
♣ x x	♣ x x x
1 ♠	1 NT
2 ◇	4 ♠
Pass	

3.

Opener	Responder
♠ A K Q J 7 5 4	♠ 3 2
♡ 10 4	♡ Q J 7 6 5
◇ K 6	◇ A 9 5
♣ K 4	♣ J 3 2
1 ♠	1 NT
3 NT (1)	Pass (2)

(1) I have a solid major (usually seven, but occasionally six or eight cards in length).
(2) I prefer notrump.

4.

Opener	Responder
♠ x	♠ Q J x x x
♡ A K Q J x x x	♡ x x
◇ A x x	◇ Q x x
♣ Q x	♣ K x x
1 ♡	1 ♠
3 NT (1)	Pass

(1) Solid hearts

2. RESPONSES TO MINOR SUIT OPENING BIDS

Bidding after minor suit openings can be as simple as you like. Following are some recommendations:

A. Rules for One-Level Responses

1) Playing five-card majors, it is mandatory that responder bid any four-card major he has, regardless of quality. Opener can have four cards in either or both spades or hearts, so it is worthwhile to explore for the all-important eight-card major suit fit.

There are only two instances where the major suit is suppressed:

a) After a 1 ♣ opening, responder can bid 1 ◇ with five diamonds and a four-card major, as long as he plans to force the bidding to game.

Examples:

1♣ — ?

♠ A x x x ♡ x x x x ◇ A J x x ♣ x	Bid 1♡
♠ A Q x x ♡ A K x ◇ A J x x ♣ x x	Bid 1♠
♠ x x ♡ A 9 x x ◇ K 10 x x x x ♣ x	Bid 1♡
♠ A K J x ♡ x x ◇ A Q 10 x x ♣ x x	Bid 1◇ (bid spades later)

b) After a 1◇ opening, responder can bid 2♣ with five or more clubs and a four-card major if he has game-going values.

Examples:

1◇ — ?

♠ A Q x x ♡ x x x ◇ x ♣ A J x x x	Bid 1♠
♠ A Q x x ♡ x x x ◇ x ♣ A K J x x	Bid 2♣

2) A 1 NT response shows 6-10 HCP and denies a four-card major. The hand is balanced or, after a 1◇ opening, contains long clubs and insufficient values for a 2♣ response.

Examples:

1◇ — ?

♠ A x x ♡ K x x ◇ x x x x ♣ J x x	Bid 1 NT
♠ A x x ♡ J x x ◇ x ♣ Q 10 x x x x	Bid 1 NT
♠ K x x ♡ A x x ◇ x ♣ Q J 10 x x x	Bid 2♣

B. 1◇ — 2♣

There is only one two-over-one auction after a minor suit opening: 1◇ — 2♣. 2♣ is game forcing unless responder rebids 3 ♣ on the next round. 10 HCP with six or more clubs is a minimum 2 ♣ response — with a weaker hand prefer a 1 NT response. For those who prefer a more detailed method, see the "Advanced" section below.

Advanced Sequences — Minor Openings

Any structure of minor suit raises you prefer is playable with Romex. A system of "graded raises" is recommended after a minor suit opening as was recommended after major suit openings. These raises, and a few other ideas, are presented below. The requirements are expressed in points rather than Cover Cards because the hand is often played in notrump.

Minor Suit Raises

Sequence	Hand Quality	Trump Support	Side Suit Distribution	Sequence "Label"
1♣ — 3♣ or 1◇ — 3◇	0-7 points	Four or more trumps	No four-card major	"Preemptive Jump Raise"
1◇ — 3♣ or 1♣ — 2◇	A good 7- a poor 11 HCP	Five or more trumps	No four-card major	"Two-Way Constructive Raise"
1♣ — 2♣ or 1◇ — 2◇	A good 11-15 points	Four or more trumps, usually five or more	No void; no four-card major	"Inverted Minor Raise"
1♣ — 3◇ 3♡ or 3♠ or 1◇ — 3♡ 3♠ or 4♣	A good 11 points or more	Five or more trumps	Void in the bid suit; no four-card major	"Void-Showing Splinter"
1♣ — 2 NT or 1◇ — 2 NT	16 or more points; five or more Cover Cards; five or more Controls	Five or more trumps (rarely four good trumps)	No void; no four-card major	"Maxi-Raise"

For a full discussion of some of these raising sequences, refer to The Inverted Minor Raise and The Maxi-Raise After a Minor Opening.

1. The Preemptive Jump Raise

The preemptive jump raise shows a weak hand and five or more trumps. The hand should contain no more than seven bad HCP and no four-card major. It is possible to raise 1 ◇ to 3 ◇ with only four diamonds because 1 ◇ is much less likely than 1 ♣ to be opened with a three-card suit.

Examples:

1 ◇ — ?

♠ A x x	♡ x	◇ J x x x x	♣ x x x x	Bid 3 ◇
♠ x	♡ x x	◇ K 10 x x	♣ Q x x x x x	Bid 3 ◇

2. Two-Way Constructive Raise

A jump shift in the other minor is a two-way bid — either a good seven to a poor 11 points with a fit for opener's suit OR a normal, strong jump shift. Naturally opener must assume the weaker hand, leaving it up to responder to clarify his hand if he has the strong jump shift.

Examples:

1 ♣ — ?

♠ A x x	♡ x	◇ K x x x	♣ K x x x x	Bid 2 ◇
♠ A x x	♡ x	◇ A K Q J x x	♣ K x x	Bid 2 ◇

If opener is not interested in game, he returns to three of the agreed minor. If he is interested in game, he makes any other bid.

1 ◇ — 3 ♣
3 ◇ — Pass = Constructive Raise
   — Other = Strong jump shift with clubs

1 ◇ — 3 ♣
3 ♡ — 4 ♣ = Strong jump shift with clubs
   — Other = Constructive Raise

191

Examples:

1. Challenge the Champs, 1982.

Opener	Responder
♠ 9 8 5 2	♠ 6
♡ A K J 4	♡ Q 7
◇ A K 10 8	◇ Q J 9 5
♣ 7	♣ K J 10 9 6 3

Opener	Responder
1 ◇	3 ♣ (1)
3 ♡ (2)	5 ♣ (3)
5 ◇ (4)	Pass

(1) Two-Way Constructive Raise - either a good 7 to a poor 11 points or a strong jump shift
(2) Game try; heart stopper
(3) Maximum constructive raise without a spade stopper; long clubs. Notice that responder cannot rebid 4♣ as this would show a strong jump shift in clubs.
(4) I prefer to play in diamonds rather than clubs.

2. Challenge the Champs, 1979.

Opener	Responder
♠ A Q 8 3	♠ J
♡ Q J 4	♡ 7 2
◇ A Q 7 5	◇ K 10 8 6 4 3 2
♣ K 9	♣ J 6 3

Opener	Responder
1 ◇	3 ♣ (1)
3 NT (2)	Pass

(1) With seven-card trump support, responder is too good for a preemptive raise to 3 ◇
(2) An easy decision with a balanced 18 HCP and all suits stopped

Both pairs stopped at 3 ◇ .

Developments after the strong jump shift are discussed in the chapter "The Strong Jump Shift."

3. The Void-Showing Splinter Raise

A double jump in a new suit shows a game-going raise (or better) in opener's minor with a VOID in the bid suit. These splinter raises deny a four-card major and promise at least five-card support. The HCP requirements can be lowered to as little as 10 — if the playing strength is exceptional. (For a discussion of the splinter concept, see Splinter Bids.)

Examples:

$1 \diamondsuit$ — ?

♠ A x x ♡ — ◇ A K x x x ♣ J x x x x		Bid 3 ♡
♠ A x x ♡ — ◇ A Q x x x x x ♣ x x x		Bid 3 ♡
♠ A Q x x ♡ K x x ◇ A x x x x x ♣ —		Bid 1 ♠

Following are three other sequences after a minor suit opening bid:

1. The 3 NT Response

This response always shows a balanced hand (usually 4-3-3-3) with no four-card major and a good 12 to 14 HCP.

Examples:

$1 \clubsuit$ — ?

♠ K x x ♡ Q J x ◇ A Q x x ♣ Q x x		Bid 3 NT
♠ Q J x ♡ Q J x ◇ K Q x ♣ Q 10 x x		Bid 3 NT

2. Bidding After a Two-Level Reverse or Jump Shift by Opener

Romex defines responder's bids quite carefully in this situation to allow for sign-offs, invitations, creating a game force, and relays. (See Part 3 for discussion of relays.)

A 2 NT bid by responder requests that opener bid 3 ♣ (opener can do otherwise with unusual shape). Responder uses this bid to:

      a) Sign off in 3 ♣ or
      b) Sign off in opener's first bid suit or
      c) Invite game in opener's second suit or
      d) Invite game in responder's suit

Example:

1 ◊ — 1 ♠
2 ♡ — 2 NT
3 ♣ — Pass with ♠ 10 x x x ♡ x x ◊ A ♣ Q J x x x x
      Bid 3 ◊ with ♠ J x x x ♡ x x ◊ A J x ♣ x x x x
      Bid 3 ♡ with ♠ K J x x x ♡ J x x x ◊ J x x ♣ x
      Bid 3 ♠ with ♠ K J 10 x x x ♡ x x ◊ x x ♣ Q J x

A direct raise of opener's suit is natural and game-forcing. If relays are being used, these are the relevant sequences:

      a) A direct raise of opener's second suit is a game-forcing relay that sets that suit as trump.
      b) A bid of the fourth suit is an artificial relay, forcing to game and sets opener's first suit as trump.

3. Advanced Sequences After 1 ◊ — 2 ♣

A 2 ♣ response can be made with 11 HCP and 3-3-3-4, 2-3-3-5, 3-2-3-5 or 3-3-2-5 distribution. Since opener could have a balanced hand with a good 12 or 13 HCP, some poor 3 NT contracts would be reached using the "basic" methods. The following structure is recommended:

$1 \diamondsuit - 2 \clubsuit$

$2 \diamondsuit$	= Five or more diamonds
2 NT	= 14-15 HCP or 18 HCP; balanced; one round force
$3 \clubsuit$	= Four or more clubs; game force
$3 \diamondsuit$	= Six or more strong diamonds; good hand
$3 \heartsuit$	= Void in hearts; four or more clubs (splinter raise)
$3 \spadesuit$	= Void in spades; four or more clubs (splinter raise)
3 NT	= 16 or 17 HCP; balanced
$4 \clubsuit$	= Key Card Blackwood; clubs is the Key Card suit

What about $2 \heartsuit$ and $2 \spadesuit$ rebids? We recommend this novel twist:

$1 \diamondsuit - 2 \clubsuit$

$2 \spadesuit$	= A ''Real'' reverse showing at least five diamonds and four spades; four or five Losers.
$2 \heartsuit$	= ''Three-way'' showing:

     1. ''Real'' reverse or

     2. A good 12 or 13 balanced HCP or

     3. A good 12 or 13 points with club support; not strong enough to force to game

Examples:

$1 \diamondsuit - 2 \clubsuit$
?

♠ xxx	♠ Qxx	♠ Axx	♠ AKxx
♡ A10x	♡ A10x	♡ A10x	♡ Axx
◇ KQxx	◇ KQxx	◇ KQxx	◇ AQxxx
♣ AJx	♣ AJx	♣ AJx	♣ x
Bid 2 NT	Bid 3 NT	Bid 2 NT	Bid 2 ♠

♠ xx	♠ xx	♠ KJxx	♠ xx
♡ Kx	♡ AKxx	♡ Kxx	♡ Qxx
◇ AQxxx	◇ AQxxx	◇ AQx	◇ AQxx
♣ AKxx	♣ Ax	♣ xxx	♣ KJxx
Bid 3 ♣	Bid 2 ♡	Bid 2 ♡	Bid 2 ♡

Some notes:

1. The 2♣ response is game-forcing unless responder bids 2 NT or 3♣ on the second round.
2. Opener treats a 4-4-4-1 hand with a club singleton as a balanced hand.
3. After the auction 1◇ — 2♣/2♡ responder can bid 2♠ to request clarification:

1◇ — 2♣
2♡ — 2♠
2 NT = A good 12 or 13 balanced HCP
3♣ = A good 12 or 13 HCP with club support
Any other bid = A "Real" reverse

Examples:

1.

Opener	Responder
♠ Q x	♠ K x x
♡ K x x x	♡ Q x x
◇ A 10 x x	◇ Q x x
♣ K J x	♣ A 10 x x

1◇ — 2♣		1◇	— 2♣
2♡ — 2 NT	OR	2♡	— 2♠
Pass		2 NT — Pass	

2.

Opener	Responder
♠ x x	♠ x x x
♡ K x	♡ Q x x
◇ A 10 x x x	◇ K Q x
♣ K Q x x	♣ A 10 x x

1◇ — 2♣
2♡ — 2♠
3♣ — Pass

3.

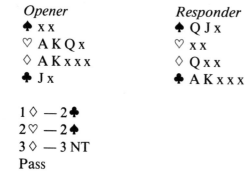

Opener	Responder
♠ x x	♠ Q J x
♡ A K Q x	♡ x x
◇ A K x x x	◇ Q x x
♣ J x	♣ A K x x x

1◇ — 2♣
2♡ — 2♠
3◇ — 3 NT
Pass

4.

Opener	Responder
♠ K x x	♠ Q J x
♡ x x x	♡ Q x x
◇ A Q x x x	◇ x
♣ K x	♣ A J 9 8 x x

1◇ — 2♣
2◇ — 3♣
Pass

Those who wish to do so may use the Romex relay path: Distributional clarification; Key Cards; Spiral, etc.

4. FOURTH SUIT FORCING AND ARTIFICIAL

Most players these days play a version of "Fourth Suit Forcing," which means that responder's bid of the fourth suit on the second round of bidding is artificial and forcing.
Examples:

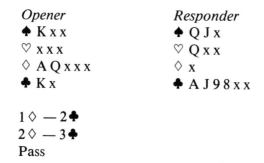

1◇ — 1♠	1♣ — 1◇	1♣ — 1♡	1♡ — 1♠
2♣ — 2♡	1♡ — 1♠	1♠ — 2◇	2♣ — 2◇

The last bid in each of the above auctions is Fourth Suit Forcing.

Following are suggested specific understandings about the Fourth Suit Forcing and Artificial principle. Responses in the discussion below are to auctions that start at the one-level. A bid of the fourth suit by responder after a two-over-one response is, of course, forcing to game.

1. Responder's second round jumps to 2 NT or three of a bid suit are always "limit" bids, i.e., invitational to game.

Examples:

1 ◇ — 1 ♡
1 ♠ — ?

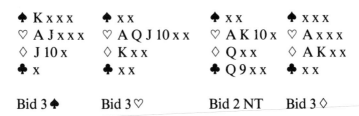

♠ K x x x	♠ x x	♠ x x	♠ x x x
♡ A J x x x	♡ A Q J 10 x x	♡ A K 10 x	♡ A x x x
◇ J 10 x	◇ K x x	◇ Q x x	◇ A K x x
♣ x	♣ x x	♣ Q 9 x x	♣ x x
Bid 3 ♠	Bid 3 ♡	Bid 2 NT	Bid 3 ◇

2. Responder uses the fourth suit to set up a forcing situation. A bid of the fourth suit followed by 2 NT or a bid in an "old" suit is game-forcing:

Examples:

1 ◇ — 1 ♡
1 ♠ — 2 ♣
2 ◇ — ?

♠ A K x x	♠ J x x	♠ x x	♠ J x x
♡ A Q x x x	♡ A Q 10 x x x	♡ A K x x	♡ A Q J x x
◇ Q x	◇ A J x	◇ A Q x x	◇ K x
♣ x x	♣ x	♣ Q x x	♣ A Q x
Bid 2 ♠	Bid 2 ♡	Bid 3 ◇	Bid 2 NT

3. The fourth suit is game-forcing, with one exception:

   1♣ — 1◊
   1♡ — 1♠ is not game-forcing only if responder passes opener's rebid.

4. Opener must not raise the fourth suit to game:

Example:

1◊ — 1♠
2♣ — 2♡
?
   ♠ x
   ♡ AKxx
   ◊ AKxx
   ♣ Q10xx

Bid only 3♡. 2♡ is forcing to game, but doesn't promise any holding in hearts. If responder shows interest in slam you will be happy to cooperate.

5. Opener bids as naturally as possible after responder's fourth suit forcing bid. Following is a list of priorities, i.e., if opener's hand fulfills the first priority, he makes the appropriate bid; if his hand does not fulfill the first priority, but does fulfill the second priority, he makes the bid appropriate to this priority; and so on:

   1. With a three-card fit for responder's first bid suit, opener bids that suit.
   2. With a balanced hand after a fourth suit bid at the two-level, opener bids 2 NT with a good 12 to 15 HCP; 3 NT with 16 or 17 HCP; or 2 NT to be followed up with strong action later with 18 HCP.
   3. With other distributions, opener bids as naturally as possible.

Examples:

1.

Opener	Responder
♠ A K x x	♠ x x x
♡ x	♡ A Q 9 x x
◇ x x x	◇ A J 9
♣ A Q 10 x x	♣ K x
1 ♣	1 ♡
1 ♠	2 ◇ (1)
3 ♣ (2)	3 NT (3)
Pass	

(1) Fourth Suit Forcing and Artificial — game force
(2) Natural — five or more clubs
(3) Settling for 3 NT when no 5-3 heart fit comes to light

2. Bermuda Bowl, 1977.

Opener	Responder
♠ A Q J 7	♠ K 2
♡ 10 2	♡ A 9 7 5
◇ K 7 4	◇ A 10 8
♣ A Q 7 6	♣ K 10 9 2
1 ♣	1 ♡
1 ♠	2 ◇ (1)
3 NT (2)	4 ♣ (3)
4 ♠ (4)	4 NT (5)
5 ◇ (6)	6 ♣ (7)
Pass	

(1) Fourth Suit Forcing and Artificial — game force
(2) 16-17 HCP; balanced
(3) Trying for a club slam
(4) Spade ace; no red suit ace
(5) Club ace or king
(6) Diamond king
(7) This excellent slam was missed by both teams.

Chapter 10

THE ROMEX APPROACH TO CUE-BIDDING

Romex tends to use cue-bidding freely, especially on those hands where the partners are roughly equal in strength. Most cue-bidding situations arise after a one-bid, when each partner has substantial assets and the combined strength justifies a slam probe.

Romex cue-bids are used for trump control. The cheapest available notrump bid shows a trump honor. However, there is one important consideration here: THE ACE AND KING OF TRUMP ARE TREATED AS EQUALS. Thus, a bid of notrump in a cue-bidding sequence shows EITHER the ace or king of trump.

Otherwise, the traditional approach to cue-bidding is followed. It is more orderly first to bid all first-round controls before starting to show second-round controls. If there is a choice of cue-bids, the cheapest available cue-bid is made. If a suit is skipped, it denies the appropriate control in that suit.

In the light of experience, however, there is one exception to the last principle. When you hold a trump control and the like club control, experience has shown that IT IS MORE ECONOMICAL TO FIRST SHOW THE CLUB CONTROL, leaving the trump cue-bid for the next convenient opportunity.

In brief, the following rules apply:

1. The cheapest cue-bid is made when a cue-bid is offered, except that you should cue-bid a club control in preference to a trump control.
2. The first minimum cue-bid of notrump in a cue-bidding sequence shows the ace or king of trump; the second minimum bid of notrump shows the missing trump control.
3. The first cue-bid of a suit shows first-round control; the second cue bid of the same suit, second round control

unless the cue-bidder has already denied this value.

4. 3 NT is a cue-bid only in certain specific circumstances — where the 3 NT bidder cannot wish to suggest notrump as the final contract.

5. 4 NT is never a cue-bid UNLESS it has been preceded by other cue-bids to set up the sequence. To clarify this — where 4 NT is the first move in a slam-going sequence is Key Card Blackwood — it never starts a cue-bidding sequence.

6. In a minor suit sequence, 3 NT is almost always natural and not forcing; i.e., not a cue-bid.

7. The king in partner's suit may be shown as the ace in exceptional cases.

There is one sequence where 3 NT is a trump cue-bid:

$$1 \spadesuit — 2 \heartsuit$$
$$3 \heartsuit — 3 \, NT$$

A 3 ♠ bid after the 3 ♡ bid would start a relay sequence. A 3 NT bid, not being needed in a natural sense, is a trump cue-bid.

In many sequences a player has a choice of using relay (See Part 3) or a cue-bidding sequence. How should he decide which method to employ?

Cue-Bid or Relay?

Cue-bidding is best when:	Relays are best when:
The strength is divided evenly between the partners	The relayer has the better hand
Lots of information is needed	The situation is well defined (strength and distribution), and/or less information is needed
The player has a void	Relayer has no void
When slam interest is only mild	There is possibility of a grand slam.

Examples:

1. Blue Ribbon Pairs, 1980.

Opener	Responder
George	Eddie
Rosenkranz	Wold

♠ A 9 8 7 5 4	♠ Q J 6
♡ A J 10 2	♡ K Q 8 6
◇ A	◇ K J 9
♣ J 7	♣ A 8 3

Opener	Responder	
1 ♠	2 ♣ (1)	
2 ♡	3 ♡ (2)	
3 ♠ (3)	4 ♣ (4)	Double
4 ◇ (5)	4 NT (6)	
5 ◇ (7)	6 ♡ (8)	
Pass		

(1) A difficult hand to bid. A waiting move instead of a Maxi-Raise with only three-card support.

(2) Setting the trump suit for cue-bidding

(3) Cue-bid

(4) Cue-bidding the ace of clubs before the trump feature

(5) Cue-bidding the ace of diamonds and denying second-round club control. Redouble would show second-round club control.

(6) Trump cue-bid (ace or king).

(7) The crucial bid, showing second round diamond control.

(8) Partner must have the singleton ace of diamonds as I have the king. His aggressive bidding indicates ten cards in the major suits. He cannot be bidding like this without the ace of trump. The king of diamonds will serve to discard the losing club.

2.

Opener	Responder
♠ Q J 7 4 3	♠ A K 5
♡ K Q J 8 5	♡ A 7
◇ K Q	◇ J 10 7 5 4
♣ 8	♣ A 7 6

1 ♠	2 ◇
2 ♡	3 ♠ (1)
4 ◇ (2)	4 ♡ (3)
4 ♠ (4)	5 ♣ (5)
5 ♡ (6)	5 ♠ (7)
6 ♠ (8)	Pass

(1) Strong hand; good spade fit, feature in at least one side suit

(2) Exceptionally the king in partner's suit can be shown before other values if convenient. Slam interest, but no high trump honor as opener could bid 3 NT.

(3) Cue-bidding the ace of hearts

(4) Non-forcing

(5) In spite of opener's sign-off, responder still has slam interest. Cue-bidding the ace of clubs.

(6) Second round heart control but no diamond control beyond that already shown
(7) Responder is still not able to bid the slam
(8) With excellent playing strength opener bids the slam.

3. Bermuda Bowl. U. S. vs. Sweden, 1953.

Opener	Responder
♠ A 9 7 5 2	♠ K Q 10 4 3
♡ A K J 6	♡ —
◇ 9 5 4	◇ A K 10
♣ J	♣ A 9 6 4 3
1 ♠	2 ♣ (1)
2 ♡	3 ♠ (2)
3 NT (3)	4 ♣ (4)
4 ♡ (5)	4 NT (6)
5 ♣ (7)	5 ◇ (8)
5 ♡ (9)	7 ♠ (10)
Pass	

(1) Planning to show the heart void by making a delayed splinter
(2) Change of plans. 4 ♠ would be non-forcing, though showing the heart void. Responder cannot risk a pass, so the slammish 3 ♠ bid is made.
(3) Cue-bid showing a high trump honor
(4) Club ace
(5) Heart ace
(6) Trump honor; no singleton or king in clubs
(7) Second-round club control
(8) Diamond ace
(9) Heart king
(10) I can count 13 tricks!

Neither Bermuda Bowl team reached this excellent grand slam.

4. Canadian Nationals, 1981.

Opener	Responder
♠ A 7 4	♠ Q 5
♡ 5 2	♡ K Q 9
◇ K Q 7 3	◇ A 6 4
♣ A 10 8 2	♣ K J 7 6 3

1 ◇	2 ♣
3 ♣	3 ♡ (1)
3 ♠ (2)	3 NT (3)
Pass	

(1) Cue-bid showing a control or a stopper
(2) Cue-bid
(3) To play since 3 NT could be (and is) the final contract

5. Mexican Nationals. Open Pairs, 1972.

Opener	Responder
♠ K Q 7 5 4	♠ 8 5
♡ A 6 4 2	♡ K J 10 9 5 3
◇ A 8 6	◇ K Q 4
♣ 2	♣ A 5

1 ♠	2 ♡
3 ♡	4 ♣ (1)
4 ◇ (2)	4 NT (3)
5 ♣ (4)	5 ◇ (5)
6 ♡ (6)	Pass

(1) Cue-bid, initiating a slam investigation. Preferable to starting a relay sequence with 3 ♠ .
(2) Delighted. First round diamond control
(3) Trump honor; no spade ace; no second round club control
(4) Still exploring. Second round club control
(5) I can show a second round diamond control
(6) That should suffice

6. Challenge the Champs.

Opener	*Responder*
♠ Q 5	♠ J
♡ J 10 6 4 3	♡ A K Q
◇ A Q 10 4	◇ 7 5 3
♣ K 3	♣ A Q 10 9 6 2
1 ♡	2 ♣
2 ◇	2 ♡
3 ♣ (1)	4 ♣ (2)
4 ◇ (3)	4 ♠ (4)
5 ♣ (5)	6 ♡ (6)
Pass	

(1) Natural
(2) Club ace; no first round control in diamonds or spades
(3) Diamond ace
(4) Spade king or singleton
(5) Club king
(6) A difficult slam to bid!

Chapter 11

THE JUMP SHIFT

The jump shift is a valuable part of the Romex arsenal. Accurate auctions on hands that would be troublesome otherwise are possible by making certain restrictions on the bid.

The key feature of a Romex Jump Shift is the quality of the suit. The suit must be at least semi-solid, i.e., a suit that can play opposite a singleton for at most one loser.

The requirements for a Romex Jump Shift:

1. Either:
    1. A six-card or longer semi-solid suit, OR
    2. A five-card or longer semi-solid suit and a fit for opener's suit
2. 16 or more HCP; perhaps less with exceptional distribution
3. Usually five or more Controls
4. No more than five Losers
5. No four-card side suit is allowed other than a fit for opener's suit. (Two-suited hands make a simple response and show the second suit later.) Later we will see how this prohibition smooths the cue-bidding path.

Opener's rebids follow an exactly prescribed order of priorities:

1. With a top honor in responder's suit, opener must give a direct raise even with a singleton honor. There are two ways to raise:
    1. Direct raise. The usual method.
    2. Void-showing jump. A jump in a new suit shows a void in that suit.

2. Lacking a trump honor:
   1. Opener shows concentration in a suit (at least two of the top three honors). He does this by bidding, in order of priority:

      Rebidding his suit — does not promise extra length. Bidding a new suit to show concentration in that suit — does not promise length in the suit.

   2. Opener can jump rebid his suit to show at least a semi-solid six-card or longer suit. The bid shows extra strength and is forcing.

3. If unable to do any of the above, opener must make the cheapest bid in notrump. Such a bid does not necessarily show a balanced hand.

Responder's Second Bid
A. Opener Raised The Jump Shift Suit

1. Raising opener's suit is Key Card Blackwood with opener's suit as trump. This applies even at the game level. In theory this establishes opener's suit as trump, though responder may do this when intending to choose his own suit as trump.

2. New suits are cue-bids — recognizable as such, as responder can't have length in a new suit. The trump suit is ambiguous, but for the purpose of the cue-bidding sequence, opener's suit is trump. This is because the jump shift suit is known to be solidified and the notrump cue-bids can establish the solidity of opener's suit.

B. Opener Has Denied a Top Honor in the Jump Shift Suit

1. Game bids in notrump, the jump shift suit or opener's suit are non-forcing — showing five Losers. Opener is free to continue with extra values by placing the contract or Romex Cue-Bidding.

2. 4 NT is Key Card Blackwood for opener's suit. It

makes no sense to use Key Card Blackwood in the jump shift suit as opener has already denied a top honor.

3. Rebidding the jump shift suit sets responder's suit as trump. Romex Cue-Bidding follows.

4. The rebid of a new suit starts a Romex Cue-Bidding sequence, with opener's suit as trump. If responder is unable to rebid his suit below game, the trump suit he intends to play is ambiguous. However, this has no effect on the cue-bidding sequence, from opener's perspective, except that he must not sign off in his suit at the six-level unless responder has actually raised it.

The jump shift into a minor over an opening bid in the other minor is a two-way bid — opener assumes it is an artificial raise of his minor, with a good 7 to a poor 11 HCP, but it could also be a genuine jump shift. To clarify the latter responder follows with strong action on the next round. The Romex Jump Shift procedure just outlined would then be in effect.

Examples:

1. Olympiad. Italy vs. Canada, 1968.

Opener	Responder
♠ Q	♠ A K J 9 5 3
♡ 8 3	♡ A K 6
◊ Q 10 9 3	◊ A 5
♣ A K J 9 6 2	♣ 8 4
1 ♣	2 ♠ (1)
3 ♠ (2)	4 ♣ (3)
4 ♠ (4)	4 NT (5)
5 ♣ (6)	5 ◊ (7)
5 ♡ (8)	5 NT (9)
6 ♣ (10)	6 ♠ (11)
Pass	

(1) Ideally should have ♠ 10, but the jump shift rates to be the most effective approach
(2) Mandatory raise with a top spade honor
(3) Key Card Blackwood with clubs as the trump suit. A tactical move to discover how useful opener's clubs will be.
(4) Two Key Cards; no club queen
(5) Spiral (See Part 3) for kings. The king of spades is not counted because the suit is known to be solid.
(6) First step = no heart king
(7) Go on
(8) No diamond king
(9) Spiral for queens. 5 ♠ would have been non-forcing.
(10) No heart queen. The club queen was denied by the response to Key Card Blackwood.
(11) You sure had a poor opening bid!

2. Mexican Trials, 1980.

Opener	Responder
Sol	George
Dubson	Rosenkranz

♠ K Q 10 8 4	♠ A 6
♡ —	♡ Q 4 3
◇ Q 8 5	◇ A K J 10 7 2
♣ A J 10 6 4	♣ K 3

1 ♠	3 ◇ (1)
4 ♡ (2)	4 ♠ (3)
5 ♡ (4)	7 ◇ (5)
Pass	

(1) Book bid with semi-solid six-card suit; six Controls; five Losers
(2) Diamond honor and heart void
(3) Key Card Blackwood in spades
(4) Two Key Cards and the spade queen
(5) I was operating

211

3.

Opener	Responder
♠ K Q x x x	♠ A
♡ x x	♡ A Q x
◇ A x x	◇ K Q J 10 x x
♣ K Q x	♣ J x x

1 ♠	3 ◇ (1)
4 ◇ (2)	4 ♡ (3)
6 ◇ (4)	Pass

(1) Ideal jump shift: 17 HCP; five Controls; five Losers; semi-solid six-card suit
(2) Immediate raise is mandatory with a top diamond honor
(3) Cue-bid agreeing spades for the moment. Club weakness is a strong possibility.
(4) Opener indicates no problem in the black suits by bidding 6 ◇. He knows that responder's five Controls must include at least two aces. The ace of clubs is denied when opener fails to cue-bid it.
(5) Responder would correct with a spade fit.

4. Olympiad. U. S. vs. France, 1980.

Opener	Responder
♠ —	♠ A K Q 10 9 3
♡ A K J 10 3	♡ Q 7 6 2
◇ K 10 5 4	◇ A 9
♣ A Q 8 6	♣ 2

1 ♡	2 ♠ (1)
3 ♡ (2)	4 NT (3)
5 ♣ (4)	7 ♡ (5)
Pass	

(1) Book Jump Shift: Semi-solid suit; five Controls; four Losers; and a fit for opener
(2) No fit. The honor concentration in hearts is shown in preference to the concentration in the side club suit.

212

(3) Key Card Blackwood with opener's suit as the Key Card suit.
(4) Zero or three Key Cards
(5) Bidding what he knows he can make

5. Olympiad. Canada vs. Holland, 1968.

Opener	Responder
♠ A K Q 6	♠ 5 3
♡ 7	♡ A K Q J 10 5 2
◇ Q 9 7 6 4	◇ A
♣ K Q 9	♣ 8 5 3

1 ◇	2 ♡ (1)
2 ♠ (2)	3 ♡ (3)
3 ♠ (4)	4 ◇ (5)
4 ♠ (6)	4 NT (7)
6 ♡ (8)	Pass

(1) Five Controls; five Losers; solid suit
(2) No heart honor; fewer than two top diamond honors; at least two of the top three spade honors
(3) Setting hearts as trumps and requesting cue-bidding
(4) Spade ace
(5) Diamond ace; denies the club ace
(6) Spade king; no other ace
(7) Trump cue-bid; no club control
(8) Since responder is still interested, knowing the club ace is missing, he must have solid hearts and the ace of diamonds.

Both pairs missed the laydown slam.

6. Challenge the Champs. The Bridge Circus vs. The Aces, 1979.

Opener	*Responder*
♠ 10 8	♠ A K Q J 3 2
♡ A 9 6 5 3	♡ 10
◇ A K 10	◇ J 5 3
♣ K 9 7	♣ A Q J
1 ♡	2 ♠ (1)
3 ◇ (2)	3 ♠ (3)
4 ◇ (4)	5 ♣ (5)
5 ♡ (6)	5 NT (7)
6 ♣ (8)	6 ♡ (9)
7 ♠ (10)	Pass

(1) All the requirements for the Romex Jump Shift fulfilled: solid six-card suit; five Controls; five Losers
(2) No honor in partner's suit; less than two of the top three heart honors; two of the top three diamond honors
(3) Setting spades as trumps; asks for cue-bidding
(4) Diamond ace; no club ace
(5) Club ace
(6) Heart ace
(7) Top trump honor; no other king
(8) Club king
(9) Heart singleton — he has already denied the heart king
(10) With the king and ten of diamonds and the ten and eight of spades in reserve, opener accepts the grand slam try

Neither the Aces nor the Bridge Circus reached this odds-on grand slam.

7. Olympiad, 1972.

Opener	Responder
George	Miguel
Rosenkranz	Reygadas

♠ A K Q 10 x x	♠ x x
♡ A Q 10 x	♡ x x
◇ x x	◇ A K x
♣ x	♣ A K Q J 10 x

1 ♠	3 ♣
4 ♠ (1)	4 NT (2)
5 ♣ (3)	5 ◇ (4)
5 ♠ (5)	7 ♣ (6)

(1) At least a semi-solid spade suit
(2) Key Card Blackwood with spades as trump
(3) Three Key Cards
(4) Do you have the queen of spades?
(5) I have the spade queen but I don't have the king of hearts
(6) Should be the safest grand. Would try 7 NT at match-points.

8.

Opener	Responder
♠ K J 10	♠ Q x
♡ x	♡ A K Q J 10 x
◇ K J 10 x	◇ A Q x
♣ K J 10 x x	♣ x x

1 ◇	2 ♡
2 NT (1)	3 ♡ (2)
3 NT (3)	Pass(4)

(1) A long list of denials: no top heart honor; no concentration in diamonds; no concentration in either side suit.
(2) Setting hearts as trump and requesting a cue-bid.
(3) No ace. Cannot be a trump cue-bid, given his previous bid.
(4) An easy pass!

9.

Opener	Responder
♠ K x x	♠ A Q
♡ —	♡ K Q J 10 x x
◇ A J x x x	◇ K Q x x
♣ K Q J x x	♣ x
1 ◇	2 ♡
3 ♣ (1)	3 ♠ (2)
3 NT (3)	4 ◇ (4)
4 ♡ (5)	4 NT (6)
5 ♣ (7)	5 ◇ (8)
6 ◇ (9)	Pass

(1) Two or three top club honors; no top heart honor; denies two top diamond honors
(2) Agrees diamonds; 3 ♡ was available to agree hearts
(3) Trump cue-bid (ace or king); no club ace because the club ace would be cue-bid first
(4) Waiting; denies the heart ace
(5) Heart void; opener has denied the ace of hearts
(6) Responder could gamble 6 ◇ now, but prefers to see if opener has extra values. The trump cue-bid denies the king of spades or the ace of clubs
(7) Club king
(8) I still can't bid it
(9) I can

10.

Opener	Responder
♠ 7 6	♠ A Q J 9 5 2
♡ K Q J 10 8	♡ A 9 7 4
◇ Q 8	◇ K J
♣ K Q J 4	♣ 5
1 ♡	2 ♠ (1)
3 ♡ (2)	4 ♡ (3)
Pass (4)	

216

(1) A good jump shift with trump support, five Controls, five Losers and a semi-solid suit.
(2) Honor concentration in hearts; no top spade honor
(3) Non-forcing; heart fit with five Losers
(4) I can pass? Great!

11. Ottawa. Open Pairs, 1983.

Opener	*Responder*
George	Eddie
Rosenkranz	Wold

♠ A Q J x	♠ K x
♡ x	♡ A 10 x
◇ Q x x	◇ A K J 10 x x
♣ A J x x x	♣ x x

1 ♣	2 ◇ (1)
3 ♣ (2)	3 ◇ (3)
4 ◇ (4)	4 ♡ (5)
4 ♠ (6)	4 NT (7)
5 ♣ (8)	5 ♠ (9)
7 ◇ (10)	Pass

(1) For the moment, assumed to be a club raise with 7-11 HCP
(2) Sign-off
(3) Surprise! I have a real jump shift in diamonds.
(4) Top diamond honor
(5) Heart ace
(6) Spade ace
(7) Trump honor (which you know) but no ace of clubs
(8) I have the ace of clubs
(9) Spade king; no heart king
(10) A heart ruff makes 13 tricks

Chapter 12

SPLINTER BIDS

Romex makes much use of one of the most popular slam conventions — "splinter" bids. They are so named because a player bids a suit in which he has a "Splinter," i.e., a suit in which he has either a singleton or a void. The splinter bid is made by a single or double jump in the short suit.

A splinter bid does more than announce shortness in the bid suit. It also declares:

1. A fit for partner's suit. This means a fit for his last bid suit, unless otherwise noted.
2. Slam interest if partner has extra values and/or losers in the "splinter suit" that will be covered by trumping.
3. A splinter bid by opener at his second turn shows four Losers, a fit for partner's major and two quick losers in the fragment suit (the fourth suit).

Romex uses this valuable tool in many sequences. Here are a few examples:

$$1 \spadesuit - 4 \clubsuit \qquad 1 \, NT - 2 \spadesuit \qquad 1 \spadesuit - 2 \clubsuit$$
$$3 \heartsuit \; - 5 \clubsuit \qquad 2 \heartsuit - 4 \diamondsuit$$

In some auctions a splinter bid promises a VOID in the bid suit. An alternative sequence is available to show a singleton (See the next Chapter, "Special Void-Showing Sequences.")

The reader can learn the various sequences employing splinter bids gradually as he reads the advanced section.

Here are some examples to show the value of a splinter bid:

1.

Opener	Responder
♠ A Q x x x x	♠ K J x x
♡ K x	♡ A x x x
◇ A x x x	◇ x
♣ x	♣ A x x x

1 ♠	4 ◇ (1)
4 NT (2)	5 ♣ (3)
7 ♠ (4)	Pass

(1) Splinter raise in spades: singleton or void in diamonds; four or more spades; slam interest; and usually no good, long side suit
(2) Key Card Blackwood
(3) Zero or three Key Cards. Obviously three in view of the slam try.
(4) Perfect! The grand is excellent even with a trump lead.

2. Mexican Nationals. Swiss Teams, 1979.

Opener	Responder
Edith	Sol
Rosenkranz	Dubson

♠ K Q 6 5	♠ A J 10 4 2
♡ Q 10 4	♡ 8 5
◇ 8	◇ A Q J 4
♣ A K Q 4 3	♣ 10 2

1 ♣	1 ♠
4 ◇ (1)	4 ♠ (2)
Pass	

(1) Spade fit; four Losers; diamond shortage; two quick losers in hearts.
(2) Too bad — two quick losers in the fourth suit

3. Bermuda Bowl. U. S. vs. Sweden, 1953.

Opener	*Responder*
♠ K Q 10 8 7 6 3	♠ A 9 5 2
♡ 8	♡ J 9 4 2
◇ A 7 6 2	◇ 10
♣ K	♣ A Q 7 2
1 ♠	4 ◇ (1)
4 NT (2)	5 ♡ (3)
6 ♠ (4)	Pass

(1) Splinter raise with short diamonds
(2) Key Card Blackwood for spades
(3) Two Key Cards; no trump queen
(4) One Key Card is missing

Neither team reached the laydown small slam.

Chapter 13

SPECIAL VOID-SHOWING SEQUENCES

Romex uses a number of sequences to show a void when the opening bid was one of a suit. The immediate distinction between a singleton and a void is quite valuable: partner can evaluate the ace of the short suit, and the splinter-bidder does not have to waste a round of bidding to show the void on the next round.

Below is a summary of these void-showing sequences:

A) After a Minor Suit Opening

1. A double jump in a new suit shows a void and a fit in the minor:

    1♣ — 3◇ , 3♡ or 3♠

2. A three-level bid in a new suit after an inverted raise shows a void:

    1◇ — 2◇
    3♣, 3♡ or 3♠

3. A double jump after a one or two-level response in the other minor shows a void:

1♣ — 1◇	or	1◇ — 2♣
3♡ or 3♠		4♡ or 4♠

B) After a Major Suit Opening

1. A jump after a single raise shows a void:

    $1\heartsuit - 2\heartsuit$
    $3\spadesuit$, $4\clubsuit$ or $4\diamondsuit$

2. A double jump after a forcing 1 NT response shows a freak one-suiter with a void:

    $1\heartsuit - 1$ NT
    $3\spadesuit$, $4\clubsuit$ or $4\diamondsuit$

    To show a heart void, opener jumps to $4\spadesuit$:

$1\spadesuit - 1$ NT	$1\spadesuit - 1$ NT
$4\heartsuit$ is natural	$4\spadesuit$ shows a heart void

    Opener must open 1 NT, $4\diamondsuit$ or $4\spadesuit$ with a hand with which he would like to open $1\spadesuit$ and follow with $4\spadesuit$ in the normal sense.

3. Responder can make a void-showing splinter in support of opener's major after a two-over-one response:

    a) A single jump shows a void:
       $1\spadesuit - 2\diamondsuit$
       $2\heartsuit - 4\clubsuit$

    b) To show a void in opener's second suit responder gives a double jump raise of opener's first bid suit:
       $1\spadesuit - 2\diamondsuit$
       $2\heartsuit - 4\spadesuit$ = Heart void; spade fit

4. Opener can make a void-showing splinter after a two-over-one response by jumping:
    $1\heartsuit - 2\clubsuit$
    $3\spadesuit$ or $4\diamondsuit$

5. Opener may show a void after a limit raise by jumping to the five-level.

$1\,\heartsuit - 3\,\heartsuit$

$5\,\clubsuit$

A maximum of four Losers and adequate controls are required.

C) After the auction has begun: $1\,\clubsuit$ or $1\,\diamondsuit - 1\,\heartsuit$ or $1\,\spadesuit$

2 of Responder's Major

responder's jumps show voids:

$1\,\diamondsuit - 1\,\heartsuit$

$2\,\heartsuit - 3\,\spadesuit, 4\,\clubsuit$ or $4\,\diamondsuit$

Note that opener's splinter after a response of one of a major is "normal," i.e., a singleton or void. He does, however, tell whether or not he controls the fourth suit:

$1\,\diamondsuit - 1\,\heartsuit$	$1\,\diamondsuit - 1\,\heartsuit$
$4\,\diamondsuit$ = A heart raise with four Losers and both unbid suits controlled	$4\,\clubsuit$ = A heart raise with four Losers, at most one club and no spade control

D) After a Jump Shift

Opener shows a void and the missing top honor in responder's suit with a jump:

$1\,\spadesuit - 3\,\clubsuit$

$4\,\diamondsuit$ = Diamond void and a top club honor

Examples:

1. International Popular Bridge Magazine. October, 1982.

Opener	Responder
♠ A 10 6 3	♠ K Q 9 8 4
♡ 4 3	♡ A Q J 7 2
◊ Q 7 5 2	◊ —
♣ A K 7	♣ J 10 8

1 ◊	1 ♠
2 ♠	4 ◊ (1)
5 ♣ (2)	5 ♡ (3)
6 ♣ (4)	6 ♠ (5)
Pass	

(1) Diamond void
(2) That's good news. I have the ace of clubs. I don't have the heart ace.
(3) Heart ace
(4) Club king and sufficient values to bid a slam. In this case — the ace of spades.
(5) No king of hearts

2. Le Bridgeur, 1982.

Opener	Responder
♠ A 8 6 4	♠ K 9 5 3
♡ 8 3	♡ K Q J 10 9 4
◊ A K Q 9 3	◊ 10 8 2
♣ 10 5	♣ —

1 ◊	1 ♡
1 ♠	4 ♣ (1)
4 ◊ (2)	4 ♠ (3)
6 ◊ (4)	6 ♡ (5)
Pass	

(1) A minimum for this bid but a lot of tricks and a fit in spades
(2) Cue-bid
(3) I don't have the heart ace and I have told my story.
(4) Natural. Responder can choose the slam.
(5) OK

3. Mexican Nationals. Men's Pairs, 1975.

Opener	Responder
Roger	George
Bates	Rosenkranz

♠ A K Q	♠ 10 9 3 2
♡ Q 6 5 4	♡ A K 10 2
◊ Q J	◊ A K 5 4 2
♣ 10 6 4 2	♣ —

1 ♣	1 ◊
1 ♡	4 ♣ (1)
4 ♠ (2)	5 ◊ (3)
5 ♡ (4)	6 ♡ (5)
Pass	

(1) A void in partner's first bid suit
(2) No wasted values, good for a cue-bid
(3) Diamond ace
(4) I have done my duty — my hearts are bad. I don't want to overbid by cue-bidding 5 ♠.
(5) OK, but I hope we didn't miss a grand.

The hearts were 4-1 but the diamonds behaved.

4. Mexican Trials, 1978.

Opener	Responder
George	Sol
Rosenkranz	Dubson

♠ A K 7 4 2	♠ Q 10 8 6
♡ 10 9 4	♡ —
◇ K 5	◇ A J 10 6
♣ Q J 6	♣ A K 9 8 2

1 ♠	2 ♣ (1)
2 ♠ (2)	4 ♡ (3)
4 NT (4)	5 ♠ (5)
7 ♠ (6)	Pass

(1) Starting the delayed splinter
(2) Minimum hand with seven Losers, not worth a 3 ♣ bid
(3) Delayed splinter: heart void; spade support
(4) Key Card Blackwood. Suddenly my seven Loser hand has become a four Loser hand. Your auction says that you should cover at least three of my four Losers.
(5) Two Key Cards and the trump queen
(6) You cover my three top-card Losers. If you have the club king, we are laydown. If you don't have the club king, you may have the AQJx of diamonds. The grand slam should be at worst on a finesse and it is likely to be laydown.

5. *Win With Romex,* 1975.

Opener	*Responder*
♠ K Q 10 5 2	♠ A 3
♡ —	♡ Q 6 4
♢ Q 6 4	♢ A K J 10 9 7
♣ A J 7 3 2	♣ K 4

1 ♠	3 ♢
4 ♡ (1)	4 ♠ (2)
5 ♡ (3)	7 ♢ (4)
Pass	

(1) Diamond honor and heart void
(2) Key Card Blackwood in spades
(3) Two Key Cards and the trump queen
(4) What do you know!

6. Mexican Nationals. Women's Pairs, 1983.

Opener	*Responder*
Edith	Maria
Rosenkranz	Cespedes
♠ K Q 10 8 6 2	♠ A J 4
♡ —	♡ K J 8 5 2
♢ A J 5	♢ 10 4
♣ Q J 7 4	♣ 10 9 2

1 ♠	2 ♣
4 ♡ (1)	4 ♠ (2)
Pass	

(1) Heart void. To show a long heart suit opener bids 2 NT to initiate the Long Suit Slam Try.
(2) Sign-off

7. Puerto Vallarta, 1982.

Opener	Responder
George	Luis
Rosenkranz	Attaguile

♠ K Q J 9 7 6 5 2	♠ 4
♡ —	♡ Q J 9 4
◊ Q J 5	◊ 10 7 4 2
♣ A 2	♣ Q J 8 4

1 ♠	1 NT (1)
4 ♠ (2)	Pass (3)

(1) Forcing
(2) Showing a heart void and four Losers
(3) The heart void doesn't excite me at all.

Opener cannot rebid 4 ♡ which would be natural.

8. Mexican Nationals. Knockout Teams, 1977.

Opener	Responder
Sol	Edith
Dubson	Rosenkranz

♠ A K 10 8 7 4	♠ 6
♡ K Q J 10 2	♡ 9 7 3
◊ 3	◊ A 9 6 4
♣ 10	♣ Q 9 8 5 2

1 ♠	1 NT (1)
4 ♡ (2)	Pass

(1) Forcing
(2) Natural with four Losers

228

9. St. Moritz. Mixed Pairs, 1978.

Opener	Responder
George	Edith
Rosenkranz	Rosenkranz

♠ —	♠ Q 7 6 4
♡ K Q 9 7 6 2	♡ 8
◇ K 8 6	◇ A Q J
♣ A Q 9 2	♣ K J 10 7 4

1 ♡	2 ♣
3 ♠ (1)	4 ◇ (2)
4 NT (3)	6 ♣ (4)
Pass	

(1) Spade void; club fit; four or five Losers
(2) Cue-bid showing the diamond ace
(3) Romex Cue-Bid showing the ace of trump and denying the ace of hearts
(4) Should have a good play

10. North American Championships. Honolulu, 1983.

Opener	Responder
♠ A K 10 7 4	♠ Q J 9 5
♡ K 9 6 5	♡ A Q J 7
◇ —	◇ 9 7 3
♣ K Q 10 9	♣ 6 2

1 ♠	3 ♠
5 ◇ (1)	6 ♠ (2)
Pass	

(1) Four Losers; diamond void
(2) Three working Cover Cards and plus values. A grand slam is out of the question in light of opener's limited opening bid. Opener cannot hold the ace-king of spades, the king of hearts, the ace-king of clubs and a diamond void.

11. North American Championships. Honolulu. Men's
Board-A-Match, 1983.

Opener	Responder
George	Eddie
Rosenkranz	Wold

♠ Q	♠ K 6 2
♡ A Q 10 3	♡ K J 9 8 7
◇ 8 7	◇ K 10 3
♣ A K Q 10 8 3	♣ 5 4

1 ♣	1 ♡
3 ♠ (1)	4 ♡ (2)
Pass	

(1) Singleton or void in spades; four Losers; denies a diamond
control. With a diamond control, opener would have bid
4 ♣.
(2) Not enthusiastic with spade duplication and an aceless hand

12. *Win With Romex,* 1975.

Opener	Responder
♠ 2	♠ K J 6 4
♡ K Q 7 4	♡ J 8 6 5 3
◇ K Q J 10 3	◇ 4
♣ A Q 5	♣ J 4 2

1 ◇	1 ♡
4 ◇ (1)	4 ♡ (2)
Pass	

(1) Heart fit; four Losers, guarantees control in both black suits
(2) Not interested. Lack of controls and probable misfit.
Opener is limited to a maximum of 17 HCP as he failed to
open 1 NT.

Chapter 14

PASSED HAND BIDDING

"Light" opening bids in third seat, after partner has passed, are a reality of modern tournament bridge. Light openings attempt to direct a lead, compete for the part-score, and/or make life difficult for the opposition. Properly used, such bids can achieve these aims and be quite successful in the long run.

There are a few potential stumbling blocks to the partnership employing light third hand openings:

1. Most important of all — don't open light indiscriminately. The hand should have some redeeming features to justify bidding, such as:

    1. A suit you want led
    2. Good distribution
    3. Near opening strength in high cards
    4. Length in one or both majors
    5. Advantageous vulnerability. It is best to be adventuresome when not vulnerable.

2. Responses to third seat openings cannot logically have the same meaning as responses by an unpassed hand. The limit on responder's hand means most responses will be nonforcing.

Let's begin by looking at some possible third hand openings:

None vulerable

Pass — Pass — ?

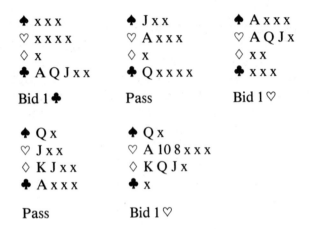

♠ x x x	♠ J x x	♠ A x x x
♡ x x x x	♡ A x x x	♡ A Q J x
◇ x	◇ x	◇ x x
♣ A Q J x x	♣ Q x x x x	♣ x x x
Bid 1 ♣	Pass	Bid 1 ♡

♠ Q x	♠ Q x
♡ J x x	♡ A 10 8 x x x
◇ K J x x	◇ K Q J x
♣ A x x x	♣ x
Pass	Bid 1 ♡

Responses to third and fourth seat major suit openings are discussed in the Chapter "Reverse Romex Drury." Following is a list of responses that change when faced with a third seat minor suit opening:

1. Non-jump new suit responses are not forcing. A two-over-one response is still sound — five-card or longer suit and near opening bid strength. However opener may pass.
2. A 2 NT response is natural, not a Maxi-Raise. Do not overuse this bid, as it makes life very difficult for opener if he doesn't like notrump and doesn't have a hand good enough for game. Thus the following rules are recomomended:

> Never bid 2 NT with a four-card major
> Keep the bid "up to strength"—a good 11 or 12 HCP

3. Raises are otherwise unchanged:

> 1♣ (or 1◇) — 2♣ (or 2◇) = Inverted; usually 10-12 HCP; not forcing
>
> 1♣ (or 1◇) — 3♣ (or 3◇) = Weak; maximum of 7 HCP
>
> 1◇ — 3♣ OR 1♣ — 2◇ = "Inbetween" raise: A good seven to a poor 10 HCP and at least five trumps. Opener can sign off in the agreed suit at the lowest level if he lacks game ambitions.

4. One hand type is particularly troublesome: a near-opening hand with good distribution; a good fit for opener's minor and a five-card or longer major: For example:

Pass — Pass — 1◇ — Pass	♠ A 10 x x x x
???	♡ x
	◇ K Q x x
	♣ x x

It would be difficult to express the full value and distribution of the hand after a 1♠ response. Game or slam could easily be missed.

The solution is to use a jump shift to show such a hand: at least a fair five-card or longer major; at least four cards in opener's minor; good distribution (a short suit somewhere); and near opening high card strength. This bid is "nearly" forcing.

Opener bids as naturally as possible: three of the agreed minor is a sign-off. With a better hand it is often a good idea to temporize with a new suit bid to give responder a chance to rebid a six-card major.

Examples:

1.

Opener	Responder
♠ x	♠ A Q x x x
♡ K x x	♡ x
◇ A Q 10 x x	◇ K x x x
♣ 10 x x x	♣ J x x

	Pass
1 ◇	2 ♠ (1)
3 ◇ (2)	Pass

(1) At least a fair five-card suit, at least four diamonds, near opening strength
(2) This is as far as we go

2.

Opener	Responder
♠ Q x	♠ A 10 8 x x x
♡ A 10 x	♡ x
◇ A K x x	◇ Q J x x
♣ J x x x	♣ K x

	Pass
1 ◇	2 ♠ (1)
3 ♣ (2)	3 ♠ (3)
4 ♠ (4)	Pass

(1) At least a fair five-card suit, at least four diamonds, near opening strength
(2) New suit giving responder a chance to define his spade length
(3) I have at least six spades
(4) Then we have a good play for game

Players using the Romex relay methods described in Part 3 could enjoy a result like this:

Opener	Responder
♠ A x x	♠ x x x
♡ K Q x	♡ A J 8 x x x
◇ J x x	◇ —
♣ A Q 10 x	♣ K J x x

	Pass
1 ♣	2 ♡ (1)
2 ♠ (2)	3 ♡ (3)
3 ♠ (4)	4 ◇ (5)
7 ♣ (6)	Pass

(1) Five or more hearts; four or more clubs; near opening strength
(2) Relay, game force. Asks for distribution.
(3) Fourth step = a diamond void
(4) Relay asking for Key Cards
(5) Third step = two Key Cards; no queen of clubs
(6) We have arrived!

Now let us turn our attention to third and fourth hand preempts. First and second chair preempts will be discussed in Chapter 16.

Third and Fourth Hand Preempts

The discipline necessary for first and second seat preempts is unnecessary in third seat — partner cannot have a big hand. Opener looks at the vulnerability, his suit and perhaps his opponents, and does what seems best.

The only change worth making special note of is that in third seat, an opening bid of three of a minor no longer promises a seven-card suit to the AKQ or AKJ. Fourth seat preempts are rare, and should follow the character of first and second seat preempts, perhaps relaxing the standards a little. Of course, the weaker preempts should be passed out.

Examples:

Not Vulnerable

Pass — Pass — ???

♠ A x x	♠ x	♠ Q J 9 7 4 3 2
♡ Q J 9 x x x	♡ Q x	♡ —
◇ x	◇ K J 10 8 6 x	◇ K 8 6 3
♣ Q 10 x	♣ K 9 8 x	♣ J 4
Bid 2 ♡	Bid 3 ◇	Bid 3 ♠

Both vulnerable

Pass — Pass — Pass — ???

♠ A J 10 x x x	♠ x	♠ x x
♡ x	♡ A Q 9 8 x x	♡ x x x
◇ K Q x	◇ J x x	◇ x
♣ x x x	♣ x x x	♣ A K Q x x x x
Bid 2 ♠	Pass	Bid 3 ♣

♠ x x
♡ x
◇ Q x x
♣ A J 9 x x x x

Pass

Responses to Passed Hand Preempts

Responses to passed hand preempts are much simplified:

New suit	= Natural and non-forcing
Raise	= Preemptive
2 NT	= Game interest. Opener's rebids are the same as if he were an unpassed hand.

Examples:

Pass — Pass — 2♡ — Pass

♠ x x	♠ A 10 8 x x x	♠ x x
♡ K x x x	♡ —	♡ A x x x
♦ A x x x	♦ Q J x x	♦ A K x
♣ x x x	♣ Q x x	♣ x x x x
Bid 3 ♡	Bid 2 ♠	Bid 2 NT

Chapter 15

REVERSE ROMEX DRURY

Shaded third hand openings are an often occurring, inevitable necessity in the life of the successful tournament bridge competitor regardless of the type of game (board-a-match, IMPs or matchpoints) being played. These bids are desperately needed to set the stage for the killing lead or a profitable sacrifice, yet no one wants to pay the price — getting too high (or too low) probing for game. The key question: can you have your cake and eat it too?

Of all the light third-hand openings, a bid of one of a major is the most attractive. Effective preemption and a fair shot at profitably buying the contract are big plusses. The disadvantages of light third hand openings of one of a major — inaccurate game and slam bidding — are handled by the Romex version of Reverse Drury (''Reverse'' because the meaning of the 2 ◇ bid and the bid of two of a major are reversed from those assigned by Doug Drury, the inventor of the Drury Convention.) Following is a new and improved approach.

What is Drury?

Drury is an artificial 2♣ response used by a passed hand responding to a third or fourth seat opening bid of one of a major. This bid promises three or more cards in opener's suit and at least limit raise values. More specifically:

> At least three cards in opener's suit
> 10-12 HCP or the distributional equivalent
> 3 - 3 1/2 Cover Cards

Opener's Rebids

Opener can transmit four basic messages with his rebid:

subminimum opening; full opening (but uncertain about game); game values; and slam interest. This is the schedule:

Drury Rebids

1♡ or 1♠ — 2♣

Subminimum Rebids: Eight Losers	Two of opener's major = Subminimum opening; could be weak with a four-card major
	2♡ after opening 1♠ = Subminimum opening; natural; could be 4-4 in the majors.
Full Opening Rebids: Six or Seven Losers	2♢ = Artificial; full opening bid but doubt about how high to bid. Usually bid with game interest, occasionally with mild slam interest.
	Four of opener's major = Full opening bid but no slam interest. This leap to game makes the defenders do some guesswork.
Slam Try Rebids	2 NT = 17-18 HCP; no singleton or void; slam interest
	New suit at the three-level or 2♠ after a 1♡ opening bid = Natural; slam try; guarantees a singleton somewhere in the hand
	New suit at the four-level or 3♠ after a 1♡ opening bid = Void in the bid suit; slam interest; 5-4-4-0
	3 NT = Demands a cue-bidding sequence. Opener usually has a strong hand with a void.
	Three of opener's suit = TAB

Subsequent Auctions

A. Opener made a subminimum rebid

Responder knows game is very unlikely. If he ventures beyond the two-level he shows a hand too strong for a limit raise.

B. Opener rebids 2 ◇

Responder's rebids are designed to cater to a possible game or slam:

1 ♡ — 2 ♣	1 ♠ — 2 ♣
2 ◇ — 2 ♡ (1)	2 ◇ — 2 ♡ (5)
— 2 ♠ (2)	— 2 ♠ (1)
— 2 NT (3)	— 2 NT (3)
— 3 ♣ (2)	— 3 ♣ (2)
— 3 ◇ (2)	— 3 ◇ (2)
— 3 ♠ (4)	— 3 ♡ (2)
— 4 ♣ (4)	— 4 ♣ (4)
— 4 ◇ (4)	— 4 ◇ (4)
	— 4 ♡ (4)

(1) Minimum; no singleton or void
(2) Singleton
(3) Extra values; no singleton or void
(4) Void and less than 9 HCP. With a
    better hand responder would splinter
    directly over the opening bid.
(5) Natural with five or more hearts

After the auctions 1 ♡ — 2 ♣   or 1 ♠ — 2 ♣
                 2 ◇ — 2 ♡ or 2 NT   2 ◇ — 2 ♠ or 2 NT
a bid of a new suit by opener is a short suit game try.

C.   Opener makes a slam try

1. 2 NT rebid:
   1 ♡ or 1 ♠   — 2 ♣
   2 NT   — 3 of a new suit = Five-card suit; Qxxxx or
                                 better
               — 4 of a new suit = short suit
               — 3 ♡ or 3 ♠   = Four card or longer sup-
                                 port; no side suit single-
                                 ton or void
               — 3 NT   = Three-card support; no
                                 singleton or void

2. New suit rebid:
   Responder will normally bid the first step as a relay, with
   responses to show the shape as in the Maxi-Raise structure.
3. Opener rebids 3 NT:
   Opener is demanding a cue-bidding sequence.
4. Opener rebids 3 ♡ or 3 ♠ :
   TAB — the responses are:
       First step   = xxx
       Second step   = Axx, Kxx or Qxx
       Third step   = xxxx or xxxxx
       Fourth step   = Axxx, Kxxx, Qxxx, Axxxx, Kxxxx, or
                       Qxxxx
       Fifth step   = Two of the three top honors with three,
                       four or five-card length

Non-Drury Raises

Responder doesn't always respond 2 ♣. His hand might be
too weak, or he may prefer a more descriptive strong raise:

1 ♡ or 1 ♠   —2 ♡ or 2 ♠   = 8-9 HCP; or the distribu-
Weaker   butional equivalent
Raises   —3 ♡ or 3 ♠   = Preemptive raise
            —4 ♡ or 4 ♠   = Preemptive raise
            —1 NT followed by two of opener's major =
                  6-8 HCP or maybe a little more if
                  holding only two-card trump support.
                  The 1 NT response by a passed hand is
                  intended as forcing but opener may
                  pass if he lacks an opening bid.

Strong   —Jump in a new suit other than clubs =
Raises   "Flower" bid, i.e., four or more
                  trumps; five or more cards in the bid
                  suit; a short suit; and game-going
                  values opposite a full opening bid.
                  After a Flower Bid opener can sign-off
                  in three or four of his original major
                  or bid the first available step to start
                  the Romex relay process.
            —Double jump in a new suit = Void; 10 or
                  more HCP. With less bid 2 ♣ (Re-
                  verse Drury) and follow with a splinter.

Other Sequences

1 ♡ or 1 ♠   —Two-over-one = 11 or 12 HCP; a good
                  five-card or longer suit; fewer than
                  three cards in opener's major
         —3 ♣ = Six or more clubs; game invitational
                  strength
         —2 NT = At least five cards in each minor;
                  9 or more HCP

1 ♡ — 1 NT 2 ♡ = *or* 1 ♠ — 1 NT 2 ♠ =	A full opening bid. With a subminimum opening bid and a six-card suit, opener must open with a weak two bid.

After Interference

1 ♡ or 1 ♠ — Double —Redouble = Any good hand that lacks a fit

            —2 ♣ = Romex Drury with the same structures as described above

            —2 NT = Preemptive raise with one defensive trick (ace or king-queen)

1 ♡ — 1 ♠ — 2 ♣ = Romex Drury with the same structures as described above

Examples:

1.

Opener	Responder
♠ A J 10 x x	♠ K x x x
♡ K J x	♡ A Q x
◊ Q x x	◊ x x x
♣ x x	♣ x x x
	Pass
1 ♠	2 ♠ (1)
Pass	

(1) Semi-constructive; 8 or 9 HCP. With any additional value responder would have bid 2 ♣, Romex Drury.

2.

Opener	Responder
♠ A J 10 x x	♠ K x x x
♡ K J x	♡ Q x x
◊ Q x x	◊ A x
♣ x x	♣ Q x x x

	Pass
1 ♠	2 ♣ (1)
2 ♠ (2)	Pass

(1) Romex Reverse Drury
(2) Subminimum opening

3.

Opener	Responder
♠ A J 10 x x	♠ Q x x x
♡ K x	♡ A Q x x
◊ Q x x	◊ K x x
♣ A x x	♣ x x

	Pass
1 ♠	2 ♣
2 ◊ (1)	2 NT (2)
4 ♠ (3)	Pass

(1) Full opening bid
(2) Something extra; no singleton
(3) I will take a chance

4.

Opener	Responder
♠ A Q x	♠ K x x
♡ A J x x x	♡ K Q x x
◇ K Q x x	◇ A x x
♣ x	♣ x x x

	Pass
1 ♡	2 ♣
3 ◇ (1)	3 ♡ (2)
3 ♠ (3)	3 NT (2)
4 ◇ (4)	4 ♠ (2)
4 NT (5)	6 ♡
Pass	

(1) Five-Losers; unbalanced slam try; at least four diamonds
(2) Relay
(3) 5-4 in the two anchor suits. Note that opener cannot be balanced for this bid. With a balanced 17 or 18 HCP his second bid would have been 2 NT.
(4) Second step = Low singleton (3-5-4-1)
(5) Three Key Cards in the two anchor suits

5.

Opener	Responder
♠ A Q x x x	♠ K x x x
♡ x	♡ K J x
◇ A x	◇ K Q x
♣ A J x x x	♣ x x x

	Pass
1 ♠	2 ♣
3 ♣ (1)	3 ◇ (2)
3 ♠ (3)	4 ♠ (4)
Pass	

(1) Unbalanced slam try with at least four clubs
(2) I don't like it, but I can relay

(3) Second step = 5-1-2-5 or 5-0-3-5
(4) Terrible duplication
(5) Too bad!

6.

Opener	Responder
♠ A	♠ 10 x x x
♡ A Q J x x	♡ K x x
◊ J x x x	◊ x
♣ Q J x	♣ A K 10 x x

	Responder
	Pass
1 ♡	2 ♣ (1)
2 ◊	3 ◊ (2)
3 ♠ (3)	4 ♣ (4)
4 ♡ (5)	5 ♣ (6)
6 ♡ (7)	Pass

(1) Romex Reverse Drury
(2) Singleton diamond
(3) Mild slam try — cue-bidding the ace of spades
(4) I am interested — cue-bidding the ace of clubs. Remember that the club feature is shown before the trump honor.
(5) I've shown my slam interest. Now it's time to show I'm willing to stop in game.
(6) One more try: I have the king of clubs but not the king of spades
(7) That is sufficient. I know you must have the king of hearts to justify your bidding

7.

Opener	Responder
♠ A K 10 x x	♠ Q J x x
♡ J x x	♡ x
◇ K x x	◇ A x x x
♣ A Q	♣ K J x x

	Pass
1 ♠	2 ♣
2 NT (1)	4 ♡ (2)
4 NT (3)	5 ◇ (4)
6 ♠	Pass

(1) Balanced; 17 or 18 HCP
(2) Jump in a new suit = a singleton or void in the bid suit, in this case — hearts
(3) Key Card Blackwood
(4) One Key Card

8.

Opener	Responder
♠ A K 10 x x	♠ Q J x x x
♡ x x x x	♡ —
◇ x x	◇ A K x x
♣ Q x	♣ x x x x

	Pass
1 ♠	4 ♡ (1)
4 ♠ (2)	Pass

(1) Heart void and an excellent hand
(2) Still no slam

9.

Opener	Responder
♠ Q x x x	♠ A K x
♡ A K x x x	♡ 10 x x x x x
◇ A	◇ Q 10 x x
♣ x x x	♣ —

	Pass
1 ♡	2 ♣
2 ◇	4 ♣ (1)
4 ◇ (2)	4 ♠ (3)
4 NT (4)	5 ♠ (5)
5 NT (6)	7 ♡ (7)
Pass	

(1) Club void
(2) Cue-bid = Ace of diamonds and slam interest
(3) Ace of spades
(4) Trump honor
(5) Spade king
(6) Trump cue-bid = Second trump honor and interest in a grand slam
(7) Don't worry about the queen of hearts, I have enough length

10.

Opener	Responder
♠ K J x x x	♠ Q 10 x x
♡ Q x	♡ K x x
◇ A J x x	◇ x
♣ K x	♣ A J x x x

	Pass
1 ♠	2 ♣
2 ◇ (1)	3 ◇ (2)
4 ♠ (3)	Pass

(1) Full opener

(2) Singleton diamond
(3) Good fit but no slam

11.

Opener	Responder
♠ A K x x x x	♠ Q J x
♡ Q J x x x	♡ A K x x
◊ —	◊ x x x
♣ A x	♣ x x x

Opener	Responder
	Pass
1 ♠	2 ♣
3 NT (1)	4 ♡ (2)
5 ♣ (3)	5 ♡ (4)
7 ♡ (5)	Pass (6)

(1) Start cue-bidding
(2) Heart ace
(3) Club ace
(4) Heart king but no diamond ace
(5) Is hearts a better trump suit?
(6) Yes!

12. Olympiad. Valkenburg, 1980.

Opener	Responder
George	Sol
Rosenkranz	Dubson

Opener	Responder
♠ Q 10 8 6 3 2	♠ 9 7 5 4
♡ A	♡ K Q 3
◊ A K J 7 6 2	◊ 8 5
♣ —	♣ K Q 10 2

Opener	Responder
	Pass
1 ♠	2 ♣
3 ♠ (1)	4 ◊ (2)
4 ♠ (3)	Pass

(1) TAB

(2) Third step = Extra length; no trump honor

(3) Maybe we will get a big swing on this hand! (We did — our opponents at the other table were in 6♠.)

Chapter 16

PREEMPTIVE OPENINGS

Preemptive openings by an unpassed hand in Romex are "disciplined" — they show a good suit and adequate playing strength for the level and vulnerability. They are also restricted with respect to side suit strength and distribution. The result of this definition and discipline is that Romex preempts become doubly effective weapons:

1. They rob the opponents of bidding space when it is "their" hand, and
2. They give responder valuable information with which to explore your best contract when the hand belongs to your side.

Romex players can further improve their bidding after preempts by using a few special tools which allow opener to define his holding quite precisely. Most of these methods have been discussed in detail in *Win With Romex* and *Modern Ideas in Bidding,* so these concepts will merely be summarized here along with any changes and additions.

Romex Preemptive Openings

These are the preemptive openings used in Romex:

2♡ or 2♠ = Weak two-bids. Requirements:

1. Six to eight Losers
2. Exactly a six-card suit
3. At least KJ9 in the suit
4. 7-12 HCP
5. Fewer than four cards in the other major
6. No freaks — 6-6, etc.

7. No void

3 ♣ or 3 ♢ = Solid minor preempts. Requirements:

1. A seven-card suit headed by the AKQ or AKJ
2. At most a queen on the side
3. No four-card major
4. No "freaks" — 7-5, 7-6, etc.

3 ♡ or 3 ♠ = Standard "Rule of Two and Three" preempts. Requirements:

1. A seven-card suit (on rare occasion, an eight-card suit) of good quality
2. Seven Losers when not vulnerable; six Losers when vulnerable
3. No outside ace; at most one outside king
4. No more than three cards in the other major
5. No freaks — 7-5, 7-6, etc.

3 NT = A normal 4 ♣ or 4 ♢ preempt. (4 ♣ and 4 ♢ openings are Romex Namyats. See Opening Four-Bids.)

1. A long minor, usually eight cards
2. Six Losers if not vulnerable; five Losers if vulnerable
3. No four-card major

4 ♣ , 4 ♢ , 4 ♡ or 4 ♠ : See Opening Four-Bids.
4 NT = Ultra-sound opening of five of a minor. Requirements:

1. Two or three Losers
2. A very long powerful minor, usually nine cards
3. At most one ace or king on the outside, with perhaps an additional queen
4. Fewer than two quick losers in any suit

5 ♣ or 5 ♢ = Normal preempt: Long suit; five Losers if not vulnerable; four Losers if vulnerable.

Weak Two-Bids

The Romex apporach to weak two-bids was covered in detail in *Modern Ideas in Bidding*. Following is a brief summary with recent changes in the system noted.

Responses:

1. A raise to any level is to play
2. 3 NT or game in a new suit must be passed
3. A new suit is natural and forcing
4. A jump in new suit is CAB
5. 2 NT is an artificial force, asking for specialized responses. They are slightly modified from *Modern Ideas In Bidding*.

2♡ or 2♠ — 2 NT	(1) Minimum: eight Losers
3♣ (1)	
3♢ (2)	(2) Seven Losers; broken suit
3 of original major (3)	
3 of other major* (4)	(3) Seven Losers; semi-solid suit
3 NT (5)	
4♣ or 4♢ (6)	(4) Six Losers; no four-card minor headed by a top honor
* Indicates a change from *Modern Ideas in Bidding*	(5) Six sure tricks with a running major, either KQJ10xx with a side ace or AKQJxx
	(6) Six Losers; four cards to a top honor in the bid suit

You could leave it at that and have very accurate bidding as shown in the next example from a recent championship in Mexico:

253

Opener	*Responder*
George	Mauricio
Rosenkranz	Smid
♠ A Q 10 6 4 2	♠ K J 5 3
♡ 9	♡ A 5
◇ K 8 6 3	◇ A Q J 8
♣ 4 2	♣ A 6 3
2 ♠	2 NT
4 ◇ (1)	7 ◇ (2)
Pass	

(1) Six Losers; 6-4 in spades and diamonds
(2) The advantage of disciplined weak two bids. Opener must
     have the ace-queen of spades and the king of diamonds

If you are unfamiliar with the methods used in Part 3, you
may want to skip this section. Responder's bid of the cheapest
available step over opener's rebid would be a distributional
relay, with the Spiral Cue-Bid in effect thereafter.

What is the cheapest available step? It is the next step except:

1. 3 NT is always to play
2. Three of opener's major is non-forcing, except in this
   sequence:

      2 ♠ — 2 NT
      3 ♡ — 3 ♠

In this sequence, 3 ♠ is Key Card Blackwood as 3 ♡ was
the most encouraging bid opener could make.

Follow-ups are in accord with Spiral Cue-Bid principles. Here
is a convincing example from a recent tournament in Mexico
City:

Mexican Nationals, 1983.

Opener	Responder
George	Eddie
Rosenkranz	Wold

♠ Q x x	♠ A K x x
♡ K Q 9 x x x	♡ A 10 x x
◇ A x x	◇ K x
♣ x	♣ A Q x

2 ♡	2 NT (1)
3 ♠ (2)	4 ♣ (3)
4 NT (4)	5 ♣ (5)
5 NT (6)	6 ♣ (7)
6 ♡ (8)	7 ♡ (9)
Pass	

(1) Forcing
(2) Six Losers; not 6-4
(3) Relay for distribution
(4) Fourth step = 3-6-3-1
(5) Relay asking responder how many Key Cards he holds
(6) Fourth step = Two Key Cards and the queen of hearts
(7) Do you have the queen of spades? Opener cannot have the ace, king and queen he has already shown plus a side king. (This is an "inferential exclusion." See Relay Methods in Part 3.)
(8) Yes, I have the queen of spades
(9) Match this!

If responder bids a new suit, opener replies as naturally as possible:

1. Raise with a fit (three or four cards). Honor doubleton is also acceptable with a "suit-oriented" hand.
2. With a minimum and insufficient fit for a raise, rebid his major at the three-level.
3. With a maximum, and insufficient fit for a raise:

Jump to game in the major with a solid or semi-solid suit.

Bid 3 NT with something in each side suit or if no attractive alternative bid is available.

Bid a new suit at the three-level to show a feature (ace or king) in that suit.

This structure will suit some just fine. However, one more refinement is suggested:

2♡ or 2♠ — New suit

A new suit at the four-level (with or without a jump) = A singleton in the bid suit and a fit for responder's suit.

Examples:

1.

Opener	Responder
♠ K Q J 10 x x	♠ x
♡ x x x	♡ A K J x x x
◇ A x x	◇ K 9 x
♣ x	♣ K J x
2♠	3♡
4♣ (1)	4♡
Pass	

(1) Heart fit, club singleton

2.

Opener	Responder
♠ J x x	♠ K x x
♡ A Q 10 8 x x	♡ x x
◇ x	◇ A K J x x x
♣ J x x	♣ K x
2♡	3◇
3♡ (1)	Pass

(1) Minimum with no fit for responder's suit.

3.

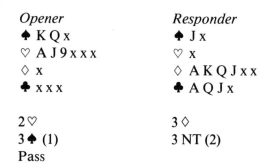

Opener	Responder
♠ K Q x	♠ J x
♡ A J 9 x x x	♡ x
◊ x	◊ A K Q J x x
♣ x x x	♣ A Q J x
2 ♡	3 ◊
3 ♠ (1)	3 NT (2)
Pass	

(1) Maximum with no fit for partner's suit; spade feature
(2) Our best shot for game

4.

Opener	Responder
♠ Q x	♠ A K J x x
♡ A J 10 x x x	♡ K x
◊ K x x	◊ A x x x
♣ x x	♣ A Q
2 ♡	2 ♠
3 ♠ (1)	4 ♣ (2)
4 ♡ (3)	4 NT (4)
5 ◊ (5)	5 NT (6)
7 ♠ (7)	Pass (8)

(1) A raise with Qx is all right if the hand is otherwise suitable
(2) Cue bid. Inititiates a Romex cue-bidding sequence
(3) Heart ace
(4) Ace or king of spades
(5) Diamond king
(6) Interested in the Grand Slam; second trump cue-bid
(7) You must be looking for the trump queen
(8) Perfect!

5.

Opener	Responder
♠ x x x	♠ A x
♡ A K 10 x x x	♡ x
◇ Q 10 x	◇ A K J x x x x
♣ x	♣ A x x
2 ♡	3 ◇
4 ♣ (1)	4 NT (2)
5 ◇ (3)	5 ♠ (4)
6 ◇ (5)	7 ◇ (6)
Pass	

(1) Club singleton and diamond support
(2) Key Card Blackwood for diamonds
(3) One Key Card
(4) Spiral. 5 ♡ could be too easily misinterpreted.
(5) Third step = Diamond queen and heart king
(6) Magic!

Opening Three-Bids

Romex uses opening bids of three of a minor to show a solid or near solid minor with no ace or king outside. Opening bids of three of a major are "standard" preempts by an unpassed hand, i.e., they follow the Rule of Two and Three. It turns out that a 3 ♣ opening is best considered in a class by itself, due to some specialized responses that can be used after that opening.

A. Responses to 3 ◇ , 3 ♡ and 3 ♠ Openings

   1. Raises, 3 NT and non-jump game bids in a new suit are sign-offs
   2. A bid in a new suit, except a 4 ♣ bid, is natural and forcing promising a good five-card or longer suit
   3. A jump in a new suit is CAB

Opener rebids over a new suit in much the same way as over a weak two-bid:

1. A raise shows a doubleton, hopefully doubleton honor
2. A new suit shows three-card support with a singleton in the bid suit
3. With no fit, opener rebids his suit or bids 3 NT (especially attractive after a 3 ◇ opening bid).

Examples:

1.

Opener	Responder
♠ K x	♠ A Q J 10 x
♡ A J 9 x x x x	♡ x
◇ x	◇ A J x
♣ x x x	♣ A Q J 9
3 ♡	3 ♠ (1)
4 ♠ (2)	Pass (3)

(1) Natural and forcing
(2) Doubleton
(3) Slam cannot be a good proposition

2. Guadalajara. Swiss Teams, 1972.

Opener	*Responder*
Sol	George
Dubson	Rosenkranz

♠ K 3	♠ J 10 4
♡ Q 10 9 6 5 4 2	♡ A K 8
◇ Q 6 5	◇ A 2
♣ 3	♣ A K Q J 5

3 ♡	4 ♠ (1)
5 ♣ (2)	6 ♡ (3)
Pass	

(1) CAB in spades
(2) Second step = Second round control
(3) 12 tricks for the taking.

On a diamond lead, opener took all 13 tricks when clubs broke 4-3.

With immediate slam interest responder has two bids available:

1. 4 ♣

A 4 ♣ response is an artificial trump asking bid. Responses after an opening bid of three of a major:

4 ◇	= No ace or king in the trump suit
4 ♡	= Ace or king of trump, but not both
4 ♠	= Ace and king, but not the queen
4 NT	= Ace, king and queen of trump

Responder can continue in Spiral Cue-Bid fashion, by bidding the next available step. Opener shows, in order:

   a) The trump queen. Needed only after a 4 ♡ response. In all other cases the queen will already have been shown or denied by the first rebid or is irrelevant. Side suit distribution is unlikely to be important, so it is not shown.
   b) Side suit kings
   c) Side suit queens

Example:

Opener	Responder
♠ x x	♠ A J 10 x
♡ A Q 10 x x x x	♡ K x
◇ K x	◇ A Q J x
♣ x x	♣ A 10 x
3 ♡	4 ♣ (1)
4 ♡ (2)	4 ♠ (3)
5 ♣ (4)	5 ◇ (5)
5 ♠ (6)	7 NT (7)
Pass	

(1) Trump asking bid
(2) Second step = ace or king
(3) Spiral
(4) One step skipped = heart queen but no spade king
(5) Go on
(6) Diamond king but no spade queen. Opener cannot have the ace-queen and two side kings as he would have been too strong to open 3 ♡.
(7) Bridge is a wonderful game!

When the opening bid is 3 ◇, the responses to the 4 ♣ trump asking bid are simpler than after an opening bid of three of a major.

$3 \diamond - 4 \clubsuit$
$4 \diamond$ = AKJ of trump
$4 \heartsuit$ = AKQ of trump

Inferential Spiral follow-ups follow the response to the 4♣ trump asking bid. Side suit queens are shown first, then side suit jacks.

2. 4 NT

As 4♣ is available to ask about trumps, 4 NT is Blackwood, not Key Card Blackwood, (only directly over the preempt).
Examples

Opener	Responder
♠ K Q J 10 9 x x	♠ x
♡ x x	♡ A K Q J x x x x
◇ x x	◇ A K Q
♣ K x	♣ A
3 ♠	4 NT
5 ♣	6 ♡
Pass	

B.   Responses to a 3♣ Opening

There are two important changes in the responses to a 3♣ opening:

1) The trump ask is 4◇, not 4♣ (which is a preemptive raise)
2) A 3◇ response is artificial, asking opener to bid a three-card major
   Purpose: to explore a 5-3 major suit fit
   As a result, a response of three of a major promises a six-card or longer suit.
3) The jump in a new suit is still CAB, except that you cannot ask directly about a control in diamonds

```
        3♣ — 3◇              3♣ — 3♡ or 3♠
        3♡ or 3♠ (1)          3 NT (3)
        3 NT (2)              Raise (4)
                             New Suit (5)
```

(1) Three-card suit
(2) No three-card major
(3) Short in responder's major
(4) Doubleton trump
(5) Three-card support; singleton or void in the bid suit

Examples:

1.

Opener	Responder
♠ x x x	♠ A Q J x x
♡ x x	♡ A K x
◇ x	◇ J x x
♣ A K Q x x x x	♣ x x

3♣	3◇ (1)
3♠ (2)	4♠ (3)
Pass	

(1) Asking for a three-card major
(2) I have three spades
(3) Avoiding the 3 NT trap. Will anyone else play it from your side?

2.

Opener	Responder
♠ J x x	♠ A K 10 x x x
♡ x	♡ K Q x
◇ x x	◇ K x x
♣ A K J x x x x	♣ x

3♣	3♠ (1)
4♡ (2)	4♠ (3)
Pass	

(1) At least six spades
(2) Three spades; singleton heart
(3) No good for slam

For the stout at heart, one additional suggestion:

    3♣ — 3♡ or 3♠
    4♣ = Raise with a doubleton honor
    4 of responder's suit = Raise with a doubleton; no honor

Example:

Opener	*Responder*
♠ Q x	♠ A K J x x x
♡ x x	♡ K x x
◇ x x	◇ A x
♣ A K Q x x x x	♣ J x
3♣	3♠ (1)
4♣ (2)	6 NT (3)

(1) At least six spades
(2) Qx or Jx in spades; must be Qx in this case.
(3) Opener must have AKQxxxx of clubs as responder has ♣J.
    6 NT must be safer than 6♣ or 6♠.

3 NT and 4 NT Openings

Openings of 3 NT and 4 NT show a preempt in an unspecified minor at the next level. A 4 NT opening also promises super-sound values, as a 5♣ or 5◇ opening is available to show the weaker preempt.

Some responses can be treated the same over either opening.

Pass = Desire to play notrump (almost always passing 3 NT). Not common as opener's hand is not oriented towards play in notrump.

Clubs at any level = "I want to play here if your suit is clubs." Responder may plan to bid on if opener has diamonds instead of clubs.

Diamonds at any level = "I want to play here if your suit is diamonds. Please correct if your suit is clubs." In this case it is clear that responder has a good hand for clubs.

Examples:

1.

Opener	Responder
♠ —	♠ Q 10 x x x
♡ x x	♡ K 9 8 x
◊ K J 10 8 x x x x	◊ x
♣ Q J x	♣ 10 x x
3 NT (1)	4 ♣ (2)
4 ◊ (3)	Pass (4)

(1) Four-level preempt in a minor
(2) Pass if your suit is clubs
(3) It isn't
(4) High enough

265

2.

Opener	Responder
♠ x	♠ K Q x x
♡ x	♡ A Q x x x
◇ x x x	◇ x
♣ K Q J 10 x x x x	♣ A x x
3 NT	4 ◇ (1)
5 ♣ (2)	Pass

(1) To play, if you have diamonds
(2) Good news! My suit is clubs.

Some responses depend on the opening:

a) After 3 NT:
   4 NT is Key Card Blackwood. Responder can follow with
   6 ♣ or 7 ♣ to allow opener to pass or correct to diamonds.
   4 ♡ or 4 ♠ is to play.
b) After 4 NT:
   5 ♡ is Key Card Blackwood. If responder follows with 6 ♣
   or 7 ♣ he is expecting a correction if opener has diamonds.
   5 NT asks if opener's suit is totally solid (even opposite a
   void).

Example:

Opener	Responder
♠ —	♠ A x x
♡ x	♡ A K Q x x x
◇ A K Q J 9 8 x x x	◇ —
♣ K x x	♣ A 10 x x
4 NT	5 NT (1)
7 ◇ (2)	Pass

(1) Is your suit totally solid?
(2) Yes

5♣ and 5♢ Openings

The only artificial responses are:

5♣ — 5♢ = Key Card Blackwood
5♢ — 5♡ = Key Card Blackwood

Examples:

1.

Opener	Responder
♠ —	♠ A x x x
♡ x x	♡ A K Q x x
♢ K J x	♢ A x
♣ K Q 10 x x x x x	♣ J x

5♣	5♢ (1)
5♠ (2)	6♣ (3)
Pass	

(1) Key Card Blackwood
(2) One Key Card
(3) Too bad

2.

Opener	Responder
George	Miguel
Rosenkranz	Reygadas

♠ A 5	♠ K Q J 4
♡ 8 5	♡ A K 8 7 6
♢ K Q J 10 8 6 5 3 2	♢ A
♣ —	♣ A 5 3

5♢	5♡ (1)
6♢ (2)	7♢ (3)
Pass	

(1) Key Card Blackwood
(2) Two Key Cards and the trump queen
(3) At matchpoints responder may gamble that opener does not have the singleton ace of spades or that the opening lead will not be a spade and bid 7 NT.

Handling Interference after Opening Preempts

The disciplined nature of Romex preempts gives responder a big head start when the opponents compete. Romex uses standard methods when the opponents compete after an opening preempt except when the opening preempt has been doubled.

1. When a Weak Two-Bid is Doubled

This is the structure:

2 ♡ or 2 ♠ — Double

— Raise	= To play
— 2 NT	= Romex 2 NT bid, requesting further information
— New Suit	= "Please lead this suit on defense."; forcing to three of opener's suit
— Redouble	= Transfer to the next step. Responder is "Bailing out" into his own long suit with a bad hand.

Examples:

Opener		*Responder*	
♠ J x		♠ K 10 9 8 7 x	
♡ K Q x x x x		♡ —	
◇ Q 10 x		◇ K 9 x x	
♣ x x		♣ J x x	
2 ♡	Double	Redouble (1)	Pass
2 ♠ (2)	Pass	Pass (3)	Pass

(1) Forcing; a "transfer" to 2 ♠
(2) Obliging
(3) Averting a possible disastrous penalty in a heart contract

2. When Other Opening Preempts are Doubled

The idea is the same:

> Redouble is a transfer to the next step, for sign-off purposes
> A new suit is a forcing "lead director"
> Game in a new suit is to play
> 3 NT or a raise is to play

3. When the Opponents Overcall

We have only one novel suggestion to add to standard practice here:

> Double is for penalty
> Raises and 3 NT are to play
> A cue-bid is a strong raise and creates a forcing situation if the opponents take a save over a game bid by the opener's side.
> A new suit is natural (and forcing, if under-game) except a bid of the cheaper unbid minor. A bid of the cheaper unbid minor is an artificial bid showing slam interest and asking the opener to describe his hand. Opener describes his hand naturally. For example:

269

$2\heartsuit — 2\spadesuit — 3\clubsuit — $ Pass

$3\diamondsuit$ = Diamond control

$3\heartsuit$ = Solid suit

$3\spadesuit$ = Spade control (presumably a singleton)

3 NT = Ace or king of spades

$4\clubsuit$ = Club control

$4\diamondsuit$ = Splinter bid: singleton diamond

$4\heartsuit$ = Minimum

Opening Four-Bids

Romex employs the "modern" approach of using all four-level suit openings to show a long major suit and a preemptive type hand. More specifically:

Opening Four Bids

Opening	Meaning	Requirements	Name
4♡ or 4♠	Long suit; preemptive	Seven, eight or nine-card suit; five Losers if vulnerable; six Losers if not vulnerable	Preemptive Opening
4♣ or 4♢	Constructive Preempt 4♣ = long hearts 4♢ = long spades	Seven, eight or nine-card suit; four or four and one half Losers where the queen of trump is one half a Loser; fewer than five Controls; one or two aces; one or two Key Cards; must have the trump queen if he has only one Key Card; no void	Romex Namyats (Stayman spelled backwards)

The opening bids of four of a minor (Romex Namyats) attempt to do two things:

1. Preempt the opponents, if the hand belongs to them
2. Describe opener's holding accurately if the hand belongs to his side. Responder should be well placed to judge slam prospects.

The relatively rare natural openings of four of a minor can be shown by a 3 NT opening.

Examples:

1.

♠ x
♡ A K J x x x x x
◇ x x
♣ K x

Bid 4 ♣
(Four and one half
Losers; four Controls;
an ace)

2.

♠ K Q J x x x x x x
♡ x
◇ A x
♣ x

Bid 4 ◇
(Four Losers; three Con-
trols; an ace)

3.

♠ x x
♡ K Q J 10 x x x
◇ x x
♣ K x

Bid 4 ♡ if not vulnerable
or 3 ♡ if vulnerable
(Not 4 ♣ with six Losers)

4.

♠ Q J 10 x x x x x
♡ K x x
◇ —
♣ x

Bid 4 ♠
(Not 4 ◇ with five Losers,
no Key Cards and a void)

5.

♠ K Q J 10 x x x
♡ —
◇ A Q J
♣ K Q x

Bid 2 ♣
(Too strong for a preempt
with 18 HCP and three
Losers)

6.

♠ A Q J x x x x
♡ K J x
◇ A
♣ x

Bid 1 NT
(Not 4 ◇ with five
Controls)

7.

♠ A K x x x x x
♡ K J
♢ Q J
♣ x x

Bid 1 ♠
(Too many Losers for
4 ♢ , too much defense
for 4 ♠)

Responding to Romex Namyats

Responding to Romex Namyats is a relatively simple task, as opener's hand is quite limited. Responder needs at least three Cover Cards (opener has four Losers), AND at least two Key Cards (opener promises one or two Key Cards) to consider slam. Responder has three options:

A. Signoff in opener's anchor major (4♡/4♣ or 4♠/4♢). This denies slam interest and opener must pass.
B. Bid the next step (4♢/4♣ or 4♡/4♢) as Key Card Blackwood. This bid promises at least second round control of all side suits (see option #3 for an explanation).

Responses to Key Card Blackwood are modified due to the narrow limits on opener's hand:

4♣	— 4♢ (1)	(1) Next step	= Key Card Blackwood
4♡ (2)	—	(2) First step	= One Key Card and trump queen
4♠ (3)	—	(3) Second step	= Two Key Cards and no trump queen
4 NT (4) —		(4) Third step	= Two Key Cards and trump queen

This response structure depends on the Romex Namyats opener having either two Key Cards or one Key Card and the queen of trump.

273

Examples:

1.

Opener	Responder	Cover Cards
♠ A K J x x x x x	♠ Q x x	1
♡ K x x	♡ x	1
◇ x	◇ K Q x x x	1 1/2
♣ x	♣ K Q J x	1 1/2
		5
4 ◇ (1)	4 ♠ (2)	
Pass		

(1) Excellent spade preempt with slam possibilities (four and one half Losers; four Controls and two Key Cards)
(2) In spite of the five possible Cover Cards, responder has to sign off because he lacks the required two Key Cards. Opener cannot have two aces and a void.

2.

Opener	Responder	Cover Cards
♠ x	♠ x x x x	0
♡ A K J x x x x	♡ Q x	1/2
◇ x x	◇ A K Q x x	2 1/2
♣ K x	♣ x x	1/2
		3 1/2
4 ♣ (1)	4 ♡ (2)	
Pass		

(1) Romex Namyats with long hearts
(2) Mandatory sign-off lacking two Key Cards

3.

Opener	Responder	Cover Cards
♠ A Q J 10 x x x x	♠ K x x	1
♡ A Q x	♡ x	1
◇ x	◇ A K Q x x x	2 1/2
♣ x	♣ K Q x	1 1/2
		6
4 ◇	4 ♡ (1)	
5 ♣ (2)	6 ♠ (3)	
Pass		

(1) Key Card Blackwood
(2) Third step = Two Key Cards + the queen of spades
(3) Placing the contract; a small slam is the limit despite responder's six Cover Cards.

In some instances responder will wish to continue the Key Card sequence in the SPIRAL fashion (See Spiral Scan). The Spiral Scan is modified due to the limits on opener's hand. It starts with the king of the other major, followed by the king of diamonds, king of clubs and down the lines for queens in the same order.

The Spiral Scan lists looks like this:

1. Extra trump length or the trump queen
2. King in partner's second suit
3. King in partner's remainder suit
4. Queen in partner's second suit
5. Queen in partner's remainder suit
6. Jack in the trump suit
7. Jack in partner's second suit
8. Jack in partner's remainder suit

The Spiral will normally be used on hands where responder is searching for a thirteenth trick. Thus he will know opener cannot have any side suit kings if opener showed two aces (Romex Namyats denies five Controls). Of course, opener might have a king if his two Key Cards are an ace and the king

of trumps, so he must Spiral for kings in that case.
Example:

1.

Opener	Responder	Cover Cards
♠ A K Q J x x x x	♠ x x	0
♡ K x	♡ A Q x x	1 1/2
◇ x x	◇ A x x	1
♣ x	♣ A x x x	1
		3 1/2
4 ◇	4 ♡ (1)	
5 ♣ (2)	5 ◇ (3)	
5 NT (4)	7 NT	
Pass		

(1) Key Card Blackwood
(2) Two Key Cards and the trump queen
(3) Start Spiralling with extra length, heart king
(4) I have the first two items on the shopping list
(5) That is enough!

The very first time the author used the Romex Namyats convention the following outrageous freak came up:

2.

Opener	Responder	Cover Cards
George Rosenkranz	Sol Dubson	
♠ Q J x x x x x x x	♠ A	1
♡ K	♡ A Q x x x	1 1/2
◇ K x	◇ A x	1 1/2
♣ A	♣ K Q J x x	1 1/2
		5 1/2
4 ◇	4 ♡ (1)	
4 ♠ (2)	4 NT (3)	
5 ♠ (4)	6 NT (5)	
Pass		

(1) Key Card Blackwood
(2) One Key Card and the trump queen
(3) Extra length?
(4) Fourth step = Extra length; heart king; diamond king
(5) We have one loser and we may as well play the hand at notrump

C) If responder lacks second round control of a side suit, he can use a special version of Key Card Blackwood devised by my teammate Eric Rodwell:

4♣ — 4♠ = Key Card Blackwood; lacking a spade control (first available step)

4♣ — 4 NT = Key Card Blackwood; lacking a diamond control (4 NT = lacking control of the relay suit)

4♣ — 5♣ = Key Card Blackwood; lacking a club control

4♦ — 4 NT = Key Card Blackwood; lacking a heart control

4♦ — 5♣ = Key Card Blackwood; lacking a club control

4♦ — 5♦ = Key Card Blackwood; lacking a diamond control

The bids are called "KEY CARD LACKWOOD" — Key Card Blackwood lacking control of a specified side suit.

Responses and follow-ups after Key Card Lackwood are the same as after Key Card Blackwood, except that the cheapest bid in opener's major is a signoff, denying a control in the Key Card Lackwood suit. It is not part of the usual Key Card Blackwood scheme.

Example sequence:

4♣ — 4♠ = Key Card Lackwood in spades

4 NT = Spade control; one Key Card and the trump queen

5♣ = Spade control; two Key Cards without trump queen

5♦ = Spade control; two Key Cards and the trump queen

5♡ = Signoff — no spade control

Examples:

1.

Opener	Responder	Cover Cards
♠ A Q J 10 x x x	♠ K x x	1
♡ x	♡ A K Q x	2 1/2
◊ A	◊ K x x	1
♣ Q J 10 x	♣ x x x	0
		4 1/2
4 ◊	5 ♣ (1)	
5 ♠ (2)	Pass	

(1) Key Card Lackwood in clubs
(2) No club control

If responder held ♠ Kxxxx ♡ Qxx ◊ Qxx ♣ AK the bidding would go:

4 ◊	4 NT (1)
5 ♡ (2)	6 ♠ (3)
Pass	

(1) Key Card Lackwood in hearts. 4♡ would be Key Card Blackwood.
(2) Heart control; two Key Cards and the queen of trump
(3) Fine! Only one Key Card is missing.

2.

Opener	Responder	Cover Cards
♠ A Q x x x x x x	♠ K x x	1
♡ A	♡ x x x x	0
◊ x	◊ A J x	1
♣ Q x x	♣ A K x	2
		4
4 ◊	4 NT (1)	
5 ♡ (2)	5 ♠ (3)	
6 ♣ (4)	6 ◊ (5)	
6 ♡ (6)	7 NT (7)	
Pass		

(1) Key Card Lackwood in hearts
(2) Heart control; two Key Cards and the queen of trump
(3) Asking for a Spiral Scan — cannot be a signoff in view of the maximal response
(4) Extra length (the eighth spade) but no heart feature. As opener has shown two aces, he cannot have an additional king which would be five Controls, the features to be shown are queens.
(5) How about the diamond queen?
(6) I don't have it
(7) Excellent! You must have the queen of clubs or nine spades to have only four losers. Either way we have 13 tricks at notrump.

3.

Opener	Responder	Cover Cards
♠ x x	♠ x x x	0
♡ A K J x x x x x	♡ Q x	1/2
◇ K Q	◇ A x x x	1
♣ K	♣ A Q J x	1 1/2
		3
4♣	4♠ (1)	
5♡ (2)	Pass (3)	

(1) I need help in spades
(2) Sorry!
(3) I am sure the opponents are going to cash the ace and king of spades. That's the price you pay for precision bidding.

There is one more wrinkle:
The response of 5 NT is a modified Grand Slam Force, asking opener to bid seven of the anchor major with the ace and king of trump.

This is used when responder has a void, both side aces and a source of tricks. Such a hand actually came up in a recent Mexico City club game.

	Opener	Responder
	♠ A K J 9 8 6 5 4	♠ 7 3 2
	♡ K 4	♡ —
	◇ 7 6	◇ A 5 4 3
	♣ 8	♣ A K Q J 9 6
	4 ◇	5 NT (1)
	7 ♠ (2)	Pass

(1) Modified Grand Slam Force, asking for the ace and king of spades
(2) I have them

Responses to 4♡ or 4♠ Opening

Responses to a 4♡ of 4♠ opening are identical to those used after Romex Namyats:

4♡ or 4♠ —	First step .	= Key Card Blackwood
	Second, third or fourth step	= Key Card Lackwood
	4 NT	= Key Card Lackwood in the relay suit

There is one critical difference — all Key Card Blackwood and Key Card Lackwood responses revert to normal. Opener's hand isn't well enough defined for the modified responses.

Examples:

1.

Opener	Responder
♠ K Q J x x x x	♠ A x x
♡ x	♡ A K x
◇ A 10 x x	◇ K Q J x x
♣ x	♣ x x
4 ♠ (1)	5 ♣ (2)
6 ♣ (3)	6 ♠
Pass	

(1) Vulnerable 4 ♠ opening
(2) Key Card Lackwood in clubs (a slight risk)
(3) Fourth step (excluding 5 ♠) = Two Key Cards, club control and the trump queen

2. Olympiad. Lebanon vs. Thailand, 1968.

Opener	Responder
♠ 8 6	♠ A 10 9 5
♡ A K Q 10 9 8 6 4	♡ J 7
◇ Q 3	◇ J 7
♣ 5	♣ A K Q 10 4
4 ♡	5 ◇ (1)
5 ♡ (2)	Pass

(1) Key Card Lackwood in diamonds
(2) No control

3.

Opener	Responder
♠ —	♠ K Q x x
♡ K J 10 9 x x x	♡ A
◊ K J x x	◊ Q x x
♣ x x	♣ A K J x x

4♡ (1)	Pass (2)

(1) Non-vulnerable preempt
(2) Too many Key Cards missing for a slam try

Interference after a 4♣ or 4◊ Opening

Interference over Romex Namyats could take any of several forms:

1. Double. This probably shows high cards and a balanced hand.
2. Cue-bid of opener's major at the four-level. This would likely be a take-out bid showing a two or three-suiter.
3. Overcall a new suit. Presumably natural.

In case #1, all bids retain the same meaning except:

1. Pass is a proposal to play that contract.
2. Redouble is Key Card Lackwood in that minor.

In case #2, the cheapest step is Key Card Blackwood; the next three steps are Key Card Lackwood. Also:

1. Pass says, "I want to defend."
2. Double says, "I want your cooperation. You may bid five of your major if you think it advisable." Opener will bid on with a singleton in the enemy suit. Otherwise he will pass or double.

283

Examples:

1. Mexican Nationals, 1981.

Opener	Responder
Mauricio	George
Smid	Rosenkranz

♠ K J 10 9 7 6 5 4	♠ 8 3 2
♡ A	♡ Q 7 5 3 2
◇ K 8 2	◇ 10 4
♣ 4	♣ K J 7

4 ◇	Double	4 ♠ (1)	Pass
Pass			

(1) Willing to play 4 ♠. With ♠ 3 ♡ Q 7 ◇ Q J 10 9 7 6 5 ♣ K J 7, responder would pass.

2.

Opener	Responder
♠ A K J x x x x x	♠ x x x
♡ K x	♡ A x x
◇ J x	◇ A K x x
♣ x	♣ K x x

4 ◇	4 ♠	4 NT (1)	Pass
5 ◇ (2)	5 ♡ (3)	6 ♠ (4)	Pass
Pass	Pass		

(1) Key Card Blackwood
(2) Second step = Two Key Cards; no trump queen
(3) Long hearts — willing to sacrifice
(4) Let's stop this nonsense

Finally here is Eric Rodwell's favorite gadget in action in a situation that required delicate cooperation.

Opener		*Responder*	
♠ A K J x x x x x		♠ Q x x	
♡ x x		♡ A	
◇ x		◇ A K J x x	
♣ K x		♣ J x x	

4 ◇	4 ♡ (1)	5 ♣ (2)	Pass
5 ♡ (3)	Pass	6 ♣ (4)	Pass
6 ♠ (5)	Pass	Pass	Pass

(1) Natural
(2) Key Card Lackwood in clubs
(3) Second step = Club control; two Key Cards; no trump queen
(4) Bid 6 ♠ to protect your king of clubs if that is your club control
(5) OK

Chapter 17

COMPETITIVE BIDDING: OPENING ONE BIDS — WITH COMPETITION

Interference bidding by the opponents creates problems in any system. It is inevitable that some wrong decisions will be made, BUT — with a little preparation your partnership can be well equipped to make the right decision most of the time. The suggestions in this chapter will prepare you to deal effectively with competition with the use of a few conventions and treatments that are natural and straightforward.

Responder's actions when partner has opened and the next player has overcalled in a suit will be discussed first. Actions after a takeout double, a 1 NT overcall and Blackwood sequences will be discussed later.

Responder Bids a New Suit

New suit bids by responder follow these simple rules:

1. A non-jump bid in a new suit (''free bid'') is forcing. Free bids are treated just like new suit responses without competition:

   a) A free bid at the two or three-level is still strong. Game must be reached unless responder rebids his suit at the three-level.

   b) Free bids at the one-level can be made on as few as a good five HCP. All subsequent bids, except cue-bids of the opponent's suit, mean the same as if there had not been any competition.

2. One important free bid modification is recommended:
   After the auction 1♣ or 1♢ — 1♡ a 1♠ response promises at least a five-card suit.

This treatment is used because responder can make a
"negative double" of 1♡ to show exactly four spades. This
"spade length" distinction is very valuable, especially if the
opponents compete further.

3. A jump shift in a new suit is preemptive. Responder
   promises at least a six-card suit but insufficient values for
   a free bid. This applies only to a single jump in a new suit
   to the two or three-level. (A jump to four of a minor would
   be a splinter raise; a jump to four of a major would be to
   play.) The requirements depend on the level and, to a lesser
   extent, vulnerability:

   Two-level jump = Very weak hand; maximum of 6 HCP.
   When vulnerable it is advisable to have some intermediates in your suit.

   Three-level jump = Up to 9 HCP. A good six or a seven-
   card suit is advisable.

Examples:
1♢ — 1♡ — ?

♠ A 9 8 x x x ♡ x ♢ x x x ♣ x x x	Bid 2♠	
♠ Q 10 x x x x ♡ x x ♢ J x x ♣ x x	Bid 2♠	
	(not vulnerable)	
♠ x x ♡ x x ♢ Q x ♣ A J 9 8 x x x	Bid 3♣	

This treatment is called Weak or Preemptive Jump Shifts in
Competition.

Responder Doubles

The use of "negative doubles" are strongly recommended.

This recommendation is especially true for those partnerships playing five-card majors. It is assumed that you are familiar with the fundamentals of the convention. Therefore the following discussion will be limited to refinements and clarifications.

1. The negative double should be used to show distribution, rather than a particular point-count range. The emphasis is on the unbid major suit.

   a) If one major is unbid, the double promises at least four cards in that major. With exactly four cards in that major, the hand can be any strength. After a 1♠ or higher overcall, make a negative double with five or more cards in the unbid major when the hand is too weak to make a free bid. After a 1♡ overcall, pass with a hand that is too weak to make a free bid at the one-level.

Examples:

1♢ — 1♠ — ???

♠ A x x ♡ K x x x ◇ Q x x x ♣ A x			Double
♠ A x x ♡ K x x x x ◇ J x x x ♣ x			Double
♠ A x x ♡ K x x x x ◇ A Q x ♣ x x			Bid 2♡

   b) If both majors are unbid, the negative double promises length in both majors. Usually this is 4-4 or 5-4 though 6-4 or 5-5 are possible if responder lacks the values for a free bid. In a pinch 4-3 is possible, if there is no other bid.

Examples:

1♣ — 1◇ — ?
  ♠ A J x x ♡ K x x ◇ J x x x ♣ x x   Bid 1♠
  ♠ A J x x ♡ Q x x x x ◇ x x ♣ x x   Double

1◇ — 2♣ — ?
  ♠ K 9 x x x ♡ Q J x x x ◇ x x ♣ x   Double

    c) If neither major is unbid, the double shows length in both minors.

Example:

1♡ — 1♠ — ?
  ♠ x x x ♡ x x ◇ A Q x x ♣ Q x x x   Double

2. There is one use of the negative double that is riskier, but justified in many cases — the one-suit negative double!

With an unbid suit at least five cards long, it is permissible to make a negative double without support for the other suit, as long as:

    a) Responder does not double an overcall in one major without length in the other major.
    b) Responder is willing to risk the possibility that opener will bid the unbid suit for which he lacks a fit.

Example:

1◇ — 2♣ — ?
  ♠ K x x ♡ Q J x x x ◇ J x x ♣ x x   Double
  ♠ x x ♡ Q J x x x ◇ J x x ♣ K x x   Pass
  ♠ Q J x x x ♡ x x ◇ J x x ♣ K x x   Double

It is much safer to make a one-suit negative double with length in the higher-ranking unbid suit, as responder can "correct," if necessary, to his suit at the same level.

3. Negative doubles are used through 3 ♠. At higher levels, a double is "card-showing" — showing values, and no good bid. No specific shape is advertised. Opener will tend to pass the double unless he has good playing strength.

Examples:

1 ♠ — 4 ◊ — ?

♠ x x	♡ A Q x	◊ J x x	♣ K Q x x x	Double
♠ x	♡ K x x x x	◊ K x x	♣ A x x x	Double
♠ Q x	♡ A Q x x	◊ x x	♣ K x x x x	Double
♠ x	♡ A x x	◊ K 10 x x	♣ Q 9 x x x	Double

Responder Bids Notrump

Bids of 1 NT, 2 NT and 3 NT are all natural and non-forcing. Such bids should deny length in unbid major suits:

1 NT = 7-10 HCP
2 NT = 11-to a good 12 HCP
3 NT = 13-16 HCP

Responder's Raises Opener's Suit

Raises after an overcall are natural limit bids:

Raises After an Overcall		
Two-level raise	= 6-10 dummy points	Downgrade
Three-level raise	= A good 10 to 12 points	dummy points
Game-level raise	= A good 12 to 14 points	when raising a
	OR preemptive	minor

Note that single raises change in character. Constructive major suit raises and inverted minor suit raises are a luxury that you can't afford in competition. Responder must make the most natural and straightforward raise available, as he may not get another chance to describe his hand.

Responder Cue-Bids the Opponent's Suit

A cue-bid shows any forcing raise in opener's suit, other than a hand suitable for a splinter bid. The purpose of the bid is to set the trump suit and force game. Because of this, it doesn't promise any control in the opponent's suit.

Examples:

1 ♠ — 3 ◇ — ?
   ♠ K x x x   ♡ A x   ◇ x x x   ♣ A K J x   Bid 4 ◇

1 ◇ — 1 ♡ — ?
   ♠ A x x   ♡ x x   ◇ K Q x x x   ♣ A Q x   Bid 2 ♡
   ♠ A x   ♡ A x   ◇ A J x x x x   ♣ x x x   Bid 2 ♡

Responder Makes a Splinter Raise

The following jumps are available as splinters:
1. 4 ♣ or 4 ◇ , as a single or double jump
2. A jump in the opponent's suit
3. A double jump in a major below the four-level

All splinters are "unclarified" — responder can have a singleton or a void in the bid suit.

Responder Bids 4 NT

An immediate jump to 4 NT is **not** Key Card Blackwood; it is regular Blackwood. Any other time 4 NT is Key Card Blackwood.

Opener's Rebids

Opener's rebids are mostly natural and commonsense, following the principles laid out earlier for non-competitive sequences where possible. A few special cases:

1. Special rebids when fourth hand overcalls

a) Double

The meaning of opener's double depends on the level of the opponent's overcall:

> One-level = Three-card support for responder's suit

Example:

After the auction 1♣ — Pass — 1♡ — 1♠ a double shows three-card heart support with undefined strength.

> Two-level = A standard strong 1 NT opening bid (16-18 HCP) without four-card support for responder's major.

Example:

After the auction 1♢ — Pass — 1♠ — 2♡, double with ♠ Kxx ♡ Axx ♢ AQxx ♣ KJx. Responder can pass the double with heart strength. Otherwise he makes the most attractive bid available.

> Three-level and higher = Penalties. Either a trump stack or a balanced strong notrump with a good trump holding.

b) 2 NT after a two-level overcall

As opener can double a two-level overcall to show a strong notrump, his bid of 2 NT, while natural, carries a special inference — opener's hand is more of a "playing hand" for notrump. He has length in the suit he opened and possibly an unbalanced hand.

Example:

After the auction 1 ◇ — Pass — 1 ♠ — 2 ♡, bid 2 NT with
♠ x ♡ Kxx ◇ AKJxxx ♣ Axx.

c) A cue-bid

Cue-bidding the opponent's suit below game shows a maximum hand, unbalanced, with three-card support for responder's suit.
Example:

After the auction 1 ♡ — Pass — 1 ♠ — 2 ♣, bid 3 ♣ with
♠ KQx ♡ AJxxxx ◇ AQx ♣ x.

This cue-bid is **not** forcing to game.

A cue-bid at the game-level shows the strongest possible raise with at least four-card support for responder's suit; usually a singleton or void in the opponent's suit.

2. Special Doubles When an Overcall is Raised

a) Game try doubles

After the auctions 1 ♡ — 2 ◇ — 2 ♡ — 3 ◇ and 1 ♠ — 2 ♡ — 2 ♠ — 3 ♡ opener has no game try available — three of a major would be competitive, not a game try. In such auctions, where there is no room for a game try, double becomes an artificial try for game.

Example:

♠ AQxxx ♡ x ◇ KQxx ♣ KJx

Opener		Responder	
1♠	2♡	2♠	3♡

Double = Game try in spades

b) Renegative Doubles

When the bidding starts

South	West	North	East
1 of a suit	Overcall	Negative	Two or three
		Double	level raise
Double			

The last bid is a Renegative Double. It says "I want to bid, but I have no clear cut bid to make." It is a type of responsive double.

This bid is discussed in detail in *Modern Ideas in Bidding*.

Responder's Second Bid

Only one sequence deserving special mention: When opener bids one of a suit, responder responds one of a suit, fourth hand overcalls and the next two players pass, a double by responder is:

Balancing (takeout) at the two level or
Card showing (cooperative) at the three-level.

Examples:

1♣ — Pass — 1♡ — 2◇
Pass — Pass — Double
 ♠ Axxx ♡ Kxxxx ◇ x ♣ xxx
 ♠ Axx ♡ Q10xxx ◇ xx ♣ Axx

If opener has a true penalty double of 2 ◇ he will pass the double.

Responder's Action over a Double and Other Overcalls

a) After a take-out double

There is little to add to standard practice:

New suit = Forcing at the one-level; non-forcing at the two-level. Weak Jump Shifts in competition.

Raises: Two-level = 6-9 points; Three-level or higher = pre-emptive; 2 NT = limit raise with 1 1/2 quick tricks in defense outside the anchor suit

1 NT or 3 NT = Natural

Splinters = At least four-card support; shortness in the bid suit; 13 or more points.

Redouble = Usually at least 10 HCP; either a desire to double the oponents or a good hand with no convenient bid

b) After a 1 NT overcall

Only one suggestion here:

1 ♣ or 1 ◇ — 1 NT — 2 ♣ = "Surrogate" negative double. Since double is for penalty, responder will be glad to have the ability to show a normal negative double-type hand.

Examples:

1 ◇ — 1 NT — 2 ♣

    ♠ Axxx   ♡ Kxxx   ◇ 109x   ♣ xx

    ♠ AJxxx   ♡ Jxxxx   ◇ x   ♣ xx

Of course, the 2 ♣ bid is 100% forcing.

c) After a 2 NT overcall

Unusual Over Unusual is the defense used against the Unusual 2 NT overcall:

$1\heartsuit - 2\,NT$
$-3\clubsuit$	= Game force; at least five spades
$-3\diamondsuit$	= Limit raise or better in hearts
$-3\heartsuit$	= Heart support; 7 to a poor 10 points
$-3\spadesuit$	= Five or more spades; non-forcing

$1\spadesuit - 2\,NT$
$-3\clubsuit$	= Game force; five or more hearts
$-3\diamondsuit$	= Limit raise or better in spades
$-3\heartsuit$	= Five or more hearts; non-forcing
$-3\spadesuit$	= Spade support; 7 to a poor 10 points

Examples:

$1\heartsuit - 2\,NT - ?$

$\spadesuit$ AQxxx	$\heartsuit$ K x	$\diamondsuit$ Axxx	$\clubsuit$ xx	Bid 3$\clubsuit$
$\spadesuit$ Axxx	$\heartsuit$ Kxx	$\diamondsuit$ Kxxx	$\clubsuit$ xx	Bid 3$\diamondsuit$
$\spadesuit$ KJ9xxx	$\heartsuit$ xx	$\diamondsuit$ xx	$\clubsuit$ AJx	Bid 3$\spadesuit$
$\spadesuit$ xx	$\heartsuit$ Kxxx	$\diamondsuit$ AJx	$\clubsuit$ xxxx	Bid 3$\heartsuit$
$\spadesuit$ Axx	$\heartsuit$ Qx	$\diamondsuit$ K10xx	$\clubsuit$ Jxxx	Double

Interference Over Key Card and Regular Blackwood

When a Blackwood 4 NT bid is overcalled the partner of the 4 NT bidder can effectively show his Key Cards while leaving open the possibility of taking a penalty from the opponents. This is true for Key Card as well as non-Key Card Blackwood. The methods, known as "DOPI/5; DEPO/6, 7" (Double = 0 or 3, Pass = 1 or 4 at the 5-level; Double = Even, Pass = Odd at the 6 or 7-level), are as follows:

DOPI/5, DEPO/6,7				
	Key Card Blackwood		Regular Blackwood	
	Five-Level	Six-Level	Five-Level	Six or Seven-Level
First Step	0 or 3 Key Cards	Even number of Key Cards	0 or 3 aces	Even number of aces
Second Step	1 or 4 Key Cards	Odd number of Key Cards	1 or 4 aces	Odd number of aces
Third Step	2 Key Cards; no trump queen		2 aces	
Fourth Step	2 Key Cards + trump queen			

PART 3

Chapter 18

RELAYS

General Concepts

The increasing popularity of relay sequences in approach forcing systems confirm the accurate vision and judgment of Romex which early on pioneered their inclusion among natural methods. Complete relay systems, starting with Monaco and followed by Alpha, Beta, Gamma, Omega, La Majeure d'abord and The Polish Strong Pass were all born in Europe. Recently Dave Cliff, Matt Granovetter, Ron Rubin, Mike Becker and Bob Danielson in the U.S.A., as well as Bose Mullick, A.D.J. Victor and others in India and groups in New Zealand and Australia have followed the lead.

All relay systems are founded on the premise that one player asking questions and getting replies is more effective than a cooperative exchange of information. The idea is that the usual descriptive dialogue between two equals is too nebulous for pinpoint accuracy.

This type of hand is a relayer's dream (Romex methods are used):

Opener A	Opener B	Responder
♠ K x	♠ J x	♠ A x
♡ A Q J x x	♡ A Q J x x	♡ K x x x
◇ J x	◇ K x	◇ A x x
♣ K Q x x	♣ K Q x x	♣ A J x x

Opener A	Responder	Opener B	Responder
1 ♡	2 NT	1 ♡	2 NT
3 ♣ (1)	3 ◇ (2)	3 ♣ (1)	3 ◇ (2)
3 ♡ (3)	3 ♠ (2)	3 ♡ (3)	3 ♠ (2)
4 ♣ (4)	4 ◇ (2)	4 ♣ (4)	4 ◇ (2)
4 NT (5)	5 ♣ (2)	4 NT (5)	5 ♣ (2)
5 NT (6)	6 NT (7)	5 ♠ (8)	5 NT (2)
Pass		6 ♡ (9)	7 ♣ (10)
		Pass	

(1) Four or more clubs
(2) Relay
(3) Exactly five hearts and four clubs
(4) Balanced hand — exactly 2-5-2-4 distribution
(5) Maximum values; one Key Card (four Key Cards is impossible)
(6) Heart queen; club king; spade king; but no king of diamonds
(7) I can count 12 tricks
(8) Queen of hearts; king of clubs; but no king of spades
(9) King of diamonds and queen of clubs but no queen of spades
(10) A diamond ruff will give us our thirteenth trick

In Sequence A, opener has given discouraging responses. His doubleton king of spades represents duplication of values, as responder also has a doubleton spade. He signs off in 6 NT since there is no advantage in playing in a suit.

In Sequence B, responder is hopeful when opener denies the

king of spades, because what he really needs is the king of diamonds. In that case an extra trick would be available provided that clubs — the 4-4 fit — become trump. Responder relays again, hoping to find opener with two cards: the king of diamonds and the queen of clubs.

Opener's 6 ♡ response shows both cards. Responder bids the grand slam; knowing it is cold. Notice that the precise information about opener's shape and high cards was critical to bidding the grand slam. Responder had to know that opener had at least five hearts, four clubs and the ace-queen of hearts, the king of diamonds and the king-queen of clubs. Magic!

Relayers hope that the spectacular successes of relays more than offset the hands where relays fail to convey the needed information in time.

However, there are many pitfalls in using relay methods:

1. **Memory.** It's more difficult to deal with artificial methods than natural methods.
2. **Applying them at the right time.** Relay methods handle some hand types much better than others.
3. **Efficiency of the method.** Getting the optimum structure, all factors included, is quite a challenge. It's like perfection — you will never get there but you can get closer and closer.
4. **Breaking the structure down into its elements.** Memory is aided tremendously when the structure is explained in the simplest terms possible. The design of the structure should facilitate this.
5. **Consistency.** It is a big strain on the memory to recall a zillion individual sequences. It is much better to be able to apply principles to as large a number of sequences as possible.
6. **Efficiency vs. simplicity.** A balance must be struck between the need for systemic efficiency and the desire for simplicity.

Balancing all these factors is quite a job. Mastering the fundamentals and understanding how these principles are applied to specific sequences make the job less difficult.

For better understanding here are some commonly used words in the relay jargon.

DEFINITIONS OF RELAY TERMS

REPLIER: The player responding to an inquiry from partner. Not limited to relay sequences.

RELAY: An artificial bid that demands a reply from a set of pre-determined responses. The cheapest available step — the cheapest step not needed as natural — is used, to save space.

RELAY STRUCTURE: A pre-planned "path," "chain" or "program" of relay/response sets to allow the "relayer" to discover the nature of partner's hand. Relay structures are limited to situations best suited to relay methods.

RELAY SYSTEM: A bidding system built around relays. With a good hand the "captain" must initiate a relay sequence. The use of natural, cooperative bidding is de-emphasized or eliminated.

CAPTAIN: The player who takes responsibility for directing the partnership to its final contract. Naturally this would be the player knowing the most about the combined hands (the player with the least limited hand). The strong hand is usually Captain. After an opening one-bid or a preemptive opening, responder is Captain. After a strong opening, opener is usually Captain.

SCANNER (Describer): Captain's partner. It is his duty to provide information to the Captain to help him choose the final contract. He provides the information in priority order — most important things first. When Captain places the contract, Scanner must pass.

CAPTAINCY TRANSFER: Captain transfers control back to partner any time he makes a natural "optional" (non-forcing) bid. He elects to describe his hand, letting partner choose the final contract.

> INQUIRER (Relayer): The player employing a relay or relay sequence. Relayer is captain unless he transfers captaincy with a non-relay bid.

When Relays are Most Effective

Relays are much better suited to some sequences than others.

1. **Relays work well for slam bidding.** Relays can perform miracles on grand slam hands and are superior on many small slam hands. Many other small slam hands are better approached with descriptive methods (natural bidding, shortness showing bids, cooperative style, asking bids, etc.). Mild slam tries are almost always better described by cooperative methods.
2. **Relays work best for well defined, well focused situations.** When one hand has described itself within fairly narrow limits with regard to HCP, controls, distributions, fit, etc., relays have a natural head start on describing the hand completely.
3. **Relay structures work best when a lot is known at a low level.** Trying to hit the bull's eye when the target is vaguely defined is practical only when there is lots of bidding space available.

Use of Relays in Romex — The Relay Process

Romex uses relay methods in the appropriate situations — hands with slam potential after a fit has been found. One or several natural paths are usually available for those times when the hand is not suited for relay methods. As a result a prudent blend of natural methods and codified sequences greatly enhances the effectiveness of the system without undue strain on the memory.

A by-product of this approach gives Romex an indirect advantage: because these relay sequences tend to begin at the three-level or higher it is less likely that the opponents will be able to interfere with our auction.

The relay process to be described can be broken down into different stages.

A. Initiation. Relayer's first relay serves to initiate the relay sequence. This first relay signals (if not already known):

1. Game forcing values with slam possibility, and
2. The use of a pre-designed relay "path" or "chain," where replier describes his hand in a pre-set order.

B. The relay "chain." The relay "chain" is the predetermined sequence of information replier transmits to relay.

Example:

In Key Card Blackwood the chain is: Key Cards first, followed by the trump queen, followed by side suit kings.

C. Phases of the relay chain. The "relay chain" consists of phases which key on a particular feature. It comes into play when specific characteristics or features are identified.

Following are examples of the phases in a Romex relay chain consisting of showing scanner's distribution; followed by identifying Scanner's Key Cards and trump queen; followed by the "Spiral Cue-Bid" (where specific lower honors — kings, queens and jacks — are shown):

Phases of Relay Chain		
Phase		What Happens
Distribution Showing		Scanner describes his distribution precisely or nearly so, with step responses
Subsets of Key Card Blackwood Phase	Key Cards	Scanner gives a step response to declare how many of the Key Cards he holds
	Trump queen	Scanner tells whether or not he has the queen of trump
Subsets of the "Spiral Cue-Bid" Phase	Side suit kings	Scanner tells exactly which side kings he has, if any
	Side suit queens	Scanner tells exactly which side queens he has, if any
	Side suit jacks	Scanner tells exactly which side jacks he has, if any

D. **The Spiral.** The "Spiral" or "Spiral Scan" is simply a relay chain where important cards can be exactly specified. This involves a long list of features to be shown or denied in a specific order, using step responses. (For details see the Chapter "Spiral Scan.")

E. Some useful adjuncts and auxiliary concepts:

1. <u>ZOOM.</u> When Replier can confirm completion of a phase, he can go to the next phase automatically in certain situations. Key Card Blackwood is a simple example:

4 NT — 5 ◇	(1) Do you have the trump queen?
5 ♡ (1) — 5 ♠ (2)	(2) No
— 5 NT (3)	(3) Yes, but I don't have the king of my longest side suit
— 6 ♣ (4)	(4) Yes, and I have the king of my longest side suit but I don't have the king of the "fragment suit"

For example, if Replier's distribution is known to be exactly 5-4-3-1, spades would be the trump suit, hearts would be the "side suit" and diamonds would be the "fragment" suit. Cards in clubs, a known short suit, would not be shown.

The trump queen is the current phase; kings are next. Responder, by showing the trump queen, confirms completion of that phase. He then "zooms on to the next phase — "Kings" — simultaneously. Zoom generally applies in the later part of a relay, when slam interest is confirmed, not early on when Relayer could want to "exit" the relay.

2. SUPER-RELAYS. A "Super-Relay" is like the fast-forward button on a tape player. Relayer employs Super-Relays by SKIPPING one relay step for each phase he wants to skip.

Example:

Replier is about to start Spiral for kings:

    4 ♠ = Start Spiral to show specific side suit kings

    4 NT = Super Relay: forget kings, start with queens

    5 ♣ = Double Super Relay: forget kings and queens; start with jacks

A Super-Relay can be used before a phase begins OR while in the middle of it. In either case the message is the same: GO ON TO THE NEXT PHASE. Super Relays can be real life-savers.

3. INFERENTIAL SKIPPING (Inferential exclusion). If Scanner has indicated his holding inferentially, he need not repeat himself in the spiral responses. A player who has shown exactly three Controls AND shows two Key Cards (they must

consist of an ace and the king of trump) is known to have no other kings. The king showing phase would therefore be skipped and the spiral would start by showing side suit queens.

E. **Termination.** Inquirer does not want to be locked in to a relay sequence. How does he exit? He has two alternatives:

1. Signoff in the agreed suit. This is comparable to the "red light" traffic signal. It generally happens after the Key Card response and is final.
2. To make a non-forcing "exit."

This is comparable to a "yellow light" and Scanner has the option to continue if he has additional values. The most frequent case occurs after the distributional description and before Key Cards are shown. Inquirer breaks the chain because he has discovered duplication. Scanner may then continue with substantial extra values. In such a case he continues bidding as though the relay is still in effect.

Example:

Opener holds:
    ♠ KQJxx ♡ AQxx ◇ — ♣ Kxxx

1♠ — 2 NT (1)	(1) Maxi-raise
4◇ (2) — 4♠ (3)	(2) Void
5♡ (4)	(3) "Yellow light"
	(4) Two key cards and the queen of trump; extra values

If Scanner now bids 5♠ over 5♡, he is saying: "No thanks" and is signing off.

Admittedly this is a lot of theory to be assimilated by the reader who is not familiar with relay concepts. However, it is important to realize that Stayman and Blackwood are simple cases of relays. Hopefully this will provide additional motivation to interested students.

After repeated reading and practice the sequences will become familiar friends. (Believe me I am speaking with the benefit of years of experience). Of particular importance is the logical structure of the Romex program which usually follows the same descriptive path:

Distribution

▼

Key Cards

▼

Trump queen

▼

Side suit kings

▼

Side suit queens

▼

Side suit jacks

Chapter 19

THE SPIRAL CUE-BID

The "Spiral Cue-Bid" (Spiral Scan) is a very valuable and often used Romex tool. It has been developed from New Zealand's Symmetric Relay System.

In many auctions the situation will be like this:

1. A fit has been found. A slam probe sequence is in effect.
2. One hand has described its distribution and strength, exactly or within close limits. This information is usually gained through relays.
3. Scanner has responded to show his Key Cards

At this point the Relayer may want to know about other cards in partner's hand. Some particularly important cards would be the trump queen or the king of Replier's longest side suit.

It is possible for Inquirer to ask for every potentially significant card in partner's hand, including jacks! The concept is fairly easily to understand and use with practice.

Here's an illustration of how it works with a hand. You hold:

♠ KQxxx   ♡ KQxx   ◊ QJx   ♣ x

Assume that spades have been agreed on as trumps. You, as Scanner, have identified your exact pattern — 5-4-3-1 — and have responded to show one Key Card (the king of spades). What exactly, and in what order, would you like to tell him? The cards that you could hold, in order of importance, are:

1. The trump queen (spades in this case)
2. The king in your longest side suit (hearts in this case)
3. The king in your "fragment" suit (diamonds in this case)
4. The side suit queen (the queen of hearts in this case)
5. The fragment queen (the queen of diamonds in this case)
6. The trump jack and so on.

The list can be extended indefinitely.
Here is the concept, offered visually:

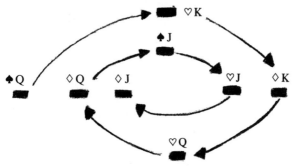

We are "spiraling in" from cards of wide significance toward lesser cards of almost invisible importance.

Returning to our example, suppose the last three bids were:

4 ◇ (1) — 4 ♠ (2)   (1) Key Card Blackwood
4 NT (3)   (2) One Key Card
                     (3) What valuable cards, in Spiral Sequence can you provide?

The response is based on this concept:

SCANNER SKIPS ONE STEP FOR EACH CONSECUTIVE CARD HE POSSESSES IN THE SPIRAL SERIES

Thus the responses to 4 NT in our example would mean:

5 ♣ = "I lack the queen of spades."
5 ◇ = "I have the queen of spades, but lack the king of hearts."
5 ♡ = "I have the spade queen and heart king, but lack the diamond king."
5 ♠ = "I have the spade queen, the heart king and the diamond king, but lack the heart queen."

And so on.

In this way a player may show a very large number of important cards with just one bid!

In our example hand you have the first two cards in the spiral (the spade queen and the heart king but lack the third card — the diamond king). Thus you skip two steps and respond 5 ♡

4 ◇ — 4 ♠	(1) Please spiral
4 NT (1) — 5 ♡ (2)	(2) I have the queen of spades and the king of hearts but lack the king of diamonds

At this point Relayer could sign-off in 5 ♠, 6 ♠, 7 ♠, 6 NT or 7 NT. If he wants to continue along the spiral, he bids the next available step — 5 NT in this case.

If Relayer were to bid 5 NT, you see that you have the heart queen and the diamond queen, but lack the spade jack. Thus you skip two steps, as you did last time:

5 NT = Continue the spiral

6 ♡ = I have the heart queen and the diamond queen, but lack the spade jack

At this point there is no more room for further relays. However, it can safely be said that Relayer should have enough information to confidently place the final contract.

Three important points should be made:

1. If the Scanner's response to Key Card Blackwood either declared or denied the trump queen, it is removed from the spiral list. The side suit king would be the first card on the list.

2. In some cases the length of Scanner's side suits won't be known exactly. In that case priority is assigned arbitrarily: The highest side suit king comes before the next lowest side suit king, etc.

3. If Replier bid a suit that may be longer than the other suits, it is considered the side suit. The common case is when opener opens 1 ♣ or 1 ◇

Example:

1♣ — 1♠
2♣

In any relay/spiral continuation the bid minor suit (in this case, clubs) is to be considered the side suit, even though it might be only a three-card suit.

Super-Relays

Try a hand from the perspective of the Relayer. Suppose you have this hand: ♠ KQxx ♡ Qx ♢ Kxx ♣ Axxx.

Through relays and Key Card Blackwood you know:

partner's pattern is exactly 5-4-3-1 and
he has three Key Cards

If you request the spiral at this point, partner would always bid the first step to deny the queen of spades. This wastes valuable bidding space.

The solution is simple. Inquirer skips a step to declare the trump queen and request the spiral starting with the side suit kings.

4♡ (1) — 4♠ (2)	(1) Key Card Blackwood
4 NT (3)	(2) Three Key Cards
5♣ (4)	(3) Please spiral
	(4) Please spiral, but I have the queen of spades. Start with the king of hearts.

These step skipping relays are called Super-Relays. They are a very valuable adjunct to Romex relay methods.

Time to try the Spiral Cue-Bid (See ''The Maxi-Raise After a Major'' for a discussion of the relay methods used in this example):

Opener	Responder
♠ K x	♠ A x x
♡ A Q J x x	♡ K x x x
◇ J x	◇ A x
♣ K Q x x	♣ A J x x
1 ♡	2 NT (1)
3 ♣ (2)	3 ◇ (3)
3 ♡ (4)	3 ♠ (3)
4 ♣ (5)	4 ◇ (3)
4 NT (6)	5 ◇ (3)
5 NT (7)	6 ♣ (3)
6 ♡ (8)	7 ♣ (9)
Pass	

(1) Strong raise
(2) Natural
(3) Relay
(4) Exactly five hearts and four clubs
(5) 2-5-2-4 pattern
(6) Maximum with one Key Card
(7) Three steps skipped = Heart queen; club king and spade king but not the diamond king. Since spades and diamonds are of equal length, spade features are shown first (because spades is the higher ranking suit)
(8) Club queen but not the spade queen
(9) Magic!

Notice how the Spiral Cue-Bid allows this "double dummy" contract to be reached with confidence. Change opener's hand to ♠ Jx ♡ AQJxx ◇ Kx ♣ KQxx and 6 NT is the limit. The long heart doesn't provide a useful pitch.

The sequence would go like this:

Opener	Responder
♠ J x	♠ A x x
♡ A Q J x x	♡ K x x x
◇ K x	◇ A x
♣ K Q x x	♣ A J x x

Opener	Responder
1 ♡	2 NT (1)
3 ♣ (2)	3 ◇ (3)
3 ♡ (4)	3 ♠ (3)
4 ♣ (5)	4 ◇ (3)
4 NT (6)	5 ♣ (3)
5 ♠ (7)	6 NT (8)
Pass	

(1) Strong raise
(2) Natural
(3) Relay
(4) Exactly five hearts and four clubs
(5) 2-5-2-4 pattern
(6) Maximum with one Key Card
(7) Skipping two steps = the heart queen and the club king but not the spade king
(8) Too bad, 6 NT is the limit

Relayer can use Super Relays later in the auction. By doing so, he says ''forget showing me our current phase. Go on to the next phase.''

Super-Relays Late in the Auction

Phase	Meaning of a Super-Replay
Trump queen	Go on and show kings
Side suit kings	Go on and show queens
Side suit queens	Go on and show jacks
Jacks	Forget one jack for each step I skipped

Example:

Opener	Responder
♠ A Q x x x	♠ K J x x
♡ A Q x x	♡ K x x
◊ Q x x	◊ A K x x
♣ x	♣ A x

. . . . (1)	5 ♣ (2)
5 NT (3)	6 ◊ (4)
6 NT (5)	7 ♠ (6)
Pass	

(1) The bidding to this point has established spades as trump. Opener's pattern is known to be 5-4-3-1.
(2) Key Card Blackwood
(3) Two Key Cards and the spade queen
(4) Super-Relay. By skipping a step, Relayer says: "Forget kings. Let's begin a scan for queens."
(5) Two steps skipped = Heart queen and diamond queen but not the spade jack
(6) Perfect!

Note how the Super-Relay saves the day.

Chapter 20

THE 2 ◇ OPENING BID

The 2 ◇ opening bid is strong and forcing for one round. It is made with any of three types of powerful hands:

TYPE A: ACOL TWO-BID; LONG MAJOR. A strong one-suited hand with a six-card or longer major.

Requirements:	17 or more HCP
	Four or five Losers
	Six or more Controls with a six-card suit; five or more Controls with a seven-card suit
	A good suit: at least three of the top five honors. This requirement can be relaxed a little with a seven-card or longer suit.

| Restrictions: | No four-card or longer side suit |
| | No void |

TYPE B: BALANCED. A balanced hand with 23-24 HCP. The hand will normally contain eight or more Controls.

TYPE C: "CLOVER." A game-forcing three-suiter: 4-4-4-1 type.

Requirements:	At most three Losers
	At least six Controls
	At least 20 HCP

Responses to 2 ◇

Responses are extremely simple, showing responder's point count in three steps:

Responses to 2 ◇

```
2 ◇ — 2 ♡   = 0 to a poor 6 HCP
     — 2 ♠   = A good 6 to 13 HCP; game forcing
     — 2 NT  = 14 or more HCP
```

Optional additional responses:

2 ◇ — 3 ♣ or 3 ◇ = Six or more cards in the bid minor and a very weak hand. The suit must be headed by the queen or queen-jack. No side ace, king, queen or void.

Opener's Rebids

Opener pinpoints his holding.

Type A (Acol Two-Bid; Long Major)

Opener makes an artificial rebid, depending on whether the response was negative or positive:

```
2 ◇ — 2 ♡                    2 ◇ — 2 ♠ or 2 NT
2 ♠ = Acol Two-Bid in        3 ♣ = Acol Two Bid in
      an unspecified                hearts
      major
                             3 ◇ = Acol Two-Bid in
                                    spades
```

The bids are forcing, of course.

Type B (23-24 HCP Balanced)

Opener bids in notrump as cheaply as possible:

```
2 ◇ — 2 ♡ or 2 ♠             2 ◇ — 2 NT
2 NT                         3 NT
```

Opener bids the suit below his shortness. This allows responder to relay at the lowest possible level by bidding opener's short suit.

The Clover bids begins where the Acol Two-Bid showing steps end:

 2♢ — 2♡
 3♣, 3♢, 3♡ or 3♠ = Clover: the bid suit is the suit below
 the singleton

 2♢ — 2♠ or 2 NT
 3♡, 3♠, 4♣ or 4♢ = Clover: the bid suit is the suit below
 the singleton

The development of the auction is discussed in two sections: Type A and Type C. Type B is discussed in Chapter "Strong Balanced Hands."

Developments After Opener Shows Type A

A. After the 2♡ negative response, the key question is "Do we have enough working Cover Cards for game?" To help answer this question, responder clarifies his holding as follows:

 2♢ — 2♡
 2♠ — 2 NT = 0-3 HCP — second negative
 — 3♣ or 3♢ = 4-6 HCP; values in the bid suit
 — 3♡ = 4-6 HCP with spade values
 — 3♠ = 4-6 HCP with heart values

The meanings of the 3♡ and 3♠ responses are reversed to allow opener to play 3♡ if he doesn't fit the spade values in responder's hand.

After $2\diamondsuit$ — $2\heartsuit$
$2\spadesuit$ — $2\,\text{NT}$

opener rebids his major at the three-level with five Losers. With four Losers, opener bids the lower minor where he needs help, i.e., Cover Cards. Responder can then evaluate his meager values.

B. When the response was $2\spadesuit$ or 2 NT, the key question is "Do we have the fit and values for slam?"

The bidding has gone: $2\diamondsuit$ — $2\spadesuit$ or 2 NT
                               $3\clubsuit$ = long hearts
                               $3\diamondsuit$ = long spades

There are now two possibilities:

1. Responder has a **fit** (two or more cards in opener's suit). In this case responder has the same "Relay Chain" available as after a Maxi-Raise:

Distribution and minimum/maximum
Key Cards
Spiral

To initiate the relay responder bids the next step. Opener then clarifies:

Whether he has four or five Losers (minimum/maximum)

If he has four Losers, opener "Zooms" to show his distribution according to the "Numerical Principle" (Steps one, two and three show singletons down the line), except that a notrump rebid by opener always shows a balanced hand.

Opener's rebids:

3 ♡ or 3 ♠ = Five Losers
3 NT = Four Losers; no short suits
First step (excluding 3 ♡, 3 ♠ and 3 NT) = Four Losers; singleton in the highest unbid suit (the other major)
Second step (excluding 3 ♡, 3 ♠ and 3 NT) = Four Losers; singleton in the middle unbid suit (diamonds)
Third step (excluding 3 ♡, 3 ♠ and 3 NT) = Four Losers; singleton in the lowest unbid suit (clubs)

Examples:

♠ A Q J 10 x x	2 ◊ — 2 ♠
♡ A x x	3 ◊ (1) — 3 ♡ (2)
◊ A K	3 ♠ (3)
♣ x x	

♠ A K Q x x x x	2 ◊ — 2 ♠
♡ K x	3 ◊ (1) — 3 ♡ (2)
◊ A J x	4 ♡ (4)
♣ x	

(1) Long spade suit
(2) Spade; relay
(3) Five Losers
(4) Four Losers; third step showing a singleton club

If opener shows five Losers, responder can continue to relay to discover distribution:

Example sequence:

2 ◇ — 2 NT   (1) Five Losers
3 ◇ — 3 ♡   (2) Relay requesting distribution
3 ♠ (1) — 4 ♣ (2)

Opener replies in a familiar way:

Cheapest notrump bid = Balanced hand — in the above hand, 4 NT

Steps one, two and three show singletons down the line (Numerical Principle). The steps exclude notrump bids, of course.

Responder can continue to relay as long as he needs further information.

2. Responder **doesn't fit** opener's major (fewer than two cards in opener's suit). In this case responder must warn opener of his lack of fit as well as show something about his distribution. This is the scheme:

3 NT = 4-4-4-1 with shortness in opener's major; or a five or six-card minor, insufficient values to bid the suit at the four-level and shortness in opener's major
New Suit = Five-card or longer suit and fewer than two cards in opener's suit. This, of course, doesn't count the "relay suit" i.e., 3 ◇ over a 3 ♣ bid by opener or 3 ♡ over a 3 ◇ bid by opener.
Three of Opener's Major = Length in the relay suit

Examples:

$2 \diamondsuit - 2 \spadesuit$
$3 \diamondsuit - ?$

♠ x ♡ AJxxx ◇ Kxx ♣ Jxxx		Bid 3 ♠ to show hearts
♠ x ♡ Qxx ◇ AJxx ♣ 10xxxx		Bid 3 NT. The clubs aren't worth bidding at four-level

Opener continues to describe his hand as follows over a new suit bid:

> 3 NT: No fit, i.e., fewer than three cards in responder's suit
>
> Four of his long major = No fit. If 3 NT is available, four of his long suit promises a solid suit.
>
> Raise = Fit, no side suit singleton
>
> New suit = Fit with a singleton in the bid suit.

Examples:

1.

Opener	Responder
♠ K Q J x x x	♠ x x x
♡ A	♡ Q x x
◇ A x x	◇ J x x
♣ K Q J	♣ x x x x
2 ◇	2 ♡ (1)
2 ♠ (2)	2 NT (3)
3 ◇ (4)	3 ♠ (5)
Pass (6)	

(1) 0-6 HCP
(2) Acol Two-Bid in hearts or spades
(3) 0-3 HCP
(4) Four Losers; needs help in diamonds
(5) No help in diamonds but one possible Cover Card in hearts.

This is not a matter of system, but of inference:

    a) With help in diamonds, responder would force to game

    b) With no help in hearts, responder would bid 3 ♡ to give opener the option of playing in 3 ♡

(6) No good, I have spades

2.

Opener	Responder
♠ K Q J x x x	♠ x x x x
♡ A	♡ Q x x x
◇ A x x	◇ x
♣ K Q J	♣ x x x x
2 ◇	2 ♡ (1)
2 ♠ (2)	2 NT (3)
3 ◇ (4)	4 ◇ (5)
4 ♠ (6)	Pass

(1) 0-6 HCP
(2) Acol Two-Bid in hearts or spades
(3) 0-3 HCP
(4) Four Losers; needs help in diamonds
(5) Two or three Cover Cards; pick the major
(6) I have spades

3. Bermuda Bowl. U.S. vs. Sweden, 1953.

Opener	Responder
♠ A K Q 8 6 4	♠ 7 2
♡ J 7 3	♡ 5 4
◇ 10	◇ K J 9 8 2
♣ A K 4	♣ J 10 7 5
2 ◇	2 ♡ (1)
2 ♠ (2)	3 ◇ (3)
3 ♠ (4)	Pass

(1) 0-6 HCP
(2) Acol Two-Bid in hearts or spades
(3) Diamond values
(4) No good

4.

The optional negative responses of 3 ♣ and 3 ◊ can be very useful in helping opener evaluate the fit.

Opener	Responder
♠ K Q J 10 x x	♠ x x
♡ x	♡ x x x
◊ A J x	◊ Q 10 x x x x
♣ A K x	♣ x x
2 ◊	3 ◊ (1)
4 ♠ (2)	Pass

(1) At least a six-card diamond suit headed by the queen; no outside values
(2) Should be good enough for game

If opener's hearts and diamonds were exchanged he would sign off in 3 ♠.

5.

Opener	Responder
♠ K Q J x x x	♠ A x x
♡ A Q x	♡ K x x x
◊ A K x	◊ Q J x
♣ x	♣ x x x
2 ◊	2 ♠ (1)
3 ◊ (2)	3 ♡ (3)
4 ♡ (4)	6 ♠ (5)
Pass	

(1) 6-13 HCP

324

(2) Long spades; four or five Losers
(3) Relay for distribution; promising a fit
(4) Third step = singleton in clubs, the lowest side suit (3 NT is not a step)
(5) All three of responder's Cover Cards are working opposite opener's four Losers

6.

Opener	Responder
♠ A K Q J 10 5 3	♠ 9 8 4
♡ 7	♡ A J 9 5
◊ A 8 6	◊ Q 9
♣ A 3	♣ K 6 4 2

2 ◊	2 ♠
3 ◊	3 ♡
4 ♣ (1)	4 ◊ (2)
4 ♠ (3)	6 ♠ (4)
Pass	

(1) Singleton heart and only four Losers
(2) Key Cards?
(3) Four Key Cards
(4) I cover three of your four Losers

In the golden days of Acol, in the finals of the Master's Pairs, only one Acol pair reached this laydown slam according to a report from Guy Ramsey.

7.

Opener	Responder
♠ K Q J	♠ A x x x
♡ A Q J x x x	♡ K x x x
◇ A K	◇ Q x x x
♣ Q x	♣ x

2 ◇	2 ♠ (1)
3 ♣ (2)	3 ◇ (3)
3 NT (4)	4 ♣ (5)
4 NT (6)	6 ♡
Pass	

(1) 6-13 HCP
(2) Long hearts
(3) I have a fit for hearts. What is your distribution?
(4) I am balanced with four Losers
(5) Key Cards?
(6) Fourth step = Two Key Cards and the queen of trump

8. U. S. Trials, 1969.

Opener	Responder
♠ A K	♠ Q J 4 2
♡ A K 10 6 5 4 2	♡ Q 9 8
◇ 6	◇ K J
♣ A 10 2	♣ Q 8 6 4

2 ◇	2 ♠
3 ♣ (1)	3 ◇ (2)
4 ♣ (3)	4 ◇ (4)
4 ♠ (5)	6 ♡ (6)
Pass	

(1) Acol 2 ♡ bid
(2) Distribution?
(3) Second step = Singleton diamond and four Losers
(4) Key Cards?
(5) Second step = Four
(6) One Key Card is missing

9.

Opener	Responder
♠ A K x	♠ Q J x x x x
♡ A K Q x x x	♡ x
◇ x	◇ A x x
♣ Q J x	♣ A x x

2 ◇	2 ♠
3 ♣ (1)	3 ♠ (2)
4 ◇ (3)	4 NT (4)
5 ♣ (5)	7 ♠ (6)
Pass	

(1) Long hearts; four or five Losers
(2) No fit; at least five spades
(3) Singleton diamond; spade fit
(4) Key Card Blackwood in spades
(5) Three Key Cards
(6) Should suffice for 13 tricks

10.

Opener	Responder
♠ K Q J x x x	♠ A x x
♡ A x x	♡ K Q J x
◇ A Q	◇ x
♣ K x	♣ A x x x x

2 ◇	2 NT (1)
3 ◇ (2)	3 ♡ (3)
3 ♠ (4)	4 ♣ (5)
4 NT (6)	5 ♣ (7)
5 ◇ (8)	5 ♡ (9)
5 NT (10)	7 NT (11)
Pass	

(1) 14 or more HCP
(2) Acol Two-Bid in spades; four or five Losers
(3) Description?
(4) Five Losers

(5) Distribution?

(6) Balanced

(7) Key Cards?

(8) Three Key Cards

(9) Spiral, please

(10) Trump queen but not the heart king

(11) Opener must have either six spades and a minor suit king or seven spades to get up to the required six Controls. Either way there are 13 tricks.

11. Vanderbilt Finals, 1982.

Opener	Responder
♠ A J 7	♠ K Q 8 6
♡ A Q J 8 6 2	♡ K 7
◇ A K	◇ 10 7 6
♣ J 6	♣ A Q 8 7

2 ◇	2 NT (1)
3 ♣	3 ◇
3 ♡ (2)	3 ♠
3 NT (3)	4 ♣
4 ◇ (4)	4 ♡ (5)
4 NT (6)	5 ♣
5 ♡ (7)	5 ♠ (8)
5 NT (9)	6 ♣
6 ◇ (10)	7 NT (11)
Pass	

(1) 14 or more HCP

(2) Five Losers

(3) Balanced

(4) Three Key Cards

(5) Spiral, please. (Forcing in view of the 2 NT response)

(6) Trump queen; no spade king

(7) Diamond king but not club king

(8) Queens?

(9) No spade queen

(10) No diamond queen

(11) Your sequence promises the jack of hearts or enough

length to make the suit solid. If you have the jack of spades, we have 13 tricks at notrump; if not, the grand slam is at worst on a squeeze or a finesse.

The laydown grand slam was bid in only one room.

12. Bermuda Bowl. U.S. vs. Italy, 1957.

Opener	Responder
♠ A J	♠ 9 4 2
♡ A K Q 10 9 8	♡ J 7 5 3
◇ A 8 4	◇ K 9 5
♣ K J	♣ A Q 4

	Pass
2 ◇	2 ♠
3 ♣	3 ◇
3 NT (1)	4 ♣ (2)
4 ♡ (3)	4 ♠ (4)
5 ♣ (5)	6 ♡ (6)
Pass	

(1) Four Losers; balanced Acol Two-Bid
(2) Key Cards?
(3) Four Key Cards
(4) Spiral, please
(5) Trump queen but no spade queen
(6) Too bad! I hoped for:

♠ A x
♡ A K x x x x
◇ A Q x
♣ K x

The laydown small slam was missed by a famous U. S. pair.

Chapter 21

STRONG BALANCED HANDS

This chapter covers all balanced hands with 19 or more HCP. These hands almost always bid 2 NT sooner or later, so we use the same structure of responses once the 2 NT bid is made. Occasionally opener will show his hand with a 3 NT bid, but the hands always have great combined strength in this case. The responses, etc., are the same — one level higher.

The system allows nice easy-to-handle two point ranges:

Expected Number of Controls in Strong Balanced Hands		
Range	Expected Controls	Sequence
19-20	6	1 NT followed by 2 NT
21-22	7	2 ♣ followed by 2 NT
23-24	8	2 ♢ followed by 2 NT
25-26	9	Open 2 NT
27-28	10	Open 2 ♢ ; follow with 3 NT
29-30	11	Open 2 NT; follow with 4 NT

Some observations make all this easy to remember:

1. The strength promised goes up by two point ranges
   The lower the opening, the weaker the hand: 1 NT is weakest, 2 NT is strongest
3. The rare 27-30 HCP hands are shown with the two highest openings and strong follow-up
4. The expected number of controls goes up by one with each increase in range. Remember the starting point: 19-20 HCP IMPLIES SIX CONTROLS.

Opener should make adjustments to his raw HCP total, promoting or demoting his hand accordingly. Look at controls (vis-a-vis expected controls), distribution and intermediates.

The responses and subsequent bidding are designed to produce accurate game and slam bidding. However, one point is so important that we emphasize it here right now:

> IF RESPONDER WANTS TO PLAY 3 NT, HE
> CANNOT BID 3 NT DIRECTLY.
> HE MUST BID 3 ♣ FIRST.

The reason for this is that a direct 3 NT bid is forcing and artificial. Let's start with a brief summary of the responses to 2 NT[1].

---

[1] The special auction 1 NT — 2 ♣ / 2 NT uses the Flint structure described later. If you prefer simplicity you can use the methods described in this chapter for this sequence also. You will not lose much — just the chance to stop short of game on occasion.

3 ♣ = Romex-Stayman. A specialized version of the Stayman convention designed to locate a five-card major in opener's hand among other things.

3 ♦ = Jacoby Transfer Bid: five or more hearts

3 ♡ = Jacoby Transfer Bid: five or more spades

3 ♠ = Transfer to clubs. Shows five or more clubs and a four-card or longer side suit.

3 NT = Transfer to diamonds. Shows five or more diamonds and a four-card or longer side suit.

4 ♣ = Exactly six diamonds; no four-card or longer side suit; slam try

4 ♦ = Exactly six clubs; no four-card or longer side suit, slam try

4 ♡ = Exactly seven clubs; no four-card or longer side suit; slam try

4 ♠ = Exactly seven diamonds; no four-card or longer side suit; slam try

Slam Procedures

Romex uses two main approaches to slam bidding after balanced openings depending on the distribution of the responding hand:

A. Balanced responding hands opposite 2 NT opening — use CONFIT

B. Unbalanced responding hands — use the Romex relay approach describing in order: distribution; Key Cards or Controls; special features.

1. **Controls.** In some auctions opener will know responder's exact number of Controls:

1 NT — 2♡ or 2♠   2♣ — 2♡ or 2♠

In these cases there is no need for a Control or Key Card response. Once the distribution is known the Spiral Scan begins. If Controls are not known from the first response and no fit is established (directly or by implication), the request for Controls is made when the distributional description is complete. The usual case for this treatment is when responder shows a three-suiter:

2 NT (1) — 3♣ (2)	(1)	25-26 HCP
3♢ (3) — 4♡ (4)	(2)	Romex Stayman
4♠ (5) — 4 NT (6)	(3)	Denies five spades or four hearts
— 5♣ (7)	(4)	Spade void
— etc. (8)	(5)	Controls?
	(6)	No Controls
	(7)	One Control
	(8)	Etc.

2. **Key Cards.** When the distributional description is complete and both partners know which suit is trump, the next available step asks for Key Cards. Usually Key Card Blackwood will be at the four, or even five, level. In one sequence 3 NT is used as Key Card Blackwood:

2 NT (1) — 3♢ (1)	(1)	Transfer to hearts
3♡ (2) — 3 NT (3)	(2)	At least three hearts
	(3)	Key Cards?

If responder has shown a two-suiter, the king of his side suit is counted as a Key Card (six Key Cards in all).

3. **The Spiral Scan.** Once distribution and Controls or Key Cards are known the relay asks responder to show his valuable cards in spiral sequence. The order of the cards shown depends on the information already conveyed.

1. In the normal case the order is: trump queen, side suit king; fragment king; etc. If the trump queen has been declared or denied already, it is removed from the list.
2. If responder shows a two-suiter, the king of his side suit was shown as a Key Card, and is removed from the list.
3. When the trump suit is known to be five or more cards in length, the jack of trump is never shown. Other jacks are more important.
4. If responder showed his Controls on the first round, opener can Super-Relay to request the Spiral Scan starting with the king of trump. This allows opener to resolve any ambiguity about the location of responder's control cards.

Relay and Escaping the Relay

If responder shows interest, opener will usually make minimum bids as relays to learn more about responder's hand. If he doesn't like what he hears he can sign off in the agreed suit. 4 NT is also available as a sign off if there is no agreed suit.

Almost all bids that sound as if they could be relays are relays. Some bids that aren't relays:

1. Any bid in the agreed suit, unless a forcing situation to a higher level has been clearly established.
2. 6 NT
3. Any bid at the six or seven level that is a plausible final contract.

In a few auctions responder will be unable to immediately clarify whether he has slam interest. In these cases, over opener's relay attempt, he merely signs off in the agreed suit to deny slam interest, using the other bids as relay steps with slam interest:

2 NT	— 3 ♣ (1)	(1) Romex Stayman
3 ◊ (2)	— 3 ♠ (3)	(2) Fewer than five spades; fewer
4 ♣ (4)	— 4 ◊ (5)	than four hearts
	— 4 ♡ (5)	(3) Five spades and four hearts
	— 4 ♠ (6)	(4) Attempted relay with spades as trumps
		(5) Slam interest; relay responses
		(6) No slam interest

Having laid the foundation for the entire method, we will examine each response individually.

Romex Stayman

Romex Stayman is used on a variety of hands:

1. A hand that wants to raise to 3 NT. Responder may discover a five-three major suit fit in the process.
2. Hands looking for a 4-4 major suit fit.
3. Five spades and four hearts — a distribution unsuited to a transfer
4. Hands with slam interest:

    1. Three-suited hands: 4-4-4-1 or 5-4-4-0
    2. Balanced hands (including all 5-4-2-2 hands). Balanced hands bid 3 ♣ to discover a fit and to use CONFIT (CON-trols-FIT). Controls are especially important when neither player has a short suit.

Opener's Rebids:

    3 NT = 4-4 in the majors
    3 ♠ = Five-card spade suit
    3 ♡ = Four or five hearts; fewer than four spades
    3 ◊ = None of the above holdings: Either exactly four spades or length in one or both minors with no four-card or longer major

Opener Rebids 3 ♠ or 3 NT

If opener bids 3 ♠ or 3 NT and responder is interested only in game, the choice will be obvious. Responder signs off naturally, with one small twist:

> 2 NT — 3 ♣
> 3 NT — 4 ◇ = Transfer to 4 ♡
> — 4 ♡ = Transfer to 4 ♠

Very often this allows the strong hand to be declarer hand. Responder can bid again to show a three-suited slam try.

After a 3 ◇ or 3 ♡ rebid things are a little more complicated.

Opener Rebids 3 ♡

3 ♡ shows four or five hearts. Responder can sign off in 3 NT or 4 ♡, or bid 4 ♣ as Key Card Blackwood. Bids of 4 ◇, 4 ♠ and 4 NT show three-suited slam tries with a heart fit.

If responder wants clarification he bids 3 ♠:

> 3 ♡ — 3 ♠
> 3 NT = Only four hearts
> 4 ♣ = 2-5-3-3   Showing the remainders
> 4 ◇ = 3-5-2-3   numerically. Responses
> 4 ♡ = 3-5-3-2   are in ascending order.

If opener bids 3 NT, showing four hearts, responder can bid 4 ♣ as CONFIT with slam interest to discover more about opener's controls and distribution.

Opener Rebids 3 ◇

Opener is now known to lack five spades or four or more hearts. Responder can sign off in 3 NT. Bids of 4 ◇ and 4 ♡ show spade shortness; 4 ♣ is CONFIT (both discussed later). Responder bids 3 ♠ to show five spades and four hearts. In this case, the only possible fit would be a 5-3 or 5-4 spade fit. Opener can sign off in 3 NT or 4 ♠. With a better hand he bids 4 ♣ as a relay:

$3 \diamond — 3 \spadesuit$
$4 \clubsuit — 4 \spadesuit$ = No slam interest
$— 4 \diamond$ = Slam interest; 5-4-1-3
$— 4 \heartsuit$ = Slam interest; 5-4-3-1

There is no step for 5-4-2-2 in any such auction because balanced hands use CONFIT.

If responder has four spades, a fit is still possible and he must bid $3 \heartsuit$ to show four spades. Opener will respond $3 \spadesuit$ to confirm a 4-4 spade fit or 3 NT to deny a fit.

In the auction:

$3 \diamond — 3 \heartsuit$
$3 \spadesuit — 3 NT$ = Three-suiter; short hearts
$— 4 \clubsuit$ = Key Card Blackwood with spades as the Key Card suit. $4 \clubsuit$ is not CONFIT as CONFIT applies only when no suit has been agreed upon
$— 4 \diamond$ = Three-suiter; short diamonds
$— 4 \heartsuit$ = Three-suiter; short clubs
$— 4 \spadesuit$ = Sign off

Examples:
1. Grand National Teams, 1982.

Opener	*Responder*
Eddie	George
Wold	Rosenkranz

♠ A K J 10	♠ 8 7
♡ K Q J 7	♡ 10 2
◇ A 4	◇ Q 10 7 6 5
♣ A K J	♣ 9 8 7 6

2 NT	3 ♣ (1)
3 NT (2)	Pass (3)

(1) Intending to play 3 NT, but forced to use Romex Stayman for sign off

337

(2) Both majors

(3) I was never interested in a major

2. Mexican Nationals, 1982.

Opener	*Responder*
George	Mauricio
Rosenkranz	Smid

♠ K J 5	♠ A Q 8 4 2
♡ Q 7	♡ K J 9 6
◇ A 6 5 4	◇ 10
♣ A K Q 2	♣ 7 4 3

1 NT	2 ♠ (1)
2 NT	3 ♣
3 ◇	3 ♠ (2)
4 ♣ (3)	4 ◇ (4)
6 ♠ (5)	Pass

(1) Three or more Cover Cards; three Controls

(2) Five spades and four hearts

(3) Spade fit. In principle, a relay.

(4) Confirming slam interest and showing the remainder numerically: one diamond and three clubs

(5) Perfect. Partner must have three of the four possible Cover Cards — spade ace and queen; heart ace and king. He can't have the singleton king of diamonds as a singleton king is generally treated as king doubleton and partner would not have confessed to a singleton diamond. Therefore I can place the contract.

Much more often the responder will bid 3 ♡ over 3 ◇ . This guarantees exactly four spades, and must be bid whenever responder has such a holding. The opener then bids 3 ♠ with a spade fit or 3 NT without a fit.

2 NT — 3 ♣	or	2 NT — 3 ♣
3 ◇ — 3 ♡		3 ◇ — 3 ♡
3 ♠		3 NT

The partnership now knows whether it has a 4-4 spade fit. If the 4-4 fit exists a 4♠ bid by responder is the only signoff. 4♣ would ask for Key Cards.

Example:

Opener	Responder
♠ A Q J x	♠ K x x x
♡ A K x	♡ J x
◇ Q x	◇ A x x x
♣ A K x x	♣ Q x x
2 ◇	2 ♠
2 NT	3 ♣
3 ◇	3 ♡ (1)
3 ♠ (2)	4 ♣ (3)
4 ◇ (4)	4 ♡ (5)
5 ♣ (6)	6 ♠ (7)
Pass	

(1) I have four spades. Do you?
(2) Yes
(3) Key Cards?
(4) Zero or three
(5) Scan please, starting with the trump queen. As I do not know about your side suit length, I expect you to scan hearts, diamonds and clubs in that order.
(6) I skip two steps, so I have two cards for you — the queen of spades and the king of hearts.
(7) Partner should have eight Controls for his first two bids. Combined with my three Controls, we have 11 Controls. We have the values, the Key Cards, the fit, the controls and the good trump suit required for a slam.

CONFIT (Acronym for CONtrols and FIT)

In almost all cases where responder bids 3♣ and follows with 4♣ he is employing CONFIT. This bid:

1. Shows that slam is likely
2. Declares a balanced hand (4-3-3-3, 4-4-3-2, 5-3-3-2, 5-4-2-2)
3. Seeks information about how many Controls opener has. This is always in relation to how many Controls opener is expected to have for his point range.
4. Asks for information about opener's minor suit distribution. Any available major suit fit will be discovered at the three-level. The information conveyed is always based on what responder already knows about opener's distribution.

Opener's response structure to the 4♣ CONFIT bid is:

1. He gives step responses to show all the basic distributional possibilities. As few as two or as many as four steps may be needed to convey the necessary information.

a) Opener has rebid 3♢ or 3♡

The basic scheme is:

4♢ = Four or five diamonds and no other four-card suit
4♡ = Four or five clubs and no other four-card suit
4♠ = No four-card minor. If this is not possible, it shows four cards in each minor.
4 NT = If opener can have neither minor or both minors, then this response shows both minors

Examples:

1.	2.	3.
2 NT — 3♣	2 NT — 3♣	2 NT — 3♣
3♢ — 4♣	3♢ — 3♡	3♡ — 3♠
4♢ (1)	3 NT — 4♣	3 NT — 4♣
4♡ (2)	4♢ (1)	4♢ (5)
4♠ (3)	4♡ (2)	4♡ (6)
4 NT (4)	4♠ (4)	4♠ (7)

(1) Four or five diamonds; no other four-card suit
(2) Four or five clubs; no other four-card suit
(3) Four spades; 4-3-3-3
(4) Four-four in the minors
(5) Four diamonds in addition to the four hearts already shown
(6) Four clubs in addition to the four hearts already shown
(7) No minor; exactly 3-4-3-3 distribution

In Sequence 1 responder knows relatively little about opener's hand. He could have four spades in a 4-3-3-3 distribution; any hand with a four or five-card minor and no other four-card suit; or a hand with two four-card minors. Therefore four steps are needed to describe all these possibilities.

In Sequence 2 opener denies a four-card major, so he must have at least one four or five-card minor. Three steps are required to show all the possible distributions.

In Sequence 3 opener can have a side four-card suit or be 3-4-3-3. Three steps are necessary to describe all the possibilities.

   b) Opener rebids 3 ♠ or 3 NT

Opener shows the remainder numerically (the basic pattern is already known):

2 NT — 3 ♣	2 NT — 3 ♣
3 ♠ — 4 ♣	3 NT — 4 ♣
4 ◇ = 5-2-3-3	4 ◇ = 4-4-2-3
4 ♡ = 5-3-2-3	4 ♡ = 4-4-3-2
4 ♠ = 5-3-3-2	

2. Opener uses steps beyond these bids to show extra control(s). He uses the same steps, starting at the next available level:

1 NT — 2 ♡
2 NT — 3 ♣
3 NT — 4 ♣
4 ◇ = Six Controls, the expected number, 4-4-2-3
4 ♡ = Six Controls, the expected number, 4-4-3-2
4 ♠ = Seven Controls; 4-4-2-3
4 NT = Seven Controls; 4-4-3-2
5 ♣ = Eight Controls; 4-4-2-3
5 ◇ = Eight Controls; 4-4-3-2

If opener has fewer than the expected number of Controls, he usually demotes the hand to the next lower range. The responses showing two extra Controls are extremely rare because the hand is usually promoted to the next category.

Bidding proceeds along natural lines. Any bid responder makes is natural unless the bidding makes this impossible. If responder lacks slam interest he must sign-off in 4 NT.

Examples:

1. U. S. Team Trials, 1969.

Opener	Responder
♠ A K 9 5	♠ J 10 2
♡ J 6	♡ A 9 2
◇ A K Q 5	◇ J 8 7 4 3
♣ A K Q	♣ 7 5
2 NT (1)	3 ♣
3 ◇	4 ♣ (2)
4 ◇ (3)	6 ◇ (4)
Pass	

(1) 25-26 HCP; balanced distribution
(2) CONFIT inquiry for minor suits; balanced
(3) Four or five diamonds; fewer than four clubs; the expected nine Controls
(4) Opener's nine Controls plus responder's two Controls = 11 Controls. The good diamond fit should produce 12 tricks.

2.

Opener	Responder
♠ A Q 10 x	♠ K x
♡ A x	♡ K x x
◇ Q x x	◇ K J 10 x x
♣ A K x x	♣ J 10 x
1 NT	2 ♠ (1)
2 NT	3 ♣
3 ◇	4 ♣ (2)
5 ◇ (3)	6 ◇ (4)
Pass (5)	

(1) Three Controls
(2) CONFIT. No interest in spades.
(3) Sixth step = Four or five clubs; fewer than four diamonds; one Control more than expected, i.e., seven Controls
(4) Suggested final contract
(5) Suits me

3.

Opener	Responder
♠ A J x	♠ K Q x x x
♡ K x x x	♡ A x
◇ A x	◇ Q J x x
♣ A K x x	♣ x x
1 NT (1)	2 ♠
2 NT	3 ♣
3 ♡	3 ♠ (2)
3 NT (3)	4 ♣ (4)
5 ♠ (5)	6 ♠ (6)
Pass (7)	

(1) It's tempting to bid 2 ♣ with eight Controls
(2) Clarify your hearts
(3) Only four
(4) CONFIT. Describe your minors
(5) Eighth step = Two extra Controls, thus eight; four clubs

343

fewer than four diamonds
(6) Five-card suit; suggesting a final contract
(7) Fine with me

If responder makes a bid that clearly cannot be natural, he is
scanning for queens. A fit for opener's minor is assumed.

2 NT — 3 ♣
3 ◇ — 4 ♣
4 ♡ — 4 ♠ = Agrees on clubs and scans for queens. 4 ♠
cannot be natural as he didn't bid 3 ♡ over
3 ◇ .

Examples:

1.

Opener	Responder
♠ A K 10 x	♠ x x x
♡ A K	♡ Q x x x
◇ Q J x x	◇ A K x x
♣ A K x	♣ Q x

2 ◇	2 ♠
2 NT	3 ♣
3 ◇	4 ♣
5 ♣ (1)	5 ♠ (2)
6 ♣ (3)	7 ◇ (4)
Pass	

(1) Four or five diamonds; fewer than four clubs; one more
Control than expected, i.e., nine Controls
(2) I cannot want to play spades — I did not bid 3 ♡ over 3 ♠ —
so this asks for a scan for queens beginning with diamonds,
the only known length
(3) Diamond queen but no spade queen
(4) I hope you have three clubs. If not we will need a little luck.

2. Challenge the Champs, 1969.

Opener	Responder
♠ A Q 5	♠ 7 6 3
♡ A Q 2	♡ K J 5 4
◇ A 10 4	◇ K 8
♣ A K Q 5	♣ J 7 6 3

2 NT	3 ♣
3 ◇	4 ♣
4 ♡ (1)	6 ♣ (2)
Pass (3)	

(1) Four or five clubs but fewer than four diamonds
(2) Club fit. With 11 Controls and 33 HCP the slam should be excellent.
(3) My hand is perfect — all aces and strong trumps

THREE-SUITED HANDS

With a three-suited hand (4-4-4-1 or 5-4-4-0) responder bids the three cheapest available steps to show his short suit numerically. In most cases the bid shows a fit for opener's major. One exception is when responder shows a short suit directly over a 3 ◇ rebid.

2 NT — 3 ♣
3 ◇ — 4 ◇ = Spade singleton
    — 4 ♡ = Spade void

With four or more spades responder bids 3 ♡ over 3 ◇. This is the only case where responder distinguishes immediately between a singleton and a void. In all other cases responder can be short in any of the other three suits.

Sample sequences:

1.
> 2 NT — 3♣
> 3♦ — 3♥
> 3♠ — 3 NT = Heart shortness with spades agreed
> — 4♦ = Diamond shortness with spades agreed
> — 4♥ = Club shortness with spades agreed

2.
> 2 NT — 3♣
> 3♦ — 3♥
> 3 NT — 4♦, 4♥ or 4♠ = Three-suiter with no agreed fit

3.
> 2 NT — 3♣
> 3♥ — 4♦ = 4-4-1-4 with a heart fit
> — 4♠ = 1-4-4-4 with a heart fit
> — 4 NT = 4-4-4-1 with a heart fit

4.
> 2 NT — 3♣
> 3♥ — 3♠
> 3 NT — 4♦ = 4-1-4-4 with no agreed fit

5.
> 2 NT—3♣
> 3♠ — 4♦ = 4-1-4-4 with a spade fit
> — 4♥ = 4-4-1-4 with a spade fit
> — 4 NT = 4-4-4-1 with a spade fit

6.
> 2 NT — 3♣
> 3 NT — 4♦
> 4♥ — 4♠ = 1-4-4-4 with a heart fit
> — 4 NT = 4-4-1-4 with a heart fit
> — 5♣ = 4-4-4-1 with a heart fit

7.
> 2 NT — 3♣
> 3 NT — 4♥
> 4♠ — 4 NT or 5♣ = Three-suited with a spade fit and
> heart shortage

This may be more easily remembered if these points are realized:

1. 3 NT is available in only one sequence (Sequence 1), where there is an agreed fit at the three-level. In other auctions 3 NT is needed as a signoff and bids showing shortness start at 4 ◇ or higher.

2. 4 ♣ is never part of the three-suiter scheme. It is CONFIT, except for two auctions where it is Key Card Blackwood:

2 NT — 3 ♣	2 NT — 3 ♣
3 ♡ — 4 ♣	3 ◇ — 3 ♡
	3 ♠ — 4 ♣

3. When opener bids 3 NT over 3 ♣, responder must transfer to the major he wants to be trump before showing his shortness because:

   a) There is no room at the four-level otherwise

   b) Opener needs to know which suit is trump

Opener's choices after hearing responder's short suit:

1. Sign off in the agreed suit in either game or slam. 4 NT is a signoff in that there is no agreed fit.

2. Bid the first available step to ask for Controls. Responder replies based on the combined number of Controls:

First step	= We have nine Controls if you have the expected number
Second step	= We have 10 Controls if you have the expected number
Third step	= We have 11 Controls if you have the expected number
Fourth step	= We have 12 Controls if you have the expected number

Example:

    2 NT — 3 ♣
    3 ♡ — 4 ◇ = 1-4-4-4, 0-4-4-5, 0-4-5-4 or 0-5-4-4
    4 ♡   = Signoff attempt
    4 ♠   = Request for Controls. A 4 NT response shows none (don't forget that 2 NT showed nine Controls); 5 ♣ shows one Control; etc.

3. Bid the second available step to ask for clarification of shortness — singleton or void.

    Responder replies:
        First step = Singleton
        Second step and beyond = Void, zooming to show combined Controls according to the formula in option 2 above.

Example:

    2 NT — 3 ♣
    3 ♡ — 4 ◇
    4 NT — 5 ♣ = Singleton
          — 5 ◇ = Void with no Controls
          — 5 ♡ = Void with one Control, etc.

If responder shows a singleton, opener can relay for the combined Controls. Once a relay sequence is in effect, the next available step starts a scan for queens. If there is an agreed fit, start with the trump queen. With no agreed fit, show queens down-the-line.

If the initial response told responder's exact number of Controls, a Spiral for queens starts directly:

2♣ — 2♠ (1)	(1) Three Controls
2 NT — 3♣	(2) Heart fit with spade shortage
3♡ — 4◇ (2)	(3) Start Spiral Scan: Heart queen,
4♠ (3)	diamond queen, club queen, etc.
4 NT (4)	(4) Do you have a singleton or
	void? Zoom to give Spiral re-
	sponse with a void.

Examples:

1. Mexican Nationals, 1982.

Opener	*Responder*
George	Mauricio
Rosenkranz	Smid

♠ A K 4 3	♠ Q J 10 7
♡ K J 5 2	♡ A Q 6 4
◇ A 5 2	◇ 10
♣ A Q	♣ K 6 4 3

2♣	2♠
2 NT	3♣
3 NT	4◇ (1)
4♡ (2)	4 NT (3)
5♣ (4)	5♠ (5)
7♡ (6)	Pass

(1) Transfer, intending to describe the 4-4-1-4 pattern with heart fit.
(2) Forced
(3) Second step = middle shortage, i.e., short diamonds
(4) As Controls are known, asks for a queen scan
(5) Third step = Heart queen and spade queen but no club queen
(6) Delighted

2. French National Open

Opener	Responder
♠ K Q 10	♠ A 8 5 4 2
♡ A K 4	♡ Q 8 7 6
◇ A K Q 3	◇ J 10 5 4
♣ Q J 9	♣ —

2♣ (1)	2♡ (2)
2 NT	3♣
3◇	3♡
3 NT (3)	4♠ (4)
5◇ (5)	5♠ (6)
5 NT (7)	6◇ (8)
7◇ (9)	Pass

(1) Enough points for 2◇, but downgraded in view of the shortage of controls and the flat distribution
(2) Two Controls
(3) Denies four spades
(4) Three-suiter; club shortage
(5) Super Relay: Do you have a void? 4 NT would have been a signoff.
(6) Second step = Club void but no spade queen
(7) Another relay for queens
(8) Heart queen but no diamond queen
(9) Splendid

3.

Opener	Responder
♠ K x x	♠ A J x x
♡ A J x x	♡ K Q x x
◇ A Q x x	◇ x
♣ A K	♣ J x x x

2♣	2♠
2 NT	3♣
3♡	4♠ (1)
4 NT (2)	5◇ (3)
6♡ (4)	Pass

(1) Heart fit and diamond shortage, partner will expect 4-4-1-4 or 5-4-0-4
(2) Start spiralling with the heart queen; I don't care about the exact nature of your shortage
(3) Second step = Heart queen but no spade queen
(4) That's it

That takes care of Romex Stayman and the large variety of hands it can handle. Next come the transfer structure and two-suited hands.

The Transfer Structure

Responses of 3 ◇ , 3 ♡ , 3 ♠ and 3 NT are all transfers:

3 ◇   = A transfer to hearts
3 ♡   = A transfer to spades
3 ♠   = A transfer to clubs
3 NT = A transfer to diamonds

Responder promises at least five cards in his suit, and in the case of transfers to a minor (3 ♠ and 3 NT), he promises a side suit and slam interest.

Though the bids are called transfers, opener will almost always be able to immediately accept or reject responder's suit:

2 NT — 3 ◇	(1) Three or more hearts
3 ♡ (1)	(2) Only two hearts; four or five
3 ♠ (2)	spades
3 NT (3)	(3) Only two hearts; fewer than four
	spades

2 NT — 3 ♡	(1) Three or more spades
3 ♠ (1)	(2) Only two spades
3 NT (2)	

2 NT — 3 ♠	(1) Club rejection
3 NT (1)	(2) Club acceptance
4 ♣ (2)	

2 NT — 3 NT	(1) Diamond rejection
4 ♣ (1)	(2) Diamond acceptance
4 ◇ (2)	

This allows responder to know, at the lowest possible level, whether there is a fit.

In the rare sequence where a game force is not established, opener responds more normally over a transfer to a major:

2 ♣ — 2 ◇
2 NT — 3 ◇
3 ♡ = Normal response with two or more hearts
Any other bid = Heart acceptance; maximum values; game force

As responder's hand is weak, slam is very unlikely. Subsequent bidding is natural. It is assumed from this point on that a game force has been established and that opener accepts the transfer with a fit or rejects the transfer without a fit.

Showing a Two-Suiter

With a two-suiter and slam interest, responder transfers to the long suit and then bids the second suit. With two suits of equal length (5-5), start by transferring at the lowest possible level: hearts, spades, diamonds and clubs in that order.

Example:

> Hearts and another suit: Bid 3 ◇ and follow with the second suit
> Spades and a minor: Bid 3 ♡ and follow with the minor
> Clubs and diamonds: Bid 3 ♠ and follow with 4 ◇

This may appear to be uneconomical, but it isn't. By showing his two suits at the lowest possible level responder allows opener to ask for the side suit length (and remainders) at the lowest possible level. The relay structure used is similar to the situation after a Maxi-Raise of one of a major. Bidding a major or minor two-suiter uneconomically denies slam interest:

2 NT	— 3 ♡	2 NT	— 3 NT
3 ♠ or 3 NT	— 4 ♡	4 ♣ or 4 ◇	— 5 ♣

Another reminder: There are two two-suiters that don't transfer — five spades and four hearts and any 5-4-2-2 hand.

There is one awkward distribution: five or more diamonds with four clubs. Responder starts by bidding 3 NT and follows with 4 ◇ (over 4 ♣) or 4 NT (over 4 ◇):

2 NT	— 3 NT	(1) Diamond rejection
4 ♣ (1)	— 4 ◇ (2)	(2) Five or more diamonds; four clubs
		(3) Diamond acceptance
2 NT	— 3 NT	
4 ◇ (3)	— 4 NT (2)	

Describing responder's distribution

As usual, opener can attempt to signoff or bid the first available step as a relay. The exact response to the relay depends on the inferences that are available about responder's suit length.

353

The basic scheme:

First step	= Only four cards in the second suit
Second step	= High shortage; at least 5-5 in the two suits
Third step	= Equal shortage; at least 6-5 in the two suits
Fourth step	= Low singleton; at least 5-5 in the two suits
Fifth step	= Low void; at least 5-5 in the two suits

The key factor for responder to clarify is whether his second suit is only four cards long or if it is five or more cards in length.

A second step response (high shortage) is further defined by the next relay:

First step	= High singleton; at least 5-5 in the two suits
Second step	= High void; at least 5-5 in the two suits

After a first step response, showing only four-cards in the second suit, the residual distribution is further defined using the same scheme as with hands that are at least 5-5:

2♣	—2♦	(1) Club acceptance
2 NT	—3♠	(2) Four or more diamonds
4♣ (1)	—4◇ (2)	(3) How many diamonds?
4♡ (3)	—4♠ (4)	(4) Only four
4 NT (5)	—5♣ (6)	(5) Remainders? Not a signoff as
	—5◇ (7)	opener has already accepted clubs
	—5♡ (8)	(6) High shortage. 5◇ would ask for
	—5♠ (9)	clarification
		(7) Equal shortage — therefore 1-1-4-7
		(8) Low singleton
		(9) Low void

In auctions where responder's distribution can be inferred, the responses are modified accordingly. The same clarification of remainders: high, equal or low shortage; and singleton/ void is given in all cases:

a) The second suit is known to be only four cards long

This occurs when the suits are bid uneconomically (minor first, major second), or in the special case of five or more diamonds and exactly four clubs:

2 NT   — 3 NT
4♣ or 4♢ — 4♡ or 4♠   = Longer diamonds. With
                                 5-5 start with a transfer
                                   to the major.

In these instances, show the remainder with the next response:

First step   = High shortage (follow with two-step clari-
                          fication)
Second step = Equal shortage
                          Etc.

A step to show only four cards in the second suit is obviously unnecessary.

    b) The second suit is known to be five cards long.

This happens in only one sequence:

2 NT   — 3 ♢   (1) Only two hearts; fewer than four
3 NT (1) — 4♠ (2)   spades
                        (2) At least five spades. No other fit
                        is possible otherwise.

In this case responder uses the usual four step scheme to clarify remainders (high shortness, equal shortness, etc.).

Note: If responder bids 4♡, 4♠ or 4 NT to show his second suit, this bid is forcing unless opener knows too many controls are missing.

Having described his distribution, responder is ready for the next phase — showing valuable cards (Controls, Key Cards, a Spiral Scan).

Showing Controls, Key Cards, and Spiraling for queens

Responder next shows his important cards. His responses depends on two factors:

1. Is a fit implied or explicit? and
2. Did responder shows his controls with the original response?

One fact is constant: cards in the second suit are especially important.

A. Responder's Exact Number of Controls is Known

In this case attention turns to responder's queens — the aces and kings have already been shown.

If a trump suit is agreed, the order is: trump queen, side suit queen, etc.

If no trump suit is agreed, the order is: longest suit queen, side suit queen, fragment queen, etc. The higher of two suits of equal length is scanned first.

In the rare case where opener wants clarification of responder's controls, he must use the Super Relay:

If no suit is agreed, responder starts spiralling with kings (the king of the longest suit comes first).

If a suit is agreed, responder gives a Key Card response. Since this is a two-suiter, six Key Cards exist. Spiral on the next round: trump queen, fragment king, side suit queen, etc.

Example:

1.

Opener	Responder
George	Eddie
Rosenkranz	Wold

♠ A K 6 2	♠ 3
♡ A K 10	♡ 9 6 2
◇ 9 4	◇ K Q J 6 3
♣ A Q J 10	♣ K 8 7 4

2 ♣	2 ♡
2 NT	3 NT
4 ♣ (1)	4 ◇ (2)
4 ♡ (3)	4 ♠ (4)
6 ♣ (5)	Pass

(1) Rejecting diamonds
(2) Five diamonds and a four-card club suit. Remember, with 5-5 in the minors, responder would transfer to clubs and show diamonds later.
(3) Interested, 4 NT would be a sign off
(4) 1-3-5-4 or 3-1-5-4
(5) Opener could scan for the diamond queen, but it is reasonable to assume that responder has that card

2.

Opener	Responder
♠ A K x	♠ Q J x x
♡ K x	♡ A x x
◇ A Q x x	◇ K J x x x
♣ A J x x	♣ x

2♣	2♦
2 NT	3 NT (1)
4◇ (2)	4♠ (3)
4 NT (4)	5♡ (5)
5♠ (6)	5 NT (7)
6♣ (8)	6♡ (9)
7◇ (10)	Pass

(1) Long diamonds
(2) Accepts diamonds
(3) Four-card spade suit. With 5-5, spades would have been shown first.
(4) Relay. Remainders?
(5) Low singleton
(6) Responder's three Controls must be the ace of hearts and the king of diamonds. I must start with 5♠ which asks for a scan for the queen of diamonds. 5 NT asks for Key Cards to clarify ambiguous holdings.
(7) No diamond queen
(8) Spade queen?
(9) Yes, but no heart queen
(10) Partner must have ♠ Qxxx ♡ Axx ◇ Kxxxx ♣ x. Responder can't have ♠ QJxx ♡ Axx ◇ xxxxx ♣ K because he wouldn't show a singleton. He would treat the distribution as 4-5-2-2.

3.

Opener	Responder
♠ A J x	♠ K Q x x x
♡ A x	♡ K Q x x x
◇ A J x x	◇ x x
♣ A K x x	♣ x

2 ♣	2 ♡
2 NT	3 ◇
3 NT (1)	4 ♠ (2)
5 ♣ (3)	5 NT (4)
6 ♣ (5)	6 ♡ (6)
7 ♠ (7)	Pass

(1) Denies three hearts or four spades, so he must be 3-2 in the majors

(2) 5-5 slam try; virtually forcing

(3) Opener Super Relays to ask about the six Key Cards. He is not particularly interested in the remainders.

(4) Two Key Cards and the queen of spades

(5) Opener still needs the queen of hearts or extra length from responder to make 7 ♠ a good proposition. Responder has already shown his two Controls so he cannot have the king of diamonds. With 6-5: ♠ KQxxxx ♡ Kxxxx ◇ x ♣ x he would know the sixth spade is enough for the grand slam.

(6) The queen of hearts. Responder knows enough about the hand to bid the grand himself if he had any extra length.

(7) Good news!

B. Responder Has Not Indicated His Controls

There will almost always be an agreed fit. The only exception is when opener rejects the transfer and responder showed only four cards in the second suit.

1. There is an agreed fit. The relay asks about the six Key Cards. The Spiral Scan order: trump queen, fragment king, side suit queen, etc. A bid of six in responder's known five-card suit is to play (if opener hasn't already

denied a fit by refusing a transfer).

2. If no suit is agreed. The relay asks for Controls; the next relay starts the Spiral Scan: long suit queen, side suit queen, etc.

Examples:

1. Australian Trials, 1976.

Opener	Responder
♠ A K 9 8 4	♠ 2
♡ A Q	♡ K 9
◇ A 8 3	◇ K Q J 9 7
♣ A Q 2	♣ K 7 6 5 3

Opener	Responder
2 ◇	2 ♠
2 NT	3 ♠
4 ♣ (1)	4 ◇ (2)
4 ♡ (3)	4 NT (4)
5 ♣ (5)	5 ◇ (6)
5 ♡ (7)	6 ♣ (8)
6 ♠ (9)	7 ♣ (10)
7 NT (11)	Pass

(1) Accepts clubs
(2) Second suit is diamonds
(3) Relay. How many diamonds?
(4) Five diamonds; high shortage
(5) Relay, not a signoff. Opener has accepted the club slam try.
(6) Singleton spade
(7) Key Cards?
(8) Two, since the king of diamonds counts, but no queen of clubs
(9) 6 ◇ would be to play as this might be a 5-4 fit. 6 ♡ would be a scan for the king of hearts. 6 ♠, the last possible scanning move, asks about the queen of diamonds. If responder does not have it, the hand will be played in 6 NT.

360

(10) I have it
(11) "Matchpoints"

2.

Opener	Responder
♠ A x	♠ K x x x x
♡ A K J x x	♡ Q x x
◊ A J x	◊ x
♣ A Q x	♣ K J x x
2 ◊	2 ♠
2 NT	3 ♡
3 NT (1)	4 ♣ (2)
4 ◊	4 ♡ (3)
4 ♠	5 ◊ (4)
5 ♡ (5)	5 NT (6)
6 ◊ (7)	6 ♡ (8)
7 ♡ (9)	Pass

(1) No spade fit
(2) Four or more clubs
(3) Exactly four clubs
(4) Low singleton; 5-3-1-4 or possibly 6-2-1-4
(5) Controls?
(6) Two Controls. Opener's bidding implies eight Controls, so the second step shows that 10 combined Controls are expected.
(7) Scan for queens. 6 ♣ would have been a signoff.
(8) No spade queen
(9) Responder is a heavy favorite to hold the queen of hearts.

Even with ♠ Kxxxxx ♡ Qx ◊ x ♣ KJxx 7♡ is best. If responder showed the spade queen opener would bid 6 NT. Responder could work out to bid on with the queen of hearts (he should bid 7♡ !)

C. A Very Special Case

On the auction:

    2 NT — 3 ◇
    3 ♠

responder has no slam try available with a spade fit (4♡ and 4 NT show heart one-suiters; four of a minor is natural; and 4♠ is a signoff). The solution — show remainders, starting with 5♣ (high shortage).

Example:

Opener	Responder
♠ A K x x	♠ Q J x x x
♡ K x	♡ A J x x x
◇ A x x	◇ Q x
♣ A K J x	♣ x
2 NT	3 ◇
3 ♠	5 ♡ (1)
5 NT (2)	6 ◇ (3)
7 ♠	Pass

(1) Opener has shown spades and rejected hearts. Now 5♡ shows a low singleton, a spade fit and slam interest.
(2) Relay for queens
(3) Spade queen, no heart queen

The One-Suited Slam Try

1. Major One-Suiters

Start with a transfer, then follow with:

4 NT = 5-3-3-2; quantitative
5 ♡ or 5 ♠ = 6-3-2-2 or 7-2-2-2; slam try
Jump in a new suit = 6-3-3-1 or 7-3-2-1; singleton in the bid
                        suit; slam try

If opener accepted the transfer, showing a fit, 3 NT is Key Card Blackwood.

2 NT — 3 ◇
3 ♡   — 3 NT = Key Card Blackwood

2. Minor One-Suiters

Responder bids to show the length of his minor:

2 NT — 4 ♣ = Exactly six diamonds, slam try
      — 4 ◇ = Exactly six clubs; slam try
      — 4 ♡ = Seven or more clubs; slam try
      — 4 ♠ = Seven or more diamonds; slam try

Opener signs off in 4 NT or bids the next available step as a relay:

If responder has already shown Controls, the relay is a scan for queens, starting with the trump queen. A Super Relay asks responder to start with the trump king.

If responder has not shown Controls, the relay asks for Key Cards and normal Spiral continuations.

After the response, 4 NT is a signoff.

Examples:

1. Bermuda Bowl. U.S. vs. Sweden, 1953.

Opener	Responder
♠ A K J 5 2	♠ Q
♡ K 10 9	♡ Q J 8 6 5 4 2
◇ A K 10	◇ 3
♣ A 9	♣ Q 10 5 2

2 ◇ (1)	2 ♠
2 NT	3 ◇ (2)
3 ♡ (3)	3 NT (4)
4 ◇ (5)	6 ♡ (6)
Pass	

(1) Only 22 HCP, but worth promotion in view of the extra Control and the strong five-card suit
(2) Transfer to hearts
(3) Accepting hearts with at least three-card support
(4) Key Cards?
(5) Four
(6) The opponents might just have the ace-king of clubs, but if they don't lead them . . .

2. Olympiad. U.S. vs. Australia, 1968.

Opener	Responder
♠ A K Q 9	♠ 10 3
♡ A 9 3	♡ Q 6 4
◇ A 7 4	◇ K 10
♣ K 10 7	♣ A 9 6 5 3 2

	Pass
1 NT	2 ♣
2 NT	4 ◇ (1)
4 ♡ (2)	4 ♠ (3)
6 ♣ (4)	Pass

(1) Slam invitation; one-suiter in clubs; exactly six clubs
(2) Controls are known, so this bid asks for a scan starting

with the trump queen
(3) No trump queen
(4) Too bad that you can't have an extra trump

3. Mexican Trials, 1976.

Opener	Responder
George	Sol
Rosenkranz	Dubson

♠ A K J	♠ Q 3 2
♡ Q J 6	♡ A K 10 9 8 4
◊ A K Q 4	◊ 8 5 2
♣ J 3 2	♣ 7

1 NT (1)	2 ♠
2 NT	3 ◊ (2)
3 ♡	5 ♣ (3)
6 ♣ (4)	6 ◊ (5)
6 ♡	Pass

(1) Demoted: only six Controls and a 4-3-3-3 pattern
(2) Intending to make a slam try in hearts
(3) Splinter bid with club shortage
(4) No relay structure here. Apparently opener is interested in a club void.
(5) I don't have it

4. Mexican Nationals. Mixed Pairs, 1982.

Opener George Rosenkranz	*Responder* Edith Rosenkranz
♠ K Q J 8	♠ A 6
♡ A J 10 4	♡ 3 2
◇ A 4 2	◇ 10 8
♣ A K	♣ Q J 10 8 7 6 3

2 ◇	2 ♠
2 NT	4 ♡ (1)
4 ♣ (2)	5 ♣ (3)
5 ◇ (4)	5 ♠ (5)
7 NT (6)	Pass

(1) One-suited slam try with seven or more clubs
(2) Key Cards?
(3) One
(4) Scan for the trump queen
(5) I have the trump queen, but I don't have the diamond king.
(6) A slight risk. If responder has the singleton ace of spades, a spade lead will defeat 7 NT. At IMPs, a 7 ♣ bid is best.

Opener Cannot Rebid 2 NT

If the response to 1 NT, 2 ♣ or 2 ◇ is 2 NT or higher, the auction is crowded. However, the partnership is known to have at least 10 combined Controls and great high card strength.

Opener has two options with a balanced hand:

1. 4 NT = Slam force; guarantees all 12 Controls; looking for a grand slam
2. 3 NT = All other hands

Responder bids over 3 NT or 4 NT with the same response structure as over 2 NT except that he is one or two levels higher.

Examples:

1. Challenge the Champs, 1970.

Opener	Responder
♠ A J 10 3	♠ K Q 9 5 4
♡ A K J 7	♡ Q 9 8
◊ K J	◊ 8 5
♣ Q 7 3	♣ A K 4

1 NT	2 NT (1)
3 NT (2)	4 ♣ (3)
4 NT (4)	5 ♣ (5)
5 ◊ (6)	6 NT (7)
Pass	

(1) Four Controls and at least three Cover Cards
(2) Fewer than eight Controls
(3) Romex Stayman
(4) 4-4 in the majors
(5) CONFIT
(6) 4-4-2-3; no extra Controls
(7) No advantage to playing spades with mirror distribution. 6 NT protects opener's diamond king.

2.

Opener	Responder
♠ A x	♠ K x x
♡ A K x	♡ Q J x x x
◊ Q x x x	◊ A K x
♣ A Q x x	♣ K x

1 NT	3 ♣ (1)
4 NT (2)	5 ◊ (3)
5 ♡ (4)	7 ♡ (5)
Pass	

(1) Five Controls
(2) I have an extra Control, so we have all the Controls
(3) Transfer to hearts

(4) At least three-card support
(5) Opener must have at least one queen, so the hand is likely to be laydown. At worst, a finesse may be required. At matchpoints, 7 NT should be bid.

Chapter 22

DEVELOPMENTS AFTER OPENER SHOWS TYPE C: "CLOVER" — THE POWERHOUSE THREE-SUITER

The bid is forcing to game in principle, though the bidding can stop in four of a minor if responder is very weak and opener is minimum.

Responder's Second Bid

Responder has such precise information about opener's hand that he will often be able to place the contract directly. His choices:

1. Attempt to place the contract in notrump or one of opener's long suits. If responder wants to play with opener's short suit as trump, he must jump in that suit.

Example:

Challenge the Champs, 1969.

Opener	Responder
♠ A K 5 3	♠ Q 7 4
♡ A	♡ K 9 6 5
♢ A K 7 2	♢ J 8 4
♣ A K 6 2	♣ J 10 5
2 ♢	2 ♠
4 ♢ (1)	4 NT (2)
Pass	

(1) 4-1-4-4 "Clover"
(2) Signoff

2. Relay by bidding opener's short suit (the next step). Responder does this when he needs to know more specifically the location of opener's honors.

The relay is particularly useful when responder has a fit and a side suit singleton. Good balanced hands may also choose to relay.

3. Responder shows a void and at least one Cover Card by making a "Splinter" jump to five of a major or six of a minor. For example:

$$2\diamondsuit - 2\spadesuit$$
$$4\clubsuit - 5\heartsuit = \text{heart void; at least one Cover Card}$$
$$- 5\spadesuit = \text{spade void; at least one Cover Card}$$
$$- 6\clubsuit = \text{club void; at least one Cover Card}$$

Development of the Auction

If responder places the contract, opener will pass unless he has enough extra values (fewer Losers) to go on.

If responder relays he is asking for opener's number of Controls. He replies:

First step   = Six Controls
Second step   = Seven Controls
Third step   = Eight Controls
Etc.

Note: It is recommended that opener discount a singleton king, i.e., that he not show it as a Control.

This can be expressed as a formula: N-5 = S

N = Number of Controls
S = Number of the steps that opener bids

Example sequence:

$$2\diamondsuit \quad - 2\spadesuit \qquad \text{(1) Controls?}$$
$$3\heartsuit \quad - 3\spadesuit \text{ (1)} \qquad \text{(2) Third step} = \text{Eight Controls}$$
$$4\diamondsuit \text{ (2)} -$$

To continue relaying responder makes the cheapest bid in notrump or in opener's short suit. This starts a scan for queens. Continuing the example sequence:

2 ◇ — 2 ♠	(1) Controls?
3 ♡ — 3 ♠ (1)	(2) Third step = Eight controls
4 ◇ (2) — 4 ♠ (3)	(3) Queens?
4 NT (4) —	(4) No queen of hearts
5 ♣ (5) —	(5) Heart queen; no diamond queen
Etc. (6)	(6) Etc. a la Spiral

Some examples of Clover in action:

1.

Opener	*Responder*
♠ x	♠ Q J 10 x x x x
♡ A x x x	♡ x x
◇ A K Q x	◇ x x
♣ A K Q x	♣ x x
2 ◇	2 ♡
3 ♡ (1)	4 ♠ (2)

(1) 1-4-4-4 powerhouse
(2) Your singleton is my playable long suit and I don't want to play 3 NT.

2.

Opener	*Responder*
♠ A K Q x	♠ x x x
♡ A x x x	♡ x x
◇ x	◇ x x x x
♣ A K Q x	♣ x x x x
2 ◇	2 ♡ (1)
3 ♣ (2)	4 ♣ (3)
Pass (4)	

(1) 0-5 HCP

(2) The four-card suit below the singleton; exactly 4-4-1-4

(3) With a fit in a minor and no sure Cover Card, responder does not want to commit himself to a five-level contract

(4) With a two Loser hand, opener would bid the club game

3.

Opener	Responder
♠ A K J 10	♠ x x x
♡ A K Q x	♡ x x x x
◇ x	◇ Q x x
♣ K Q J x	♣ 10 x x

2 ◇	2 ♡ (1)
3 ♣ (2)	4 ♡ (3)
Pass	

(1) 0-5 HCP

(2) The four-card suit below the singleton; exactly 4-4-1-4

(3) Placing the contract

4.

Opener	Responder
♠ A Q x x	♠ K x
♡ A K Q x	♡ x x x
◇ x	◇ x x x
♣ A K J x	♣ Q x x x x

2 ◇	2 ♡ (1)
3 ♣ (2)	6 ♣ (3)
Pass	

(1) 0-5 HCP

(2) The four-card suit below the singleton; exactly 4-4-1-4

(3) Two working Cover Cards assure the slam

5.

Opener	Responder
♠ A K x x	♠ Q J x x
♡ A K x x	♡ Q x
◊ A	◊ x x x x
♣ A K Q x	♣ J x x
2 ◊	2 ♡
3 ♣	6 ♠ (1)
7 ♠ (2)	Pass

(1) Two Cover Cards and a spade fit
(2) You must have both major suit queens, and I have only two losers

6.

Opener A	Responder
♠ A Q J x	♠ K x x x x
♡ A K x x	♡ x
◊ x	◊ A x x x
♣ A K Q x	♣ J x x

Opener B
♠ A Q J x
♡ K Q J x
◊ x
♣ A K Q x

Opener C
♠ A Q J x
♡ A K Q x
◊ x
♣ A K x x

A

2 ◇　　— 2 ♠ (1)
4 ♣ (2)　— 4 ◇ (3)
4 NT (4) — 5 ◇ (5)
5 ♠ (6)　— 7 ♠ (7)
Pass

B

2 ◇　　— 2 ♠ (1)
4 ♣ (2)　— 4 ◇ (3)
4 ♡ (8)　— 6 ♠ (9)
Pass

C

2 ◇　　— 2 ♠ (1)
4 ♣ (2)　— 4 ◇ (3)
4 NT (4) — 5 ◇ (5)
5 NT (10) — 7 ♠ (11)
Pass

(1) 6-13 HCP
(2) 4-4-1-4
(3) Controls?
(4) Third step = Eight Controls
(5) Queens?
(6) The queen of spades but not the queen of hearts
(7) The grand slam should be on. Opener must have the queen of clubs to have only three Losers since he has denied the queen of hearts.
(8) Six Controls
(9) We are missing two Controls
(10) The queen of spades and the queen of hearts but not the queen of clubs
(11) I can dispose of my minor suit losers

7. Mexican Trials, 1980.

Opener	*Responder*
George	Sol
Rosenkranz	Dubson

♠ A K 5 2	♠ 10 8 7 6
♡ A	♡ K Q J 8 7 6
◇ A K 6 4	◇ Q
♣ A K 4 3	♣ J 2

2 ◇	2 ♠
4 ◇ (1)	4 ♡ (2)
5 ♠ (3)	7 ♡ (4)
Pass	

(1) 4-1-4-4
(2) Controls?
(3) Sixth step = 11 Controls
(4) An excellent contract. 7 NT has no play on an opening diamond lead.

The opponents reached 6 ♠.

375

8. Acapulco Regional, 1981.

The same approach can be used with strong, balanced responding hands.

Opener	Responder
Eddie	George
Wold	Rosenkranz

♠ A K Q 2	♠ J 10 6 5
♡ A 8 6 4	♡ K Q 7 5
◇ A K 3 2	◇ 10 4
♣ A	♣ K Q 3

Opener	Responder
2 ◇	2 ♠
3 ♠	4 ♣ (1)
5 ♣ (2)	5 NT (3)
6 ◇ (4)	7 ♠ (5)
Pass	

(1) Controls?
(2) Fifth step = 10 Controls
(3) Queens?
(4) The spade queen but not the heart queen
(5) Enough for 13 tricks!

If responder jumps to 5♡ or 5♠ to show a void, opener shows the number of remaining Losers. The first step shows three remaining Losers, the next step shows two, etc.

Examples:

1.

Opener	Responder
♠ A Q x x	♠ —
♡ x	♡ A J x x x
◇ A K Q x	◇ J x x x x
♣ K Q J x	♣ x x x
2 ◇	2 ♠ (1)
4 ◇ (2)	5 ♠ (3)
6 ♣ (4)	6 ◇ (5)
Pass	

(1) 6-13 HCP
(2) 4-1-4-4
(3) Spade void. Hoping for less than total duplication. If opener has a three-Loser hand with the AKQ of spades, that is too bad. Maybe 6 ◇ will be on a diamond finesse, or maybe opener will have the ace of clubs.
(4) Second step = Two remaining Losers outside the spade suit
(5) No problem with five trumps

2.

Opener	Responder
♠ A K Q x	♠ J x x
♡ A J x x	♡ —
◇ x	◇ A J x x x
♣ A K Q x	♣ J x x x x
2 ◇	2 ♠
4 ♣	5 ♡ (1)
6 ♣ (2)	7 ♣ (3)
Pass	

(1) Heart void
(2) I have one remaining Loser
(3) I cover that

377

The bidding is easy with a superstrong responding hand.
Example:

Opener	Responder
♠ K Q J x	♠ A x
♡ A K Q x	♡ J x x x
◇ x	◇ K Q J x x
♣ A K x x	♣ Q J
2 ◇	2 NT (1)
4 ♣ (2)	4 ◇ (3)
4 ♠ (4)	6 NT (5)
Pass	

(1) At least 14 HCP
(2) 4-4-1-4 with at most three Losers
(3) Controls?
(4) Second step = Seven Controls
(5) No grand — two Controls are missing

With length and strength in responder's short suit a notrump contract will often be the best resting place.

An even more precise method has been designed by George and Roni Abrahamsohn — relentless innovators and contributors to Romex.

Their solution, which involves slightly more memorization is available on request from the author.

Chapter 23

ADVANCED COMPETITIVE SEQUENCES AFTER STRONG OPENINGS

This chapter will present some ideas that will allow you to further improve your handling of competitive sequences. Intervention over the newly-introduced 2 ◊ opening also will be discussed.

The basic concepts are the same: Responder classified his hand as WEAK, INTERMEDIATE, or STRONG. The discussion will provide refinements to these basis concepts.

Doubles, One-Step and Two-Step Overcalls

Doubles and low-level overcalls can be essentially ignored, allowing responder to make his normal response. Doubles and a one-step overcall consume so little space that there is frequently a gain in accuracy when these calls are made.

This is how it works:

1. After a double

> PASS = 0-3 HCP (but not a king)
>
> First step = At least four HCP (or a bare king), but a negative response
>
> Second step or higher = The same as without the double or overcall
>
> REDOUBLE = Good defense for the suit(s) advertised by the double AND the values for positive response

Example:

1 NT — DOUBLE (1) —
   (1) Showing the majors

♠ J x x x x	♠ K x x	♠ A x x x x
♡ J x x	♡ x x x x	♡ x
◇ x x	◇ x x x	◇ K J x x
♣ x x x	♣ x x x	♣ x x x
Pass	Bid 2♣	Bid 2◇

   ♠ K J 9 x
   ♡ Q 8 x x
   ◇ Q x
   ♣ x x x

Redouble

2. After a one-step overcall

PASS = 0-3 HCP (but not a king)
DOUBLE = At least four HCP (or a bare king), but still
            a negative response
First step or higher = The same as without the overcall

Examples:
2♣ — 2◇ — ?

♠ Q x	♠ K J x x x	♠ A J x x
♡ K x x x x	♡ x	♡ —
◇ Q x x	◇ K x x	◇ Q x
♣ x x x	♣ Q J x x	♣ K J 10 x x x x
Double	Bid 2♡	Bid 2♠
	(= Two	(= Three
	Controls)	Controls)

380

3. After a two-level overcall

PASS = Negative response
DOUBLE = Lowest positive response (2 ◇ after 1 NT or
             2 ♡ after 2 ♣)
First step or higher = The same as without the overcall

Examples:

1 NT — 2 ◇ — ?

♠ K x x	♠ A J 10 x x x	♠ A x x
♡ Q x x x	♡ x x	♡ K Q x x
◇ x x	◇ A x x	◇ x x
♣ x x x x	♣ x x	♣ Q x x x
Pass	Double	Bid 2 ♠
		= Three Controls

Subsequent bidding follows the normal Romex path.
Example:

Opener		*Responder*	
♠ A K J x x		♠ 10 x	
♡ A		♡ J x x x x	
◇ A K Q x		◇ x x x	
♣ J 10 x		♣ x x x	
1 NT	2 ♣	Pass (1)	Pass
2 ♠ (2)	Pass	Pass (3)	Pass

(1) 0-3 HCP
(2) An easy 2 ♠ bid
(3) An easier pass

Overcalls at the Three-Level and Beyond

After an overcall at the three-level or higher, it is suggested that responder "beef up" the requirements for a cue-bid. With a weaker hand that would otherwise cue-bid, make a natural bid.

The Meaning of a Cue-Bid		
Opening Bid	Two-Level Overcall	Three-Level or Higher Overcall
1 NT	Four or more Controls; three or more Cover Cards	Five or more Controls; three or more Cover Cards
2 ♣	Three or more Controls	Four or more Controls

Example:

Opener		*Responder*	
♠ A		♠ 9 7 5	
♡ A Q J 10 8 6 4		♡ K	
◇ A K		◇ 9 6 5 4 2	
♣ K Q 6		♣ A 8 7 2	

2 ♣	3 ♠	Double (1)	Pass
5 ♡ (2)	Pass	7 ♡ (3)	Pass
Pass	Pass		

(1) Three Controls are not enough for a cue-bid at this level. The diamonds aren't worth mentioning at the four-level.
(2) Very big hand with excellent hearts
(3) Two magic cards must be enough!

Responder Has Length and Strength in the Overcalled Suit

What does responder do when he wishes to make a penalty double of the overcall and/or expose a possible psyche? There are two possibilities:

1. A jump to 3 NT (only after an overcall of at least three steps) shows length and strength in the opponent's suit, with an "intermediate hand."
Example:

Opener	Responder
♠ x	♠ K Q x x
♡ A K Q x x	♡ x x
◇ A Q x x	◇ K 10 x
♣ A J x	♣ Q 10 9 x

1 NT	2 ♠	3 NT (1)	Pass
Pass (2)	Pass		

(1) Showing spade length and strength and an intermediate hand
(2) An easy pass

2. The "Penalty Pass"

Responder can pass an overcall with a trump stack, hoping for a reopening double.

Example:

Mexican Nationals, 1982.

Opener		*Responder*	
♠ 5		♠ K Q 10 8 7	
♡ A Q 4		♡ J 3	
◇ A J 10 6 3		◇ 5 2	
♣ A K Q 9		♣ J 8 6 2	
1 NT	2 ♠	Pass (1)	Pass
Double (2)	Pass	Pass (3)	Pass

(1) Hoping for a reopening double
(2) Takeout
(3) Not on this hand!

If opener reopens with a suit bid, responder shows the "stack" and a positive response with a cue-bid.

Example:

Opener		*Responder*	
♠ x		♠ A J 9 x	
♡ A Q J 8 x x		♡ K x	
◇ A K J x		◇ Q 10 x x	
♣ A x		♣ 10 x x	
1 NT	2 ♠	Pass (1)	Pass
3 ♡ (2)	Pass	3 ♠ (3)	Pass
4 ◇ (4)	Pass	4 ♠ (5)	Pass
4 NT (6)	Pass	5 ◇ (7)	Pass
5 ♡ (8)	Pass	5 NT (9)	Pass
6 ◇ (10)	Pass	7 ◇ (11)	Pass
Pass	Pass		

(1) A "penalty pass"
(2) The natural reopening call
(3) Showing a penalty pass AND some interest in higher things. Would bid 3 NT or 4 ♡ otherwise.
(4) Natural

(5) Cue-bid, showing a diamond fit

(6) TAB

(7) Second step = Minimum length with the ace, king or queen

(8) CAB in hearts

(9) Second step = Second round control

(10) I still can't bid the grand

(11) The king of hearts must be the key. A singleton heart wouldn't be nearly as good. If this isn't enough, opener would not have used the asking bid sequence.

The Opponents Use an Artificial Defense

You are unlikely to encounter artificial defenses. If you do, treat the bids the same way you do other overcalls, EXCEPT THAT there is no cue-bid unless the opponent has promised length in that suit.

Example:

1 NT — 2 ♡ (1) — Pass (2)

           — Double or any bid other than 2 ♠ (3)

           — 2 ♠ (4)

(1) Spades and a minor

(2) 0-5 HCP or a penalty double of spades

(3) Normal and natural including a bid of 3 ♡

(4) Cue-bid; four or more Controls; three or more Cover Cards

Ideas for Opener

Opener has several tools he can use. They all relate to use of the cue-bid.

1. Opener's cue-bid after a negative response.

It is suggested that a cue-bid by opener after a negative response by responder be used as a "Michaels Cue-Bid" showing 5-5 in the majors after a minor suit overcall or five cards in the unbid major and five cards in an unspecified minor after a major suit overcall. These cue-bids are forcing to game unless the opening bid was 1 NT.

Examples:

1 NT — 2♣ — Pass — Pass
3♣ = At least 5-5 in the majors

1 NT — 2♡ — Pass — Pass
3♡ = At least 5-5 in spades and a minor

These cue-bids are not forcing to game after a 1 NT opening.
Example:

Opener	Responder
♠ A K Q x x	♠ 10 x x
♡ A K 10 x x	♡ x x x
◇ Q x	◇ J x x x
♣ x	♣ x x x

1 NT	2♣	Pass	Pass
3♣ (1)	Pass	3♡ (2)	Pass
Pass (3)	Pass		

(1) Michaels Cue-Bid: at least 5-5 in the majors
(2) No interest — A worthless hand
(3) A trusting pass

Opener also can use the Michaels Cue-Bid when the overcall is on his right.
Example:

Opener	Responder
♠ A K Q x x	♠ x
♡ x	♡ x x x x x
◇ A K J 10 x	◇ Q x x
♣ K x	♣ J 10 x x

2♣	Pass	2◇	2♡
3♡ (1)	Pass	4♡ (2)	Pass
5◇ (3)	Pass	Pass	Pass

(1) A good hand with five spades and a five-card minor
(2) Bid your minor, please
(3) OK

2. Opener's cue-bid after a positive response

The meaning of opener's cue-bid after a positive response depends on the level at which the cue-bid is made:

A.   Three-level cue-bid

There are two choices:

1. Play the cue-bid as NATURAL (psyche control)
2. Play the cue-bid as "waiting" (looking for 3 NT)

Examples:

1 NT — 2♠ — 3♡ — Pass
3♠

♠ A K J 9 x	♠ x x x
♡ x	♡ A
◇ A Q 10 x	◇ A K Q x x
♣ A J x	♣ A K J x
3♠ as natural	3♠ as a probe for 3 NT

You must select one method or the other. It is recommended that the cue-bid be used as a notrump probe unless you are playing against opponents who are likely to psyche.

B.   A cue-bid at the four-level or higher

Opener's cue-bid at the four-level or higher is used to ask for the Control Count. Responder gives a step reply, starting with the lowest number of Controls he can hold:

```
1 NT   —2♠  —3♣  —Pass
4♣     —Pass —4♡  —Pass
4♠ (1) —Pass —4 NT (2)
              —5♣ (3)
              —5♢ (4)
              —5♡ (5)

1 NT   —2♠  —3♡  —Pass
4♣     —Pass —4♡  —Pass
4♠ (1) —Pass —4 NT (6)
              —5♣ (7)
              —5♢ (8)
              —5♡ (9)
```

(1) Asking for the number of controls
(2) Four Controls
(3) Five Controls
(4) Six Controls
(5) Seven Controls
(6) Zero Controls
(7) One Control
(8) Two Controls
(9) Three Controls

Examples:

1. Challenge the Champs, 1981.

Opener	Responder
♠ A Q 10 6	♠ 3
♡ A	♡ K 8 6 4
♢ A Q 7 4 2	♢ K 9 8 5 3
♣ A 5 3	♣ J 10 9

1 NT	2♠	3♢ (1)	3♠
4♠ (2)	Pass	5♢ (3)	Pass
5♡ (4)	Pass	5 NT (5)	Pass
6♢ (6)	Pass	Pass	Pass

(1) Five or more diamonds; intermediate hand
(2) Asking for controls
(3) Third step = Two Controls (the 3 ◇ bid didn't promise any Controls)
(4) CAB
(5) The heart king but no heart queen
(6) There is a club loser.

Both pairs missed this slam.

2. Challenge the Champs, 1982.

Opener		Responder	
♠ A Q 6		♠ K J 10 8 5 3	
♡ A 7 4		♡ K 8	
◇ 3		◇ A K Q 8	
♣ A K J 9 4 2		♣ Q	

1 NT	2 ◇	3 ◇ (1)	Pass
4 ♣ (2)	Pass	4 ♠ (3)	Pass
4 NT (4)	Pass	5 ♠ (5)	Pass
6 ◇ (6)	Pass	6 ♠ (7)	Pass
7 ♠ (8)	Pass	7 NT (9)	Pass
Pass	Pass		

(1) Four or more Controls; three or more Cover Cards
(2) Natural
(3) Could be a four-card suit; forcing
(4) TAB
(5) Fourth step = One top honor with extra length
(6) Control Count?
(7) Second step = Five Controls
(8) Should be enough
(9) Correct to 7 NT — 13 top tricks

If responder makes a response that specifies his Control Count, there is no need to use the cue-bid to ask for the Control Count. For example, after the auction:

Opener		*Responder*	
2♣	Pass	2♠	3♡

4♡ can be played to mean whatever you want. It is suggested that it be played as a Michaels Cue-Bid.

The Forcing Pass

Often the best thing to do in a competitive auction is to pass and let partner decide what to do. This subject is quite complex,[2] but you can use these simple rules to guide you:

1. After a 1 NT opening

The opponents may not play a contract undoubled unless:
>   Responder gave a negative response, AND
>   The opponents' contract is below game

2. After a 2♣ opening

The opponents may never play an undoubled contract.
Here is a superb hand from the Ottawa Regional of May, 1983.

[2] Eddie Kantar has written so many articles about it in the ACBL *Bulletin* that I have lost count. He has recently written an excellent book on the subject.

Opener		*Responder*	
Eddie		George	
Wold		Rosenkranz	

♠ K J 7 4		♠ Q 9 8 3	
♡ A 4		♡ 2	
◇ K 3		◇ 10 9	
♣ A K 9 8 5		♣ Q 10 7 6 4 2	

1 NT	3 ♡	Pass (1)	4 ♡
Pass (2)	Pass	4 ♠ ! (3)	Pass
Pass	Pass		

(1) 0-5 HCP
(2) Forcing pass — the opponents are in game
(3) Partner is probably interested in spades — hope for the best
(4) Happily

Result: + 450
Our teammates were + 590 in 4 ♡ doubled.

Interference After a 2 ◇ Opening

Interference after a 2 ◇ opening can be handled in the familiar way.

PASS = "weak" = 0-5 HCP
BID OR DOUBLE = "Intermediate" = 6-13 HCP
CUE-BID = "Strong" = 13 or more HCP

Responder can use the rules described at the beginning of this chapter to handle double, 2 ♡ ("one-step") and 2 ♠ ("two-step") overcalls.

Opener's Rebid

Opener rebids to show his hand type:

TYPE A: Two-Bid. A One-Suiter with a Six-Card or Longer Major. Bid your major. This applies even if it is a cue-bid of the opponent's suit.

Examples:

North-South Vulnerable

1.

Opener	LHO	Responder	RHO
2♢	2♡	Pass	Pass
3♡			

♠ x x
♡ A Q J x x x
♢ A K x
♣ A x

2.

Opener	LHO	Responder	RHO
2♢	2♠	Pass	Pass
3♠			

♠ A K Q 10 x x x
♡ x
♢ A Q x
♣ Q x

TYPE B: 23-24 HCP; Balanced

Double or bid notrump.

Examples:

None Vulnerable

1.

Opener		Responder	
♠ K x x		♠ J x x	
♡ K Q x		♡ J x x	
◇ A K J x		◇ 10 x x x	
♣ A K x		♣ x x x	
2 ◇	3 ♣	Pass (1)	Pass
Double (2)	Pass	Pass (3)	Pass

(1) 0-5 HCP
(2) Balanced hand
(3) Go for the plus score. 3 NT is unlikely to make. 3 ♣ doubled
    Should net + 100 to + 500.

2.

Opener		Responder	
♠ A K x		♠ x x x	
♡ A K J		♡ x x	
◇ K x x		◇ A J 9 x x	
♣ A J x x		♣ K Q x	
2 ◇	2 ♠	3 ◇ (1)	Pass
3 NT (2)	Pass	6 NT (3)	Pass
Pass	Pass		

(1) 6-13 HCP; five or more diamonds
(2) 23-24 HCP; balanced
(3) Should be the top spot

TYPE C: At Most Three Losers; 4-4-4-1 Type

Opener plans to bid a minor to show this hand:

South	West	North	East
2 ◇	2 ♡ or 2 ♠	Pass	Pass

3 ♣ = 4-4-4-1 with four cards in the opponent's suit
3 ◇ = 4-4-4-1 with a singleton in the opponent's suit

At higher levels, opener will double when he has four cards in the opponent's suit:

South	West	North	East
2 ◇	3 ◇	Pass	Pass

Double = Could be 4-4-4-1 with four diamonds
4 ♣ = Exactly 4-4-1-4 (Opener bids the cheaper minor to show 4-4-4-1 with shortness in the opponent's suit)

If responder bids something, then any bid in an unbid minor confirms the three-suiter.

Examples:

1.

Opener	Responder
♠ K Q J x	♠ x x x x
♡ A K Q x	♡ J x
◇ x	◇ Q x x
♣ A K x x	♣ x x x x

2 ◇	3 ◇	Pass (1)	Pass
4 ♣ (2)	Pass	4 ♠ (3)	Pass
Pass (4)	Pass		

(1) 0-5 HCP
(2) Exactly 4-4-1-4
(3) Placing the contract
(4) Trusting partner

2. Canadian Nationals, 1981.

Opponents Vulnerable

Opener	Responder
♠ A Q J 4 3 2	♠ —
♡ 2	♡ Q J 10 6 5
◇ A K 3	◇ J 10 8 7 6
♣ K 10 4	♣ 6 5 2

2 ◇	2 ♠	Pass (1)	Pass
Pass (2)			

(1) 0-5 HCP
(2) At this vulnerability it seems best to let the opponents rot in 2 ♠

Result: + 200

The other team was − 300 playing 4 ♠ doubled on these hands at the other table.

3. Bermuda Bowl. U.S. vs. Sweden, 1953.

Opener	Responder
♠ A 8	♠ K 9 3
♡ A K Q J 7 2	♡ 3
◇ 9 7 3	◇ A 10 5 2
♣ K 3	♣ 10 9 8 7 2

2 ◇	2 ♠	Double (1)	Pass
3 ♡ (2)	Pass	3 NT (3)	Pass
Pass (4)	Pass		

(1) Prefer the double to showing the weak five-card club suit
(2) Type A: Acol Two-Bid with long hearts
(3) Suggesting a contract
(4) Happily accepting the suggestion

Chapter 24

THE MAXI-RAISE OF A MAJOR OPENING

The strongest raise available after a major opening is the "Maxi-Raise," a response of 2 NT. This bid forces game and probes for slam via relays. The requirements for this response are:

1. Four or more trumps (in principle)
2. At least 13 HCP
3. At least five possible Cover Cards
4. No void

Opener's first rebid is usually natural. Exceptions occur when opener has unusual distribution — a void suit or a freakish pattern. Responder usually initiates a series of relays (the cheapest step other than game bids in the agreed major). Opener describes, in order:

1. Basic Pattern
    a) One-Suiter (5-3-3-2, 6-3-3-1, etc.)
        1) Contains no singleton or
        2) Contains a singleton
    b) Two-Suiter (5-4-2-2, 6-4-2-1, 5-5-2-1, etc.)
    c) Three-suiter (specifically 5-4-4-0, 4-6-3-0 or 4-6-0-3)
    d) One-suiter with a void (7-3-3-0, 8-3-2-0, etc.)

2. Completing the distributional picture
    a) With one-suiters
        1) Opener describes the location of any singleton
        2) With no singleton, he describes the length of his major (five, six or seven cards)
    b) With two-suiters
        1) Opener distinguishes between 5-4 and at least

10 cards in his two suits

2) Opener shows the distribution of his side suit remainders (immediately with 10 or more cards in his two suits, one round later with only 5-4)

c) With three-suiters or freaks the void is shown directly. There is no need for further distributional description.

3. Strength

Opener defines his hand as minimum or maximum:

a) A one-step response shows a minimum

b) A two-step or higher response shows a maximum and are "Zoom" responses showing Key Cards

4. Key Cards: The four aces and the king of trump

5. Spiral Cue-Bid

Opener shows his valuable cards in Spiral sequence: trump queen, side suit king, fragment king, side suit queen, etc.

Phase 1: Distributional Description

Opener bids naturally to show any four-card or longer side suit (one exception will be noted shortly). With a one-suiter he rebids three of his major or 3 NT.

The distribution-showing mechanism in four basic categories will be considered: one-suiters, two-suiters, three-suiters and freaks.

One-Suited Hands

There are two types of one-suiters to consider:

1. Balanced: No singleton or void

Opener bids 3 NT over 2 NT. In response to a 4♣ relay he shows the length of his major in steps:

    1♡ or 1♠ — 2 NT
    3 NT   — 4♣
    4◇ = Five-card suit (5-3-3-2)
    4♡ = Six-card suit (6-3-2-2)
    4♠ = Seven-card suit (7-2-2-2)

2. Unbalanced: Contains a singleton

Opener rebids his major over 2 NT. Next time he shows his side suit singleton according to the "Numeric Principle":

1♡ — 2 NT	1♠ — 2 NT
3♡ (1) — 3♠ (2)	3♠ (1) — 3 NT (2)
4♣ (3) —	4♣ (6) —
4◇ (4) —	4◇ (4) —
4♡ (5) —	4♡ (5) —

(1) One-suiter; contains a singleton
(2) Relay
(3) High singleton (spade singleton)
(4) Middle singleton (diamond singleton)
(5) Low singleton (club singleton)
(6) High singleton (heart singleton)

> **Important Note**
>
> When opener's suit is hearts, the 3 NT step is skipped. This is because 3 NT shows four spades and six hearts.

Two-Suited Hands

Show the side suit at the three-level (Exception: four spades and six hearts). In response to responder's second relay, opener's rebid depends on whether he is 5-4 or if he has 10 or more cards in the two suits.

1. 5-4 in the two suits

Opener bids the first step over the second relay to show 5-4. Example sequence:

1 ♡ — 2 NT
3 ♣ — 3 ◇
3 ♡ = Exactly five hearts and four clubs

Over the third relay, opener shows his short suit remainders "numerically":

1 ♡   — 2 NT
3 ♣   — 3 ◇
3 ♡   — 3 ♠
3 NT = One spade; three diamonds
4 ♣ = Two spades; two diamonds
4 ◇ = Three spades; one diamond

In the special case of

1 ♡ — 2 NT
3 ♠

there is no need for a step to clarify 5-4. This is because opener rebids 3 ♡ over 2 NT with four spades and six hearts. Opener shows his side suit remainders over the second relay:

1 ♡ — 2 NT
3 ♠ — 3 NT
4 ♣ = 4-5-1-3
4 ◇ = 4-5-2-2
4 ♡ = 4-5-3-1

2. 10 or 11 cards in the two suits but not four spades and six hearts

Opener has to clarify the location of the short suit and whether it is a singleton or a void.

Opener rebids starting with the second step (the first step shows 5-4 in his two suits):

1 ♡	— 2 NT	(1) Second step = High shortage
3 ♣	— 3 ◇	(1-5-2-5, 0-5-3-5, 0-6-2-5)
3 ♠ (1) —		(2) Third step = Equal shortage
3 NT (2) —		(1-6-1-5 or 1-7-1-4)
4 ♣ (3) —		(3) Fourth step = Low singleton
4 ◇ (4) —		(2-5-1-5)
		(4) Fifth step = Low void (2-6-0-5 or 3-5-0-5)

A second step response needs further clarification:

3 ♠ (1) — 3 NT
4 ♣   = spade singleton
4 ◇   = spade void
(1) Second step = high shortage

---

3. Four spades and six hearts

With a void (4-6-3-0 or 4-6-0-3) treat the hand as a three-suiter. With 4-6-2-1 or 4-6-1-2 bid 3 ♡ over 2 NT. Over the 3 ♠ relay, bid 3 NT:

1 ♡ — 2 NT
3 ♡ — 3 ♠
3 NT = 4-6-1-2 or 4-6-2-1

Over the 4 ♣ relay, show the remainders:

3 NT — 4 ♣
4 ◇   = 4-6-1-2
4 ♡   = 4-6-2-1

Three-Suited Hands

Three-suited hands include any 5-4-4-0 plus any hand with four spades, six hearts and a void. Opener jumps to the four-level in his void. To show a spade void he jumps to 4 ♡ :

        1 ♡ — 2 NT
        4 ♡ = 0-5-4-4

No further distributional clarification is necessary.

Freak Hands

Hands that don't fall into one of the three aforementioned categories are rare. There are two types of freak hands:

1. One-suiter with a void (7-3-3-0, 8-3-2-0, etc.)

Show the void immediately over 2 NT with the three lowest available steps:

        1 ♡ or 1 ♠ — 2 NT
        4 ♠   = Void in the other major (high ranking void)
        4 NT = Void in diamonds (middle ranking void)
        5 ♣   = Void in clubs (low ranking void)

Recall that 4 ♣ , 4 ◇ and 4 ♡ show three-suited hands, leaving 4 ♠ , 4 NT and 5 ♣ as the next available steps.

2. Extreme two-suiters (6-6, 7-5 or 8-4)

Bid the second suit over 2 NT. When responder relays again, the two lowest "meaningless" steps are used to show the void.

Example:

♠ A Q x x x x
♡ x
◇ A x x x x x
♣ —

1♠ — 2 NT
3◇ — 3♡
4 NT = Lower void; freak two-suiter

A 3♠ bid would show a hand with exactly five spades and four diamonds, and bids of 3 NT, 4♣, 4◇ and 4♡ would show 10 or 11 cards in spades and diamonds. Therefore 4♠ is the first meaningless step and 4 NT is the second meaningless step. The first step (4♠) bid would show the higher-ranking (heart) void. The second step shows the lower-ranking void (clubs).

Here is the distribution-showing phase in a table:

Distribution Showing Phase after a Maxi Raise of a Major

Rebid	Meaning	Completing the Distributional Message

Three of a lower-ranking suit, i.e., 3♣ or 3♦ after a 1♡ opening bid or 3♣, 3♦ or 3♡ after a 1♠ opening bid	Natural, four-card or longer suit	1) With 5-4:
		  a) Bid one step over responder's second relay
		  b) Show remainders over responder's third relay
		2) With 10 or 11 cards in the two suits:
		  a) Bid steps two through five over responder's second relay
		  b) Further clarify a two-step response after responder's third relay:
		    One step with a singleton or
		    Two steps with a void
		3) With 12 cards in the two suits:
		    Bid steps six or seven over responder's second relay to show the void

3♠ after a 1♡ opening bid	Exactly four spades and five hearts; no void	Show the side suit remainders over responder's second relay

1 ♠ — 2 NT 3 ♠	No void; no four-card side suit; contains a singleton	Show the singleton over responder's second relay
1 ♡ — 2 NT 3 ♡	One-suited hand with a suit singleton, 4-6-2-1 or 4-6-1-2.	1) With 4-6-2-1 or 4-6-1-2: a) Opener bids 3 NT over responder's second relay b) Show remainders over responder's third relay 2) With a one-suiter, opener bids 4♣, 4◇ or 4♡ to show the location of his singleton
3 NT	Balanced one-suiter; no singleton	Opener shows the length of his major over responder's second relay
4♣, 4◇ or 4♡	Three-suited hand, 4-6-3-0 or 4-6-0-3 4♡ = Void in the other major 4♣ = Club void 4◇ = Diamond void	Unnecessary
4♠, 4 NT or 5♣	One-suiter. The rebid shows the void (Numeric Principle).	Unnecessary

Phase II: Minimum or Maximum

Once opener has completed the distributional description, the next relay asks if he is minimum or maximum:

1. With a minimum, he gives a one-step reply
2. With a maximum, he bids steps two through five. Zoom responses to show Key Cards.

Example sequence:

Opener	Responder		
1 ♠	2 NT	(1)	Natural
3 ♡ (1)	3 ♠	(2)	5-4
3 NT (2)	4 ♣	(3)	5-4-2-2
4 ♡ (3)	4 NT	(4)	Minimum
5 ♣ (4)		(5)	Maximum; 0 or 3 Key Cards
5 ◇ (5)		(6)	Maximum; 1 or 4 Key Cards
5 ♡ (6)		(7)	Maximum; two Key Cards; no
5 ♠ (7)			trump queen
5 NT (8)		(8)	Maximum; two Key Cards;
			trump queen

As a general rule, 12-14 HCP is a minimum, though opener is free to use his judgment.

Phase III: Key Cards

The next stage in the relay process is for opener to show his Key Cards. He has already done so with a maximum. With a minimum he shows Key Cards over the next relay. Continuing the example:

Opener	Responder		
4 ♡	4 NT	(1)	Minimum
5 ♣ (1)	5 ◇ (2)	(2)	Key Cards?
5 ♡ (3)		(3)	0 or 3 Key Cards
5 ♠ (4)		(4)	1 or 4 Key Cards
5 NT (5)		(5)	Two Key Cards; no trump
6 ♣ (6)			queen
		(6)	Two Key Cards; trump queen

Phase IV: Spiral Cue-Bid

If responder needs more information he can request opener to show his important cards in spiral sequence. Continuing the example:

Opener	Responder
4♡	4 NT
5♣	5◇
5♠	5 NT = Please Spiral
	6♣ = Please Spiral, but forget about showing the spade queen

Opener responds:

5♠	5 NT

6♣ = No spade queen
6◇ = Spade queen but no heart king
6♡ = Spade queen, heart king but no diamond king
Etc.

Save valuable space with Super Relays

In most cases responder will want to use the full relay scheme. However, he may want to skip one or more steps for one of several reasons:

1. He knows the information gleaned would be useless. This is the case when Relayer has the trump queen:

4♠ (1) — 4 NT (2)	(1) One or four Key Cards
— 5♣ (3)	(2) Spiral, please
	(3) Spiral, please but forget about showing the queen of spades

Using the 5♣ Super Relay saves a step and a round of bidding.

2. He doesn't particularly care about the next available information.

If responder has the ace in opener's short suit, he may prefer to go directly to Key Card Blackwood, not asking for clarification:

$4\clubsuit$ (1) — $4\diamond$ (2)　(1) Diamond singleton or void
　　　　— $4\heartsuit$ (3)　(2) Singleton or void?
　　　　　　　　　　(3) I don't care if you have a singleton or void in diamonds. Tell me if you have a minimum or a maximum and if you have a maximum, tell me about your Key Cards.

3. There is a "crisis of space" and responder has to be very careful about the information he seeks:

$1\heartsuit$ — $2\,NT$	(1)	Singleton club
$3\heartsuit$ — $3\spadesuit$	(2)	Maximum; two Key Cards; no
$4\heartsuit$ (1) — $4\spadesuit$		heart queen
$5\heartsuit$ (2) — $5\spadesuit$ (3)	(3)	Spiral, starting with the spade
— $5\,NT$ (4)		king
	(4)	Super Relay, asking for queens

A normal spiral sequence would be far too slow. Responder starts a scan for queens (he has several kings in his own hand).

How does the Super Relay work? Relayer skips one step for each stage in the relay he wants Replier to skip. The stages are:

Each stage in the distribution clarifying process (one, two or three relays depending on the auction).
Minimum or maximum
Key Cards (Relayer would almost never skip Key Card Blackwood)
Trump queen
Spiral for kings
Spiral for queens

Example sequences:

1.

Opener	Responder	
1 ♠	2 NT	(1) Low singleton
3 ♠	3 NT	(2) Forget about minimum/maxi-
4 ♡ (1)	5 ♣ (2)	mum. Tell me about your Key Cards.

2.

Opener	Responder	
1 ♡	2 NT	(1) 4-6-2-1 or 4-6-1-2
3 ♡	3 ♠	(2) Side suit remainders?
3 NT (1)	4 ♣ (2)	(3) Minimum/maximum?
	4 ◇ (3)	(4) Key Cards?
	4 ♠ (4)	

The Maxi-Raise in Action

Let's see the relays at work:

One Suiters

1.

Opener	Responder
♠ K x	♠ A x x
♡ J 10 x x x	♡ A K Q x
◇ A K x	◇ Q x
♣ K J x	♣ Q 9 x x
1 ♡	2 NT
3 NT (1)	4 ♣ (2)
4 ◇ (3)	4 ♠ (4)
5 ◇ (5)	6 ♡ (6)
Pass	

(1) Balanced one-suiter; no singleton
(2) Relay
(3) Minimum suit length, i.e., five cards
(4) 4 ♡ would be a signoff, so 4 ♠ is the relay, asking for minimum/maximum

(5) 4 NT would show a minimum. With a maximum opener would show his Key Cards:

    5 ♣ = 0 or 3 Key Cards

    5 ◇ = 1 or 4 Key Cards

(6) Signoff in the small slam. One Key Card is missing.

2.

Opener	Responder
♠ K Q x x x x	♠ A J x
♡ A K x	♡ Q J x x
◇ K x	◇ A x
♣ x x	♣ A Q x x

1 ♠	2 NT
3 NT (1)	4 ♣ (2)
4 ♡ (3)	4 NT (4)
5 NT (5)	6 ♣ (6)
6 ♠ (7)	7 NT (8)
Pass	

(1) Balanced one-suiter
(2) Relay
(3) Six-card suit
(4) Relay since 4 ♠ would be a signoff
(5) A 5 ♣ response would show a minimum. Opener bids four additional steps to show a maximum, two Key Cards, and the spade queen.
(6) Relay
(7) We are no longer concerned with the spade queen, so the first items on the Spiral list are the heart king and the diamond king. I have them but lack the club king. 6 ♠ is the response, skipping two steps.
(8) Responder can count 13 tricks.

3.

Opener	Responder
♠ A Q x x x x	♠ K x x x
♡ x	♡ A x
◊ K Q x	◊ A J x x x
♣ x x x	♣ A x

1 ♠	2 NT
3 ♠ (1)	3 NT (2)
4 ♣ (3)	4 ◊ (4)
4 ♡ (5)	4 NT (6)
5 ◊ (7)	5 ♡ (8)
6 ♣ (9)	6 ◊ (10)
6 ♠ (11)	7 NT (12)
Pass	

(1) Unbalanced one-suiter
(2) Relay
(3) High singleton, therefore hearts
(4) Relay
(5) Minimum strength
(6) Relay
(7) One or four Key Cards.
(8) Spiral, please
(9) Spiral: trump queen and diamond king but not the club king
(10) Relay
(11) Diamond queen but not the club queen
(12) The diamond queen was just what was needed to count 13 tricks

1. Bermuda Bowl. U. S. vs. Italy, 1973.

Opener	*Responder*
♠ A K	♠ 10 9
♡ A Q 10 4 2	♡ K J 9 6
◇ K 10 9 4	◇ A 8
♣ 6 5	♣ A K 8 7 2

1 ♡	2 NT
3 ◇	3 ♡
3 ♠ (1)	3 NT
4 ◇ (2)	4 ♠ (3)
5 ♠ (4)	5 NT
6 ♡ (5)	7 ♡ (6)
Pass	

(1) Automatic first-step with a 5-4 hand
(2) First step would show 1-3 remainder; this second step shows 2-2
(3) 4 ♡ would be a signoff, not a relay
(4) 4 NT would be a minimum, so opener must bid 5 ♠ to show two Key Cards plus the trump queen and a maximum
(5) The diamond king and the spade king are first on the Spiral list. Skipping two steps to show the diamond and the spade king but deny the club king.
(6) 16 HCP in the opener's hand are known. He cannot have enough other cards to make 7 NT a possibility in view of his limited opening.

Both the U.S. and Italy reached the heart grand slam.

2.

Opener	Responder
♠ Q x x	♠ A 10 x
♡ Q 10 9 x x	♡ A x x x
◇ A	◇ K J x x
♣ A Q x x	♣ K x
1 ♡	2 NT
3 ♣	3 ◇
3 ♡ (1)	3 ♠
4 ◇ (2)	4 ♡ (3)
Pass (4)	

(1) Forced with a 5-4 hand
(2) The third step, therefore a 3-1 remainder, i.e., 3-5-1-4
(3) Signoff, too much duplication in the diamond suit.
(4) Virtually forced. With a super-maximum opener might move. To do so he would show his Key Cards in the usual way.

3. Bermuda Bowl. U. S. vs. Sweden, 1953.

Opener	Responder
♠ K 8	♠ A Q
♡ A 9 4 3 2	♡ K 8 7 6
◇ A Q 7 3	◇ 6 5 4
♣ Q 5	♣ A K 9 6
1 ♡	2 NT
3 ◇	3 ♡
3 ♠ (1)	3 NT
4 ◇ (2)	4 ♡ (3)
5 ♣ (4)	5 ♡ (5)
Pass	

(1) Forced with 5-4
(2) Second step = 2-5-4-2
(3) I don't like it
(4) But I have a maximum and two Key Cards without the trump queen

(5) I wasn't part of this nonsense!

The unmakable slam was reached at both tables.

4.

Opener	Responder
♠ A Q J x x	♠ K x x x
♡ K Q J x	♡ A x x
◇ K Q x	◇ A x x
♣ x	♣ A Q x
1 ♠	2 NT
3 ♡	3 ♠
3 NT (1)	4 ♣
4 ♠ (2)	4 NT
5 ♡ (3)	5 NT (4)
7 ♡ (5)	7 NT (6)
Pass	

(1) Forced with 5-4
(2) The third step showing 3-1 remainder (5-4-3-1)
(3) 5 ♣ would be a minimum, so 5 ♡ shows a maximum with one Key Card
(4) Not 5 ♠, which would be a signoff
(5) Surprise — the eighth step showing seven cards on our shopping list. They are: the spade queen, the heart king, the diamond king, the heart queen, the diamond queen, the spade jack and the heart jack.
(6) The heart jack allows us to count 13 tricks and play notrump instead of spades

5.

Opener	Responder
♠ A Q x x x	♠ K J x x
♡ A Q x x	♡ K x x
◇ Q x x	◇ A K x x
♣ x	♣ A x

1 ♠	2 NT
3 ♡	3 ♠
3 NT (1)	4 ♣ (2)
4 ♠ (3)	5 ♣ (4)
5 NT (5)	6 ◇ (6)
6 NT (7)	7 ♣ (8)
7 ◇ (9)	7 ♠ (10)
Pass	

(1) 5-4 of some kind
(2) Which kind?
(3) The third step, showing a 3-1 remainder (5-4-3-1)
(4) Super Relay: Forget minimum/maximum and show Key Cards
(5) Two Key Cards and the spade queen
(6) I need the red queens for seven, but a normal Spiral will be far too slow. So I am using the Super Relay, asking opener to forget kings and tell me about his queens.
(7) The queen of hearts and the queen of diamonds but not the jack of spades
(8) Jack of hearts?
(9) No
(10) 7 ♡ is a plausible contract, so I can't ask about the diamond jack for 7 NT

6. Olympiad. U. S. vs. Chile, 1968.

Opener	*Responder*
♠ A J 10 7	♠ 6 2
♡ K J 9 7 6	♡ A Q 8 5 4
◇ 2	◇ A K 10
♣ K J 7	♣ A 10 3

1 ♡	2 NT
3 ♠ (1)	3 NT (2)
4 ♣ (3)	4 ◇ (4)
4 ♡ (5)	4 ♠ (6)
5 ◇ (7)	5 ♠ (8)
5 NT (9)	6 ♡ (10)
Pass	

(1) 4-5 in majors
(2) Residue?
(3) First step = 4-5-1-3
(4) Size?
(5) Minimum
(6) Key Cards?
(7) Two Key Cards but no heart queen
(8) Kings?
(9) No spade king
(10) The limit

The U. S. team gained 14 IMPs when Chile was down two in 6 NT.

7.

Opener	Responder
♠ Q J x x x	♠ A K x x
♡ Q	♡ A x x x
◊ K Q J	◊ A x x
♣ K x x x	♣ A x

Opener	Responder
1 ♠	2 NT
3 ♣	3 ◊
3 ♡ (1)	3 ♠
3 NT (2)	4 ♣
4 ◊ (3)	4 ♡
4 ♠ (4)	4 NT
5 ♠ (5)	5 NT
6 ♡ (6)	7 ♠ (7)
Pass	

(1) Forced with 5-4
(2) High shortage, so 5-1-3-4
(3) Minimum
(4) Zero or three Key Cards
(5) A Spiral skip of three steps, so it shows three cards: the spade queen, the club king and diamond king but denies the club queen
(6) Skipping two steps showing the diamond queen and the spade jack
(7) Enough for seven. Without the trump jack the grand slam would be shaky, for the last ruff in either hand might promote a trump trick for the defense. However, even without the trump jack 7 ♠ would have fair play and could be bid in an attempt to retrieve a losing match.

8. England vs. Wales.

Opener	Responder
♠ K Q 6 5 3	♠ A 10 9 4
♡ A K 3	♡ Q J 9 8 6 5
◇ 9	◇ A
♣ K 9 8 3	♣ A 6

1 ♠	2 NT
3 ♣	3 ◇
3 ♡ (1)	3 ♠
4 ◇ (2)	4 ♡ (3)
5 ♡ (4)	5 NT (5)
6 ♡ (6)	7 NT (7)
Pass	

(1) 5-4
(2) Third step = 5-3-1-4
(3) Minimum or maximum?
(4) Fifth step = Maximum with two Key Cards and the trump queen
(5) Spiral, please
(6) The king of clubs and the king of hearts but not the queen of clubs
(7) I have 14 tricks at notrump

England bid 7 ♡, Wales 6 ♠!

9.

Opener	Responder
♠ A 10 x x x	♠ K Q J x
♡ Q x x x x	♡ A 10
◊ A	◊ K x x
♣ A x	♣ K Q J 10
1 ♠	2 NT
3 ♡	3 ♠
4 ♣ (1)	4 ◊ (2)
4 ♡ (3)	4 NT (4)
5 ◊ (5)	5 ♡
5 ♠ (6)	5 NT
6 ♣ (7)	7 ♣ (8)
Pass	

(1) 10 or 11 cards in spades and hearts; high shortage, i.e., in diamonds

(2) This relay asks for the nature of the shortage

(3) One step shows a singleton. Two steps would have shown a void. (An advanced partnership could agree to run on to the next stage when a void is shown, indicating Key Cards without waiting to be asked.)

(4) 4 ♠ would, of course, be a signoff

(5) A maximum with zero or three Key Cards. 14 HCP would usually be a minimum, but there are only five Losers.

(6) Denies the trump queen — no surprise to responder

(7) No heart king, the card that would be needed for 7 ♠

(8) Surprise! — All we need is a 4-3 club break and no opening spade ruff. Not a laydown, but just about worth it. It would be the bidding coup of a lifetime. If a puzzled partner retreats to the "safety" of 7 ♠, shoot him and get anyone to fill in.

10.

Opener	Responder
♠ K J 8 7 6 3	♠ A Q 9
♡ 10 6	♡ A J 4
◇ K J 7 3	◇ A Q 5 2
♣ A	♣ Q 10 8

1 ♠	2 NT (1)
3 ◇	3 ♡
4 ◇ (2)	4 ♡
4 ♠ (3)	4 NT
5 ♠ (4)	5 NT
6 ◇ (5)	7 ◇ (6)
Pass	

(1) With three strong trumps and extra strength, it is a reasonable time to break the rule that requires four-card support for a Maxi-Raise
(2) Shows 10 cards in spades and diamonds, no void and low shortage. Distribution must be 5-2-5-1 or 6-2-4-1.
(3) Minimum
(4) Nominally showing two Key Cards and the trump queen. Opener knows that his extra length is almost as good as the queen. Responder is looking at the queen and works it out. He knows that opener is 6-4, not 5-5.
(5) Diamond king, no heart king
(6) Surprise

11.

Opener	Responder
♠ A K 10 x x x	♠ Q x x x
♡ K Q x x x	♡ A x x
◇ x	◇ A Q x
♣ Q	♣ A J x
1 ♠	2 NT
3 ♡	3 ♠
4 ◇ (1)	4 ♡
5 ♡ (2)	5 ♠
6 ◇ (3)	7 ♠ (4)
Pass	

(1) Equal shortage, so 6-5-1-1 or perhaps 5-6-1-1 or 7-4-1-1
(2) This four-Loser hand should certainly be treated as a maximum, so the response is the fifth step showing two Key Cards and the trump queen (the sixth trump makes up for the missing trump queen — see the previous example)
(3) The king and queen of hearts but not the jack of spades
(4) A little lazy. At matchpoints you should relay again and find out about the heart jack. If opener has it, play in 7 NT.

12.

Opener	Responder
♠ A K Q J 9	♠ 10 8 5 4
♡ —	♡ A Q 9 7 4 3
◇ 9 8 6 2	◇ A
♣ A 8 5 4	♣ K 2
1 ♠	2 NT
4 ♡ (1)	4 NT
5 ◇ (2)	5 ♡
5 NT (3)	7 ♠ (4)
Pass	

(1) A heart void. In this case the distribution is guaranteed to be 5-0-4-4

420

(2) Solid trumps and only five Losers make this hand a maximum, even with only 14 HCP, so three Key Cards are shown

(3) Spiral, showing the trump queen but denying the diamond king. (Remember that the first focus is on diamonds rather than clubs. With equal length in two unbid suits as far as responder knows, the Spiral responses start with the higher of the two unbid suits.)

(4) That is all I need to know for seven. Without a trump lead, we can cross-ruff. With a trump lead, we can try to establish hearts. The spade jack is a useful card in opener's hand but there is insufficient time to locate it. However, opener might not have shown a maximum without that card.

13.

Opener	Responder
♠ —	♠ K x x x
♡ A Q x x x x x	♡ K x x x
◇ x	◇ A Q x
♣ K J x x x	♣ A x
1 ♡	2 NT
3 ♣	3 ◇
4 ♡ (1)	4 ♠
4 NT (2)	5 ♣
5 ♡ (3)	5 ♠
6 ◇ (4)	7 ♡ (5)
Pass	

(1) A five-step response is normally the limit. We go off the scale with freak hands containing a void. This is a six-step response showing the high-ranking void. 4 ♠ would show a diamond void. The distribution is presumably 0-6-6-1 or 0-7-1-5. 0-8-1-4 is possible.

(2) Minimum in high cards

(3) One Key Card

(4) Spiral past the heart queen and club king, denying the club queen

(5) Perfect

Chapter 25

THE MAXI-RAISE AFTER A MINOR OPENING

A 2 NT response to a minor opening is a Maxi-Raise. It is relatively uncommon — a good fit, no four-card major, and a hand too good for an inverted raise. The requirements:

1. At least 16 HCP
2. Five or more trumps or, rarely, a very good four trumps
3. Five or more Controls
4. Five or more Cover Cards
5. No void

Opener rebids as follows:

1. With a Void

Opener jumps to the four-level in a new suit to show a void:

> 1♣   — 2 NT
> 4♦ , 4♡ or 4♠ = A void in the bid suit

2. With a Singleton

Opener rebids 3♣ to show an unspecified singleton. Responder will almost always relay to discover the location of the singleton.

3. With no Short Suit

Opener has several choices, depending on his strength and stoppers:

a) 3 NT = 13-15 HCP; all suits stopped
b) 4 NT = 17-18 HCP; 4-3-3-3 distribution
c) Four of the bid minor = Maximum; unbalanced but no singleton or void; 5-4-2-2, 6-3-2-2 or 7-2-2-2 distribution.
d) 3 ♡ or 3 ♠ = Weakness in the bid suit (xx or xxx). A 3 ◊ bid shows weakness in the unbid minor. Opener also uses these rebids to describe maximum with 4-4-3-2. The doubleton is shown as though it were a weak suit, the opener continues bidding beyond 3 NT to show his extra strength.

Subsequent Bidding

If responder has slam interest he will relay at his second turn. 3 NT and any bid in the agreed minor (game or higher) are not available as relay steps. If opener has shown a minimum balanced hand, 4 NT is a signoff, not a relay.

Opener's distribution is clarified unless he rebids 3 ♣. Over a 3 ♣ rebid by opener, responder's 3 ◊ bid would ask for the singleton to be shown naturally, not numerically:

1 ♣ or 1 ◊ — 2 NT	(1)	Where's your singleton?
3 ♣ — 3 ◊ (1)	(2)	Singleton heart
3 ♡ (2) —	(3)	Singleton spade
3 ♠ (3) —	(4)	Singleton in the other minor
3 NT (4) —		

Opener's rebids fall into two groups:

If opener specified his strengh, the relay asks for Key Cards, with normal Spiral continuation. If opener's strength is unspecified, the relay asks for the usual minimum/maximum and Key Card clarifications:

1 ◇	— 2 NT	(1) Spade singleton
3 ♣	— 3 ◇	(2) Relay. 3 NT would be non-forcing
3 ♠ (1)	— 4 ♣ (2)	(3) Minimum
4 ◇ (3)	—	(4) Maximum; zooming to show Key
4 ♡ through		Cards
5 ♣ (4)	—	

If responder signs off in 3 NT, opener may continue with substantial extra values. As usual, he would do so by continuing to respond with relay replies showing Key Cards.

After responder bids 2 NT over 1 ♣ with:

♠ K J x
♡ x
◇ A Q x x
♣ A Q x x x

Here's how the bidding would continue opposite a number of opening hands:

424

1.

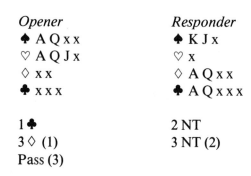

Opener	Responder
♠ A Q x x	♠ K J x
♡ A Q J x	♡ x
◇ x x	◇ A Q x x
♣ x x x	♣ A Q x x x
1 ♣	2 NT
3 ◇ (1)	3 NT (2)
Pass (3)	

(1) Weakness
(2) Bad news
(3) Would continue with a maximum

2.

Opener	Responder
♠ Q x x	♠ K J x
♡ K Q x	♡ x
◇ K x x	◇ A Q x x
♣ K x x x	♣ A Q x x x
1 ♣	2 NT
3 NT (1)	4 ♣ (2)
4 ♡ (3)	5 ♣ (4)
Pass	

(1) Balanced minimum; all suits stopped
(2) Key Cards?
(3) One of four
(4) Safe. At matchpoints you could try 4 NT, which is quite safe but not totally so.

425

3.

Opener	Responder
♠ A x x	♠ K J x
♡ A x x	♡ x
◇ K x x	◇ A Q x x
♣ K x x x	♣ A Q x x x

1♣	2 NT
3 NT (1)	4♣ (2)
4◇ (3)	4 NT! (4)
5♣ (5)	6♣ (6)
Pass	

(1) Balanced minimum; all suits stopped
(2) Relay, asking about Key Cards
(3) Zero or three
(4) Sounds good. But wait a minute. Could that be zero? The hand could be:

  ♠ Q x x
  ♡ K Q J
  ◇ K J 10
  ♣ J 10 x x

So, assuming the worst, I sign off in 4 NT.

(5) You cannot want to stop when I have three Key Cards. So I'll Spiral, denying the club queen.
(6) So it was three. Seven seems likely to depend on the spade finesse or on disposing of partner's spades on my diamonds. Partner is known to have the king of diamonds for his 3 NT bid. If I needed points, I would bid 7♣.

426

4.

Opener	Responder
♠ A Q x	♠ K J x
♡ x x x	♡ x
◊ K x x	◊ A Q x x
♣ K J x x	♣ A Q x x x
1 ♣	2 NT
3 ♡ (1)	3 ♠ (2)
3 NT (3)	4 ♣ (4)
4 ♠ (5)	6 ♣ (6)
Pass	

(1) Heart weakness
(2) Minimum or maximum?
(3) Minimum
(4) Key Cards?
(5) Two without the trump queen
(6) With nothing wasted in hearts, opener is almost sure to have the diamond king and the spade queen to justify his opening bid. At the worst, 6 ♣ will need a finesse.

5.

Opener	Responder
♠ x	♠ K J x
♡ K Q x x	♡ x
◊ K J x	◊ A Q x x
♣ K J x x x	♣ A Q x x x
1 ♣	2 NT
3 ♣ (1)	3 ◊ (2)
3 ♠ (3)	3 NT (4)
Pass (5)	

(1) Singleton somewhere
(2) Where?
(3) Spades
(4) Not good. Let's stop.
(5) Would continue with a maximum

Examples:

1.

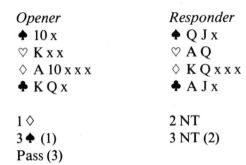

Opener	Responder
♠ 10 x	♠ Q J x
♡ K x x	♡ A Q
◇ A 10 x x x	◇ K Q x x x
♣ K Q x	♣ A J x
1 ◇	2 NT
3 ♠ (1)	3 NT (2)
Pass (3)	

(1) Spade weakness
(2) Sad. Even my 19 HCP and great fit will not produce a slam if you have spade weakness. Paradoxically, with a weaker hand I might have to bid more. Change my spades from QJx to Jxx and I would have to continue to 5 ◇.

The next few examples will allow for a lot more bidding:

---

2. Bermuda Bowl, 1970.

Opener	Responder
♠ A K 8 4	♠ Q J
♡ A K J 7	♡ 10 2
◇ 4	◇ A 10 9 8
♣ J 9 8 5	♣ A K Q 10 2
1 ♣	2 NT
3 ♣ (1)	3 ◇ (2)
3 NT (3)	4 ♣ (4)
4 NT (5)	5 ◇ (6)
5 NT (7)	7 ♣ (8)
Pass	

(1) Singleton somewhere
(2) Where?
(3) The unbid minor — diamonds
(4) Minimum or maximum?

(5) Maximum with two Key Cards but not the club queen

(6) Spiral, please

(7) Skip two steps to show the spade king and the heart king. This bid denies the spade queen, which comes as no surprise to responder.

(8) This excellent grand slam was missed by Taiwan. Romex Relays make it easy.

3. Bermuda Bowl. U.S. vs. Italy, 1957.

Opener	Responder
♠ A K 4	♠ 10
♡ Q J 3	♡ K 7 2
◇ 7	◇ A Q J 9 6
♣ K 9 7 6 5 4	♣ A J 8 3

Opener	Responder
1 ♣	2 NT (1)
3 ♣ (2)	3 ◇ (3)
3 NT (4)	4 ♣ (5)
5 ♣ (6)	6 ♣ (7)
Pass	

(1) Responder chooses to use the Maxi-Raise. A 1 ◇ response would make the bidding more difficult.

(2) Singleton somewhere

(3) Where?

(4) The unbid minor — diamonds

(5) Minimum or maximum?

(6) Maximum with two Key Cards and the club queen. The sixth club makes up for the lack of the club queen.

(7) One Key Card is missing

The U. S. missed the small slam.

4.

Opener	Responder
George	Eddie
Rosenkranz	Wold

♠ 10 8 4 3   ♠ A
♡ A K 7 6   ♡ Q 5 4
◇ K J 2   ◇ A Q 7 6 4
♣ A 9   ♣ K Q 8 2

Opener	Responder
1 ◇ (1)	2 NT
3 ◇ (2)	3 ♡ (3)
3 NT (4)	4 ♣ (5)
4 ◇ (6)	4 ♡ (7)
4 ♠ (8)	4 NT (9)
5 ◇ (10)	7 ◇ (11)
Pass	

(1) A balanced 15 HCP hand is normally a minimum, but this hand has a wealth of aces and kings so I intend to treat it as a maximum

(2) Temporarily suggesting weakness in clubs, but a strong doubleton is possible if the hand is a maximum. If I intended to treat this hand as a minimum I would bid 3 NT.

(3) Maximum or minimum?

(4) Maximum with three Key Cards.

(5) Spiral, please. (Responder, holding the diamond queen, could Super Relay with 4 ◇ asking opener to start scanning for side kings.)

(6) No trump queen

(7) Tell me more

(8) No spade king. (Spades and hearts are equal in length as far as responder knows.)

(9) Good news. Tell me more.

(10) Heart king but no club king

(11) Excellent

5.

Opener	Responder
♠ Q x x x	♠ A x x
♡ A Q x	♡ x
◊ —	◊ A K Q x
♣ A x x x x x	♣ K J x x x
1 ♣	2 NT
4 ◊ (1)	4 ♡ (2)
4 ♠ (3)	4 NT (4)
5 ♠ (5)	7 ♣ (6)
Pass	

(1) Diamond void
(2) Maximum or minimum?
(3) Minimum
(4) Key Cards?
(5) Two Key Cards and the trump queen. Opener knows there are at least 10 trumps in the combined hands and therefore treats his sixth club as the queen.
(6) That's all I need to know!

Chapter 26

OTHER RELAYS

Relays After Opener's Reverse

Opener's reverse shows a good hand: four or five Losers, but usually limited to 17 or 18 HCP. Better hands are shown by opening 1 NT or 2♣. These limitations permit playing the reverse as non-forcing.

To start a relay, responder must agree to one of opener's suits:

1. To agree opener's second suit, raise it.

> 1♣ — 1♠
> 2◇ — 3◇ = Setting diamonds as trump and beginning
>   a relay

2. To agree opener's first suit, bid the fourth suit

> 1♣ — 1♠
> 2◇ — 2♡ = Setting clubs as trump and beginning a
>   relay

Recall that a 3♣ bid would be forcing, but requests natural bidding.

Opener's first duty is to describe his pattern:

> Whether he is 5-4 or 6-4
> The distribution of his "remainders"

Using the normal relay rules:

1. The lower responses show less shapely hands, and

2. The remainders are shown in ASCENDING numerical order

Opener shows his shape as follows:

		Number of Cards in Responder's Suit	Number of Cards in Fourth Suit	Distribution
First step	=	1	3	5-4
Second step	=	2	2	5-4
Third step	=	3	1	5-4
Fourth step	=	1	2	6-4
Fifth step	=	2	1	6-4
Sixth step	=	3	0	6-4

Note two things:

1. Responder's suit is always counted first (for purposes of determining the numerical remainder). Responder's suit will be higher ranking in all cases except where spades is the fourth suit.
2. Opener should avoid reversing with a void in responder's suit. If he does so, he must bid the seventh step to show 6-4 with a void in responder's major.

Opener describes his exact pattern with this bid so further relays ask for Key Cards followed by Spiral Cue-Bids.

Example:

Opener	Responder
♠ Q x x	♠ A x
♡ A	♡ Q x x x
◊ A K x x	◊ Q J x
♣ A J 10 x x	♣ K Q x x

1 ♣	1 ♡
2 ◊	2 ♠ (1)
2 NT (2)	3 ♣ (3)
3 ◊ (4)	3 ♠ (5)
4 ♣ (6)	7 ♣ (7)
Pass	

(1) Relay, agreeing clubs
(2) Opener must look first at his holding in responder's suit, then at the fourth suit. He bids the first step showing 1-3. His distribution is now known.
(3) Key Cards?
(4) Three Key Cards
(5) Spiral, but forget the club queen
(6) I have the diamond king but not the spade king
(7) Responder places the contract with confidence

Sometimes opener's distribution will be a disappointment to responder. In that case he can attempt to signoff in 3 NT. However, opener is not barred — he can bid on with a suitable maximum (a good four Loser hand). If opener does bid on, he pretends the relay is still in effect and shows Key Cards. Responder can continue to relay, or he can sign off in either 4 NT or the agreed suit.

Examples:

1.

Opener	Responder
♠ x x	♠ Q x x x
♡ A	♡ K Q J
◇ A Q x x	◇ K J
♣ A Q J x x x	♣ K x x x

Opener	Responder
1 ♣	1 ♠
2 ◇	2 ♡ (1)
3 ♡ (2)	3 NT (3)
4 ♣ (4)	5 ♣ (5)
Pass	

(1) Relay, agreeing clubs
(2) Fifth step = 2-1-4-6
(3) Non-forcing. Opener has the wrong singleton.
(4) With only four Losers, this hand is worth another try. I will continue the relay sequence and show three Key Cards.
(5) Still signing off. We are bound to have either two spade losers or a heart and a spade loser.

2. Olympiad. Canada vs. Italy, 1968.

Opener	Responder
♠ A	♠ 6 4 3
♡ A 5 2	♡ K J 10 8
◇ A K 9 7	◇ Q 8 5 3
♣ K J 9 7 3	♣ A 10

Opener	Responder
1 ♣	1 ♡
2 ◇	3 ◇ (1)
3 NT (2)	4 ♣ (3)
4 ♡ (4)	4 NT (5)
5 ◇ (6)	6 ◇ (7)
Pass	

(1) Relay setting diamonds as trump
(2) 1-3-4-5

(3) Key Cards?

(4) Four Key Cards

(5) Forget the diamond queen and Spiral

(6) I have the club king but not the heart king

(7) Opener can't have enough for seven. If responder thought seven was a possibility, he could continue relaying asking for queens.

An interesting question arises: Is it always right for responder to relay with a good fit and slam interest?

To help answer the question, consider this deal:

Opener	Responder
♠ A x	♠ K Q x x x
♡ K Q x x	♡ A J x x
◇ A Q J x x	◇ K x
♣ x x	♣ x x
1 ◇	1 ♠
2 ♡	3 ♡
3 NT	???

Responder will not be able to find out if opener controls the fourth suit at a safe level. The slam is cold if opener's spade ace is the club ace.

What is the solution? Responder bids 2 NT, forcing opener to rebid his first suit, and follows with 4 ♡ on the next round, showing slam interest but no control in the fourth suit:

Opener A	Opener B	Responder
♠ A x	♠ x x	♠ K Q x x x
♡ K Q x x	♡ K Q x x	♡ A J x x
◇ A Q J x x	◇ A Q J x x	◇ K x
♣ x x	♣ A x	♣ x x

Sequence A	Sequence B
1 ◇ — 1 ♠	1 ◇ — 1 ♠
2 ♡ — 2 NT	2 ♡ — 2 NT
3 ◇ — 4 ♡	3 ◇ — 4 ♡
Pass	5 ♣ (1) — 6 ♡ (2)
	Pass

(1) Opener has a club control, but, with five Losers, he is still not sure. He cue-bids his club control to let responder know about the situation.
(2) Responder is happy to bid the slam

Relay After Opener's Limit Splinter

A jump reverse is used to show a four-card fit for responder's major, invitational values (four or five Losers), and shortness in the bid suit.

The sequence is always:

1 ♣ or 1 ◇ — 1 ♡ or 1 ♠
3 ◇ or 3 ♡

Responder can sign off in the agreed suit at the three-level or higher. The cheapest non-signoff step is a relay. There are four possible relay sequences:

1 ♣ — 1 ♡	1 ♣ — 1 ♠	1 ♣ — 1 ♠	1 ◇ — 1 ♠
3 ◇ — 3 ♠	3 ◇ — 3 ♡	3 ♡ — 3 NT	3 ♡ — 3 NT

Note that 3 NT can be used as a relay when a major is agreed. When the agreed suit is a minor, 3 NT is always natural.

When "Scanner" has shown shortness, the relay asks for clarification — whether it is a singleton or a void. The next stage in the relay process is Key Cards, so opener can "Zoom" to show Key Cards with a void:

1♣ — 1♠	(1)	Limit raise; short diamonds
3♦ (1) — 3♥ (2)	(2)	Relay — describe your shortness
3♠ (3) —	(3)	First step = singleton
3 NT (4) —	(4)	Second step = void; Zooming to
4♣ (5) —		show 0 to 3 Key Cards.
4♦ (6) —	(5)	Third step = void; Zooming to
4♥ (7) —		show 1 or 4 Key Cards
	(6)	Fourth step = void; Zooming to show 2 or 5 Key Cards; no trump queen
	(7)	Fifth step = void; Zooming to show 2 or 5 Key Cards; trump queen

Example:

Opener	Responder
♠ K Q x x	♠ A J x x
♥ K Q x x	♥ A x
♦ x	♦ x x x
♣ A J x x	♣ K Q x x
1♣	1♠
3♦ (1)	3♥ (2)
3♠ (3)	3 NT (4)
4♠ (5)	4 NT (6)
5♣ (7)	5♦ (8)
5♠ (9)	6♠
Pass	

(1) Game invitational spade raise; short diamonds
(2) Relay, asking opener to describe his shortness
(3) Singleton
(4) Key Cards?
(5) Two Key Cards with the queen of spades

438

(6) Spiral, please

(7) No club king. Opener's suit, though never rebid, is considered to be the side suit in the Spiral scheme.

(8) Spiral again

(9) I have the heart king but not the club queen

Relay After Opener's Jump Raise of Responder's Major

Opener's jump raise shows four trumps and game invitational values. Opener also announces that he is unable to make a limit splinter — either he is balanced or his singleton doesn't lie between opener's suit and responder's suit.

The four possible auctions fall into three categories:

1. Opener's hand is known to be balanced
2. Opener's hand is either balanced or he has shortness in a black suit
3. The "Random Raise" — opener may be balanced or have shortness in either unbid suit

In each case opener defines his distribution in the usual way, depending on the inferences responder has about his distribution.

1. Opener's Hand is known to be Balanced

This happens in only one sequence:

$$1\clubsuit - 1\spadesuit$$
$$3\spadesuit$$

Opener had 3 ◇ or 3 ♡ available if he had a singleton, so he is known to be balanced.

Further distributional description is unnecessary, so 3 NT (the relay) asks for Key Cards.

Example:

Opener	Responder
♠ A Q x x	♠ K J x x x
♡ A J x	♡ x
◇ K Q x	◇ A x x x
♣ Q x x	♣ K J x

1 ♣	1 ♠
3 ♠ (1)	3 NT (2)
4 ♠ (3)	4 NT (4)
5 ♣ (5)	5 ◇ (6)
5 ♡ (7)	6 ♠ (8)
Pass	

(1) Balanced raise; 17 or 18 HCP
(2) Key Cards?
(3) Two Key Cards with the spade queen
(4) Spiral, please
(5) No club king
(6) Go on
(7) No heart king
(8) Good news. If opener had shown the heart king, responder would have stopped in 5 ♠. The danger of a diamond loser would have been too great.

2. Balanced or Black Suit Shortage

There is only one suit between opener's minor and responder's major.

a) 1 ♣ — 1 ♡   or   b) 1 ◇ — 1 ♠
   3 ♡   3 ♠

In the first case, opener would bid 3 ◇ with diamond shortness. Thus, either he is balanced or he is short in spades.

In the second case, opener would bid 3 ♡ with heart shortness. Thus, either he is balanced or he is short in clubs.

Opener has not clarified his shape, so the relay requests distributional clarification:

First step   = Balanced
Second step = Singleton in the unbid black suit
Third step and beyond = Void in the unbid black suit and Zooming for Key Card Blackwood responses

Example:

Opener	Responder
♠ A K 8 7	♠ Q J 5 4
♡ A 7	♡ 9 6
◇ Q 9 7 5 3 2	◇ A 8 4
♣ 9	♣ A J 10 2
1 ◇	1 ♠
3 ♠ (1)	3 NT (2)
4 ◇ (3)	4 ♡ (4)
4 ♠ (5)	5 ♣ (6)
5 ◇ (7)	5 ♠ (8)
Pass (9)	

(1) Balanced or short clubs
(2) Relay for clarification
(3) Second step = Club singleton
(4) Key Cards?
(5) None or three
(6) Spiral, but omit the trump queen
(7) No side suit king
(8) I have my doubts
(9) So have I. With the heart king, I would have continued.

Both teams were down one in a spade slam against a normal heart lead.

3. The "Random Raise"

One awkward case arises when the two suits are touching:

    1 ◇ — 1 ♡
    3 ♡

Opener could be balanced or short in either unbid suit. The relay seeks:

1. Balanced?
2. The location of a short suit, and
3. How short

The structure works like this:

    1 ◇ — 1 ♡
    3 ♡ — 3 ♠
    3 NT = High suit shortage. In this case, spades.
    4 ♣ = Balanced
    4 ◇ = Low suit singleton. In this case, clubs.
    4 ♡ and beyond = Low suit void (in this case, clubs);
                      Zooming to show Key Cards

A first step response needs further clarification:

    1 ◇   — 1 ♡   (1) Singleton or void?
    3 ♡   — 3 ♠   (2) Singleton spade
    3 NT   — 4 ♣ (1)   (3) Spade void; Zooming to show
    4 ◇ (2) —   Key Cards
    4 ♡ and beyond (3) —

Example:

Opener	Responder
♠ x	♠ A x x
♡ K Q x x	♡ A 10 x x
◇ A 10 x x x	◇ K x
♣ A Q J	♣ K x x x

1 ◇	1 ♡
3 ♡ (1)	3 ♠ (2)
3 NT (3)	4 ♣ (4)
4 ◇ (5)	4 ♠ (6)
4 NT (7)	5 ♣ (8)
5 ♡ (9)	5 NT (10)
6 ♣ (11)	6 ◇ (12)
6 ♠ (13)	7 ♡ (14)
Pass	

(1) The Random Raise — no clues to the distribution
(2) Relay, asking about distribution
(3) Short spades
(4) How short?
(5) Singleton
(6) Key Cards?
(7) Zero or three
(8) Spiral, please
(9) Heart queen but no diamond king
(10) We need one minor-suit queen for seven, and opener almost surely has one to justify his 3♡ bid. I cannot find out by a normal Spiral, so I'll use the Super Relay, asking for queens.
(11) No diamond queen
(12) Do you have the queen of clubs?
(13) Yes
(14) Not a laydown, but with good chances

The sequence
    1 ♡ — 1 ♠
    3 ♠

is treated the same as

    1 ♢ — 1 ♡
    3 ♡

3 NT is a relay, with the same step responses and follow-ups.
  Example:

North American Team Trials, 1969.

Opener	Responder
♠ Q 6 4 2	♠ A J 10 9 8 7
♡ A Q 10 9 7 3	♡ K
♢ —	♢ J 10 8 5 2
♣ K 8 5	♣ A
1 ♡	1 ♠
3 ♠	3 NT (1)
4 ♣ (2)	4 ♢ (3)
4 NT (4)	6 ♠ (5)
Pass	

(1) Relay, asking about distribution
(2) High shortage. In this case, diamonds.
(3) Relay, asking opener to define his shortness.
(4) 4 ♡ would show a singleton diamond. 4 NT shows a void
    with one Key Card.
(5) The diamond void is perfect

  In real life both pairs bid to a grand slam, down one.

Similarly, relays can be used after the sequences

 1 ♣ or 1 ◊ — 1 ♡
 2 ♡
 and
 1 ♣ or 1 ◊ — 1 ♠
 2 ♠

In each case the first step (2 ♠ after a heart raise or 2 NT after a spade raise) is a relay. The responses are the same as after the auction:

 1 of a minor — 1 of a major
 3 of responder's major — 3 NT.

Relays After a Two-Level Response is Raised to the Three-Level

Relays are possible whenever a two-over-one response is raised to the three-level.

There are two cases:

a) The major suit fit:

 1 ♠ — 2 ♡
 3 ♡

b) The minor suit fit

1. The Major Suit Fit

This occurs only in the auction

 1 ♠ — 2 ♡
 3 ♡

The relay is 3♠ (used as a relay with hearts agreed). The step responses assume that opener has no void — he failed to splinter.

1♠	— 2♡	(1)	Relay, asking about distribution
3♡	— 3♠ (1)	(2)	Higher suit singleton. In this case,
3 NT (2) —			diamonds.
4♣ (3) —		(3)	4-5-2-2
4♢ (4) —		(4)	Lower suit singleton. In this case, clubs.

Further relays ask for Key Cards, followed by the Spiral. Example:

Opener	*Responder*
♠ A J x x x	♠ x
♡ K Q x	♡ A J x x x
♢ Q x x x	♢ A K J
♣ x	♣ K Q x x

1♠	2♡
3♡	3♠ (1)
4♢ (2)	4♠ (3)
5♡ (4)	6♡ (5)
Pass	

(1) Relay, asking about distribution
(2) Low singleton. In this case, clubs.
(3) Key Cards?
(4) Two Key Cards and the heart queen
(5) Should have a good play

2. The Minor Suit Fit

In cases where a minor is agreed, 4♣, the first step, is used as the relay since it is not needed in a natural sense.

Because the bidding is at such a high level, the responses are slightly modified:

First step (4 ◇) = High shortage (usually a singleton)
Second step (4 ♡) = Balanced
Third step (4 ♠) and beyond = Low shortage; Zoom to show Key Cards

Example:

Opener	Responder
♠ x x	♠ A J x
♡ A K x x x	♡ Q x
◇ A Q x x	◇ K J x x x x x
♣ J x	♣ A

1 ♡	2 ◇
3 ◇	4 ♣ (1)
4 ♡ (2)	4 ♠ (3)
5 ♡ (4)	5 ♠ (5)
6 ♣ (6)	7 ◇ (7)
Pass	

(1) Relay, asking about distribution
(2) Balanced
(3) Key Cards?
(4) Two Key Cards and the trump queen
(5) Spiral, please. I need the king of hearts for seven.
(6) I have the king of hearts, but not the king of spades.
(7) Your fifth heart will be the thirteenth trick as long as the suit is no worse than 4-2.

When the Opponents Interfere With a Relay

Any overcall after a relay is rare because the bidding is at a high level and the opponents will have had earlier opportunities to bid. There is one exception. When the bidding proceeds 1 ♡ or 1 ♠ — Pass — 2 NT, fourth hand may overcall. The usual intervention is with a double.

1. Doubles

There are two cases:

a) An opponent doubles the response to a relay bid
b) An opponent doubles a relay bid

a) An Opponent Doubles the Response to a Relay Bid

The relayer has the following options:

1. Pass. This continues the relay sequence. The Relayer usually selects this option.
2. Bid. Natural.
3. Redouble. "To play"

When Relayer passes to continue the relay, one step is saved. Scanner's replies:

> Redouble = First step
> Cheapest Bid = Second step
> Next Cheapest Bid = Third step, etc.

Example:

1 ♠	— Pass	— 2 NT (1)	— Pass
3 ♡	— Double	— Pass (2)	— Pass
Redouble (3) —			
3 ♠ (4) —			
3 NT (5) —			

(1) Maxi Raise
(2) Continue the relay
(3) First step
(4) Second step
(5) Third step . . . and so on

b) An Opponent Doubles a Relay Bid

Scanner's responses now use the following schedule:

Pass = The first step
Redouble = The second step
The cheapest bid = The third step
The next cheapest bid = The fourth step, etc.

An opponent's double of a relay bid thus saves two steps.

The following example shows the value of the extra steps made available by an opponent's double. The hand comes from the 1980 Mexican Trials, when George Rosenkranz and Sol Dubson successfully bid to the grand slam. The bidding has been updated.

Opener Sol Dubson		*Responder* George Rosenkranz	
♠ A Q x		♠ x x	
♡ K Q 9 x x		♡ A J 10 x x	
◇ x		◇ A Q x	
♣ A J x x		♣ K Q x	
1 ♡	Pass	2 NT (1)	Pass
3 ♣ (2)	Pass	3 ◇ (3)	Pass
3 ♡ (4)	Pass	3 ♠ (3)	Double
3 NT (5)	Pass	4 ♣ (3)	Pass
4 ♡ (6)	Pass	4 ♠ (3)	Pass (7)
5 ♣ (8)	Pass	5 ◇ (3)	Pass
5 ♡ (9)	Pass	5 ♠ (3)	Pass
5 NT (10)	Pass	6 ♣ (3)	Pass
6 ♡ (11)	Pass	7 ♡ (12)	Pass
Pass	Pass		

(1) Maxi-Raise
(2) Natural
(3) Relay

(4) 5-4 distribution
(5) Thank you for saving me two steps. Pass would be the first step and redouble the second, so 3 NT (instead of 4 ◇) is the third step.
(6) Maximum and zero or three Key Cards (obviously three)
(7) I have learned not to double
(8) Heart queen but no club king
(9) No spade king
(10) No club queen
(11) Spade queen
(12) One more helpful double and I could have found out about the club jack, but I want to be in 7 ♡ anyway. The double has marked the spade king in a favorable position. Even without that clue, we would bid seven. With opener as declarer, they cannot lead spades, so at worst I can draw trumps, test clubs and fall back on the spade finesse.

2. Overcalls

a) If the overcall is made on Relayer's right:

Pass is the relay. Scanner doubles to show the first step.
Double is for penalties
Other calls are natural

b) If the overcall follows a relay (made on Relayer's left):

Pass is the first step. Relayer doubles to continue the relay.
Double is the second step, bids are higher steps.

Examples:

1.

1 ♠	Pass	2 NT	Pass
3 ♣	3 ♡	Pass (1)	
		Double (2)	

(1) Relay
(2) Penalty

2.

1 ♠	Pass	2 NT	Pass
3 ♣	Pass	3 ◊	3 ♡

Pass (1)
Double (2)
3 ♠ (3)

(1) First step
(2) Second step
(3) Third step, etc.

Chapter 27

THE INVERTED MINOR RAISE

A raise of 1♣ to 2♣ or 1♢ to 2♢ is a one round force, denying a four-card major and promising at least four-card support, usually five or more. The range is a good 11 to 15 HCP. With more responder employs the Maxi-Raise response of 2 NT. The raise denies a void because responder would splinter directly with a void.

With slam potential opener usually elects to bid the next step as a relay. His options are:

With a Void

Opener always identifies a void immediately, with any hand strength. Any three-level bid in an unbid suit shows a void:

    1♢   — 2♢
    3♣, 3♡ or 3♠ = Void in the bid suit

With a Minimum Hand

Opener has two choices with a minimum (12-14 HCP), both non-forcing:

1. 2 NT shows a balanced hand
2. Three of the agreed minor shows an unbalanced hand or a good five-card or longer minor

With an Intermediate Hand

An intermediate hand is defined as follows:

Balanced   = 15-17 HCP, or 18 HCP with fewer than six Controls
Unbalanced = 15-18 HCP with six or fewer Losers

Opener's rebids:

1. 3 NT = 15-17 HCP; balanced; all suits stopped
2. 2♡ over a 2♣ raise or 2♠ over a 2♢ raise = Artificial saying, "I can't rebid 3 NT."
3. 2♠ after a 2♣ raise = Singleton spade

With a Strong Hand

Strong hands include:

> Balanced = 18 HCP with six or more Controls
> Unbalanced = Maximum with no more than five Losers

These hands bid the next step (2♢ or 2♡) as a relay.

Development of the Auction

The concepts are familiar. In some cases they are modified to fit a particular sequence.

1. After Minimum Rebids

The bidding is straightforward. A new suit at the three-level shows a stopper, probing for 3 NT.
Example:

U.S. Team Trials, 1979.

Opener	*Responder*
♠ J 10 5	♠ A
♡ K 7 6	♡ Q J
♢ Q 9	♢ K 10 8 3
♣ A K 7 6 5	♣ J 10 9 8 4 3
1♣	2♣
3♣ (1)	3♢ (2)
3♡ (3)	5♣ (4)
Pass	

(1) Minimum with long clubs
(2) Extra values with a diamond stopper
(3) Heart stopper but no spade stopper
(4) 3 NT is out

A big swing resulted to the team which avoided the 3 NT contract that was defeated by the expected spade lead.

2. Opener Shows a Void

If responder bids the next step (not three of the agreed minor or 3 NT), he initiates a relay sequence. Opener's hand strength is totally undefined, so the first stage in the relay chain is minimum/maximum. Opener Zooms to show Key Cards with a maximum.

3. Opener Shows an Intermediate Hand

If opener bids 3 NT, responder can bid 4♣ to start a relay for Key Cards. If opener bids 2♡ or 2♠ (not the relay), responder shows a singleton if he has one. Three of the agreed minor shows a singleton in the major suit bid by opener. Responder must bid 2 NT if he lacks a singleton.

1♣ — 2♣	(1)	Intermediate hand
2♡ (1) — 2♠ (2)	(2)	Singleton spade
— 2 NT (3)	(3)	No singleton
— 3♣ (4)	(4)	Singleton heart
— 3♢ (5)	(5)	Singleton diamond

Opener's follow-ups:

a) Responder showed a singleton

The next step is a relay:
If responder showed a singleton in the other minor, his shape is known to be 6-3-3-1 or 7-3-2-1. The relay asks for Key Cards because the shape is known.

454

If responder showed a singleton in a major, the next relay asks for distributional clarification.

Example:

1♣	— 2♣	(1)	Artificial; intermediate hand
2♡ (1)	— 2♠ (2)	(2)	Spade singleton
2 NT (3)	— 3♣ (4)	(3)	Relay, asking about distribution
	— 3◊ (5)	(4)	Two cards in the other major; three cards in the other minor, i.e., in diamonds. Thus 1-2-3-7 distribution.
	— 3♡ (6)		
	— 3♠ (7)		

(5) Two cards in the other major; four or more cards in the other minor. In this case, two hearts and four or more diamonds.

(6) 3-3 in the other major and the other minor. In this case, 3-3 in hearts and diamonds. Thus 1-3-3-6 shape.

(7) Three cards in the other major; four or more cards in the other minor. In this case, three hearts and four or more diamonds.

The next relay asks for Key Cards. The same remainder-showing scheme is used after the immediate relay.

b) **Responder bid 2 NT**

Opener's choices:

3 NT = 18 HCP; balanced, fewer than six Controls. 4♣ by responder would now be Key Card Blackwood.

Three of the agreed minor = 15-17 HCP; balanced; one or more suits unstopped. Responder bids: 3 NT, five of the agreed minor or three of a suit (showing his lowest stopper).

Three of a suit other than the agreed minor = A singleton in the bid suit. The next step by responder is a relay asking for Key Cards.

4. Opener Relays   1♣ — 2♣   or   1♢ — 2♢
                          2♢   2♡

Responder replies:

a) The first three steps show a singleton. 2 NT shows a singleton in the relay suit:

1♢ — 2♢	(1)	Relay, asking for a singleton
2♡ (1) — 2♠ (2)	(2)	Spade singleton
— 2 NT (3)	(3)	Singleton in the relay suit. In this case, a singleton heart.
— 3♣ (4)	(4)	Club singleton

b) Three of the agreed minor shows six or more trumps and no singleton: 6-3-2-2 or 7-2-2-2.

c) Other three-level bids show balanced hands. Three of a suit shows that suit to be unstopped (usually a weak doubleton). 3 NT shows stoppers in all the unbid suits with the possible exception of clubs when diamonds is the agreed suit.

Opener's follow-ups:

If responder shows a balanced hand, a suit at the three-level shows a stopper and probes for 3 NT. 4♣ is Key Card Blackwood.

If responder shows a singleton, the next step continues the relay. With a major suit singleton, responder must clarify the side suit remainders. He uses the same scheme as after a rebid of two of a major:

1♣ — 2♣	(1)	Relay, asking for a singleton
2♢ (1) — 2♠ (2)	(2)	Singleton spade
2 NT (3) — 3♣ (4)	(3)	Relay, asking about distribution
— 3♢ (5)	(4)	Two cards in the other major; three cards in the other minor. In this case, two hearts and three diamonds. Thus 1-2-3-7 shape.
— 3♡ (6)		
— 3♠ (7)		
	(5)	Two cards in the other major;

four or more cards in the other minor. In this case, two hearts and four or more diamonds.

(6) 3-3 in the other major and the other minor. In this case, 3-3 in hearts and diamonds. Thus 1-3-3-6.

(7) Three cards in the other major; four or more cards in the other minor. In this case, three hearts and four or more diamonds.

Let's see the Inverted Raise at work:

1.

Opener	Responder
♠ K J x x	♠ A x
♡ A x x x	♡ K Q J
◊ x	◊ J x x x
♣ A Q x x	♣ K J x x
1 ♣	2 ♣
2 ♡ (1)	2 NT (2)
3 ◊ (3)	3 ♡ (4)
4 ◊ (5)	4 ♡ (6)
4 NT (7)	6 ♣ (8)
Pass	

(1) Intermediate values
(2) Forced, lacking a singleton
(3) Singleton diamond
(4) Relay, asking about Key Cards
(5) Two Key Cards and the trump queen
(6) Spiral, please
(7) Spade king but no heart king
(8) Looks perfect

2.

Opener	Responder
♠ x x	♠ Q J 10
♡ K Q J x	♡ x x
◇ A Q 10 x	◇ K J x x x
♣ A J x	♣ K Q x

1 ◇	2 ◇
2 ♠ (1)	2 NT (2)
3 ◇ (3)	3 ♠ (4)
3 NT (5)	Pass

(1) Marking time with an intermediate hand
(2) Forced unless there is a singleton to be shown
(3) Balanced, with a weak suit somewhere
(4) I can stop spades
(5) And I can stop hearts

3.

Opener	Responder
♠ A x	♠ x x
♡ A K x	♡ Q J x
◇ J x x x	◇ K Q x x x
♣ K Q x x	♣ A x x

1 ◇	2 ◇
2 ♡ (1)	3 ♠ (2)
4 ♣ (3)	4 NT (4)
5 ◇ (5)	Pass

(1) Relay
(2) Balanced with weak spades. This implies a heart stopper, known by opener to be the queen, since responder would bid 3 ♡ with both majors unstopped.
(3) 3 NT would be to play. This relay asks for Key Cards.
(4) Two Key Cards and the trump queen
(5) The defense is almost sure to score a minor suit trick and a spade trick. A discard, even if one is available, would come too late. The responder cannot have a doubleton spade and

a doubleton heart queen, for he would not consider the hearts stopped. Notice that the obvious 3 NT contract which most pairs would reach is virtually hopeless. Unless the opponents forget to lead spades, declarer would have to hope that the suit would block.

4. Challenge the Champs, 1979.

Opener	*Responder*
♠ A 8 5	♠ 9
♡ A K Q	♡ 8 6 2
◇ Q J 8 4 2	◇ A K 9 3
♣ 7 6	♣ A K 8 5 4

1 ◇	2 ◇
2 ♡ (1)	2 ♠ (2)
2 NT (3)	3 ♠ (4)
4 ♣ (5)	4 ◇ (6)
4 ♡ (7)	4 ♠ (8)
4 NT (9)	5 ◇ (10)
7 ◇ (11)	Pass

(1) Relay. Only five Controls, but all the points are working
(2) Singleton spade
(3) Relay for distribution of remainders
(4) Fourth step = Three hearts and at least four clubs
(5) Key Cards?
(6) Zero or three
(7) Zero is impossible, for ♠ K ♡ J x x ◇ 10xxxx ♣ KQJx would not bid 2 ◇. So opener relays to start a Spiral. He could have Super Relayed for the club king.
(8) No trump queen — not a surprise
(9) Relay, continuing the Spiral
(10) The club king. Theoretically this denies the heart king, but responder cannot have another king, or even a queen, after showing ace-king, ace-king. If he had any more, he would have made a Maxi-Raise.
(11) A grand slam on only 30 HCP.

Only one of the pairs, using a club system, reached the laydown grand slam.

5. Challenge the Champs, 1978.

Opener	Responder
♠ K J 10 7	♠ A Q 5
♡ A 7	♡ 2
◇ A 10 9 4	◇ K Q J 7 6 2
♣ A 8 5	♣ 7 6 3

1 ◇	2 ◇
2 ♡ (1)	2 NT (2)
3 ♣ (3)	3 ♠ (4)
4 ♣ (5)	4 NT (6)
5 ♣ (7)	5 ◇ (8)
5 ♡ (9)	5 ♠ (10)
5 NT (11)	6 ◇ (12)
7 ♠ (13)	Pass (14)

(1) Relay, asking for a singleton
(2) Singleton in hearts, the relay suit
(3) Distribution?
(4) Third step shows 3-3 in the remainders, so the distribution must be 3-1-6-3
(5) Key Cards?
(6) Two Key Cards with the trump queen
(7) So far, so good. Spiral please.
(8) No spade king
(9) Not surprised. Tell me more.
(10) No club king either
(11) More please
(12) Spade queen but no club queen
(13) I can count only 12 tricks. Should I pass or bid 6 NT. On second thought, I won't do either. A heart ruff will give me 13 tricks in spades provided that I don't run into an opening diamond ruff.
(14) I don't know what's going on, but I suppose I have to trust you

6.

Opener	Responder
♠ A J	♠ x x
♡ A x x	♡ K Q x
◊ K Q x x x x	◊ A x x x x
♣ K x	♣ A Q x

1 ◊	2 ◊ (1)
2 ♡ (2)	3 ♠ (3)
4 ♣ (4)	4 ♠ (5)
4 NT (6)	5 ◊ (7)
5 ♡ (8)	6 ♣ (9)
7 NT (10)	Pass

(1) With 15 HCP, five Controls and five-card support, this is a super-maximum Inverted Raise. A Maxi-Raise of 2 NT would be acceptable.
(2) Relay, asking for distribution. Slam prospects are good.
(3) Balanced with spade weakness
(4) Key Cards?
(5) Two Key Cards, but no diamond queen
(6) Spiral please, starting with hearts. We both know you do not have the spade king.
(7) The heart king but not the club king
(8) How about queens?
(9) Skip two steps to show two cards: the heart queen and the club queen. (Incidently this bid denies the spade queen, which could be doubleton, because that card would give responder too many points.)
(10) Marvelous! I can count 13 tricks. In the remote event that your ace-queen of clubs is doubleton, I will shoot myself.

7.

Opener	Responder
♠ A x x x	♠ K Q
♡ —	♡ Q x x
◇ K x x	◇ A x x
♣ A K 10 x x x	♣ J x x x x

1 ♣	2 ♣
3 ♡ (1)	3 ♠ (2)
4 ♣ (3)	4 ◇ (4)
4 ♠ (5)	4 NT (6)
5 ◇ (7)	7 ♣ (8)
Pass	

(1) Heart void. It is wrong to relay with a void.
(2) Relay, asking about strength
(3) This five-Loser hand is treated as a maximum. This Zoom response shows a maximum with three Key Cards.
(4) Do you have the club queen?
(5) Yes, but not the spade king. With a known 10-card or longer fit, opener is not concerned about the queen of clubs.
(6) Continue
(7) Diamond king but no spade queen
(8) Perfect!

8.

Opener	Responder
♠ K 10 x x	♠ A Q x
♡ K x x x	♡ A Q
◇ A J x x x	◇ K x x x x
♣ —	♣ x x x

1 ◇	2 ◇
3 ♣ (1)	3 ♡ (2)
3 ♠ (3)	4 ♣ (4)
4 ♡ (5)	4 ♠ (6)
4 NT (7)	5 ♣ (6)
5 ♠ (8)	7 ◇ (9)
Pass	

(1) Club void
(2) Relay. 3 ◊ would be natural and discouraging.
(3) Minimum
(4) Relay. 3 NT would be a signoff.
(5) One Key Card, obviously the ace of diamonds.
(6) Relay
(7) No diamond queen
(8) Spade king and heart king
(9) That's all we need

9. Bermuda Bowl, 1967.

Opener	Responder
♠ A x	♠ x x
♡ A Q J	♡ K x x
◊ A x x x	◊ Q J x x x x
♣ Q 10 9 x	♣ A K

1 ◊	2 ◊
2 ♡ (1)	3 ◊ (2)
3 ♡ (3)	3 NT (4)
4 ♣ (5)	4 ♡ (6)
4 ♠ (7)	5 ◊ (8)
6 ◊ (9)	Pass

(1) Relay
(2) Six or seven diamonds; no singleton
(3) Key Cards?
(4) One
(5) Slam is now doubtful. More information is needed. Spiral please.
(6) Trump queen, but no spade king. As far as responder is concerned, the side suits are equal, so spades are described first.
(7) You surely have either the heart king or the club king, but need both to make a slam.
(8) I have both. (And incidentally, no spade queen.)
(9) Excellent

10.

Opener	Responder
♠ A 7 5	♠ 4
♡ 3 2	♡ A Q 7
◊ A K J	◊ Q 10 6 5
♣ K Q 10 4 2	♣ A J 8 6 5

1 ♣	2 ♣
2 ◊ (1)	2 ♠ (2)
2 NT (3)	3 ♠ (4)
4 ♣ (5)	4 ♠ (6)
4 NT (7)	5 ♣ (8)
5 ◊ (9)	5 ♡ (10)
5 ♠ (11)	6 ♡ (12)
7 ♣ (13)	Pass

(1) Relay, asking about distribution
(2) Singleton spade
(3) Side suit distribution
(4) Fourth step = 3-4, or just possibly, 3-5
(5) Key Cards?
(6) Two Key Cards without the club queen
(7) Spiral, please
(8) No diamond king
(9) More?
(10) No heart king
(11) All I need is the diamond queen, which is next on the program. So relay again.
(12) Not only the diamond queen, but also the heart queen and the club jack
(13) I could have found out about the diamond queen faster with a Super Relay of 4 ◊ instead of the 4 NT bid. But that would have given up the chance to find responder with the ace-king-queen of hearts and four small diamonds.

Chapter 28

THE WOLFF ADJUNCT

The Wolff Adjunct, developed by Bobby Wolff of Dallas, resembles the Jacoby, Flint and Lebensold conventions, which allow responder to sign off below game in a long suit opposite a strong balanced hand. The Romex version of the Wolff Adjunct works like this:

Wolff Adjunct

$1 \clubsuit — 1 \diamondsuit , 1 \heartsuit$ or $1 \spadesuit$　　or　　$1 \diamondsuit — 1 \heartsuit$ or $1 \spadesuit$
$2 \text{ NT} — 3 \clubsuit$ (1)　　　　　　　　$2 \text{ NT} — 3 \clubsuit$ (1)

(1)　A demand for a three-level preference with three-card support for responder's major. Otherwise opener must bid $3 \diamondsuit$.

The purposes of the Wolff Adjunct:

1. To be able to sign off in three of responder's suit or three of a lower ranking suit.
2. To create additional sequences, allowing much more accurate slam investigation. Responder can show unbalanced two-suiters or three-suiters.

Another side benefit of this is that opener can also rebid 2 NT with awkward hands containing a singleton in responder's suit. (The standard requirements are: 17-18 HCP; balanced hand; at least five Controls and no four-card fit in responder's suit.) The shape is usually 6-3-3-1 with a weakish six-card suit. After $1 \clubsuit — 1 \heartsuit$, rebid 2 NT with ♠ AKx ♡ Q ♢ AJx ♣ A109xxx.

Responder will be able to show a six-card heart suit at the three-level, so this rebid is safe.

The scheme of responses to 2 NT looks like this:

```
   Wolff Adjunct: Responses to 2 NT

1 ♣ or 1 ◇ — 1 ♡ or 1 ♠
2 NT      — 3 ♣ (1)
          — 3 ◇ (2)
          — 3 of responder's major (3)
          — 3 of other major (4)
          — 3 NT (5)
          — 4 ♣ (6)
          — 4 ◇ (7)
          — 4 of responder's major (5)
          — 4 of the other major (8)
          — 4 NT (9)

1 ♣  — 1 ◇
2 NT — 3 ♣ (10)
     — 3 ◇ (11)
     — 3 ♡ or 3 ♠ (12)
     — 3 NT (5)
     — 4 ♣ (6)
     — 4 ◇ (13)
     — 4 ♡ or 4 ♠ (14)
```

Some points to be kept in mind about the response and 2 NT rebid:

1. A 1 ◇ response denies a four-card major, in principle. The only exception is when responder has five or more diamonds and a good hand.
2. Opener should rebid a major at the one-level when possible in preference to 2 NT. An exception could occur with 4-3-3-3 and a weak major.

Some general points:

1. Responder bids 4♣, CONFIT, over 2 NT on all balanced slam tries: 4-3-3-3, 4-4-3-2, 5-3-3-2 or 5-4-2-2. As a result, there is no step in relay auctions to show 5-4-2-2 if responder shows a two-suiter.

(1) Wolff Adjunct. Any other bid is game forcing.
(2) Slam try in opener's minor
(3) Six card or longer suit
(4) Natural; at least 5-4 in his two bid suits
(5) Sign off
(6) CONFIT
(7) 5-4-4-0 with a void in the unbid minor (i.e., not in opener's minor)
(8) 5-4-4-0 with a void in the unbid major
(9) Key Card Blackwood with responder's major as the Key Card suit
(10) Wolff Adjunct: demands a 3 ◊ bid
(11) One-suited slam try
(12) Natural; slam interest
(13) Key Card Blackwood with diamonds as the Key Card suit
(14) Void in the bid major; 5-4-4-0; five diamonds; at least opening bid strength

2. When responder identifies a slam try, or possible slam try, opener can attempt to sign off, or he can relay. If responder shows two suits, opener must identify which suit he is supporting. A preference shows a fit for the first suit; the cheapest meaningless step shows a fit for the second suit:

a) 1 ♣   — 1 ♠
   2 NT — 3 ♡
   3 ♠ (1) —
   4 ♣ (2) —

b) 1 ♣   — 1 ♡
   2 NT — 3 ♡
   3 ♠ (3) —

(1) Three spades, relay attempt
(2) Four hearts; fewer than three spades, relay attempt
(3) Relay attempt

Example:

Opener	Responder
♠ A J	
♡ A J x x	
◇ K 10 x x	
♣ A x x	
1 ◇	1 ♠
2 NT	3 ♡
4 ♣ (1)	

(1) Slam try in hearts; relay for distribution

One purpose of setting the trump suit is to allow opener to use bids in the other suits as relays.

In some sequences responder has not confirmed slam interest with his rebid. Auctions a) and b) above are such cases. If he lacks slam interest he rejects the relay by signing off in the agreed suit. Other steps are relay responses showing distribution, and confirm slam interest.

3. Relay auctions follow normal Romex procedure: distribution identification, Key Cards or Controls, Spiral Scan. Some notes about sequences after a 2 NT rebid:

a) When responder shows a two-suiter, there are six Key Cards: the four aces and the kings in responder's suits.

b) If responder showed a two-suiter, he clarifies his long suit distribution. In some cases this is done before opener relays:

      1 ◇ — 1 ♠
      2 NT — 3 ♣
      3 ♠ — 3 NT = Exactly four spades and five clubs

In most cases, however, this is done after opener's relay. Responder bids the first step to show 5-4 only. Higher steps show at least 10 cards in the two suits. These higher steps "Zoom" to show the side suit residue:

468

```
1 ◊  — 1 ♠          (1) 5-4 only
2 NT — 3 ♡          (2) At least five cards in each of his
3 ♠  — 3 NT (1)           two suits; singleton diamond
     — 4 ♣ (2)      (3) At least five cards in each of his
     — 4 ◊ (3)           two suits; singleton club
     — 4 ♡ (4)      (4) At least five cards in each of his
     — 4 ♠ (5)           two suits; diamond void
     — 4 NT (6)     (5) Signoff
                    (6) At least five cards in each of his
                         two suits; club void
```

Opener can relay over the 5-4 showing step to get the same four-step reply for short suit residue. There is no step to show 5-4-2-2 because all 5-4-2-2's with slam interest use CONFIT.

4. When responder employs a specialized sequence to show a three-suiter, opener uses the first available step (i.e., that can't be an eight-card fit if responder is 5-4-4-0) to ask for controls:

First step = 4-4-4-1 with four Controls
First step = 5-4-4-0 with three Controls

With 4-4-4-1 the first step shows four Controls because opener implies five Controls and 5 + 4 = 9 combined Controls, the usual minimum combined number of Controls to consider a slam. With 5-4-4-0, the void is expected to compensate for the lower number of Controls.

After the control ask, the next relay starts a scan for queens.

Examples:

1.

Opener	Responder
♠ K x	♠ J x x x x
♡ A J x	♡ Q x x x x
◊ K Q x x	◊ J x
♣ K J x x	♣ x

1 ◊	1 ♠
2 NT (1)	3 ♣ (2)
3 ◊ (3)	3 ♡ (4)
Pass (5)	

(1) 17-18 HCP; balanced; two or three spades
(2) Wolff Adjunct
(3) Denies three spades
(4) Signoff in a lower ranking suit
(5) No need to correct

2.

Opener	Responder
♠ Q J x	♠ 10 x x x
♡ A K x x	♡ Q x
◊ K x x	◊ A x x
♣ A J x	♣ K 10 x x

1 ♣	1 ♠
2 NT	3 NT (1)
Pass	

(1) No slam interest

470

3.

Opener	Responder
♠ K Q x x	♠ A x x x
♡ x x	♡ Q x x x
◇ K Q J x	◇ x x
♣ A Q J	♣ K x x

1 ◇	1 ♡
1 ♠ (1)	2 ♠ (2)
4 ♠ (3)	Pass

(1) Don't rebid 2 NT with four spades unless you hold 4-3-3-3 with bad spades

(2) A single raise with 8-10 "dummy points." With less, responder passes as game is unlikely.

4.

Opener	Responder
♠ K 10 2	♠ Q J 3
♡ J 9	♡ K Q 10 6 4
◇ K Q 10 9	◇ J 8
♣ A K Q 2	♣ J 10 5

1 ◇	1 ♡
2 NT (1)	3 ♣ (2)
3 ◇ (3)	3 NT (4)
Pass (5)	

(1) 17-18 HCP; balanced; fewer than four hearts; less than four good spades.

(2) Wolff Adjunct

(3) Only two hearts

(4) Balanced hand with five hearts and no slam interest. This reveals that responder was merely checking for a 5-3 heart fit.

(5) Seems safer than the major suit game

5.

Opener	Responder
♠ A K x	♠ Q J 10 x x
♡ K x	♡ A Q J x
◇ Q J 10 x	◇ A x x
♣ A x x x	♣ x

1 ◇	1 ♠
2 NT	3 ♡
3 ♠ (1)	3 NT (2)
4 ♣ (3)	4 ♡ (4)
4 NT (5)	5 ♠ (6)
5 NT (7)	6 ♣ (8)
6 ♠ (9)	Pass

(1) Three-card spade support
(2) First step showing a 5-4-3-1 or 5-4-1-3 slam try. A balanced
    hand would have bid 4♣ (CONFIT) directly.
(3) Distribution?
(4) Second step = Low singleton. Distribution is 5-4-3-1.
(5) Relay for Key Cards. In this auction, there are six Key Cards
(6) Two Key Cards and the trump queen
(7) Spiral for the fragment king
(8) No diamond king
(9) It will make only a small slam

6.

Opener	Responder
♠ A J	♠ K Q 10 x x
♡ A J x x	♡ K Q x x
◇ K 10 x x	◇ A x x
♣ A x x	♣ x

1 ◇	1 ♠
2 NT	3 ♡
4 ♣ (1)	4 ◇ (2)
4 ♠ (3)	5 ♣ (4)
5 ◇ (5)	5 ♡ (6)
5 ♠ (7)	6 ♣ (8)
6 ◇ (9)	6 ♠ (10)
7 ♡ (11)	Pass

(1) Slam try in hearts; relay for distribution; fewer than three spades
(2) 5-4-3-1 or 5-4-1-3
(3) I am very interested; 4♡ would have been a "yellow light"
(4) Second step = Singleton in the lower suit, i.e., 5-4-3-1
(5) Relay for Key Cards
(6) First step = Three Key Cards
(7) Spiral please — starting with the trump queen
(8) Second step = Trump queen but no fragment king
(9) Queens?
(10) Side suit queen but no fragment queen
(11) So the grand should be bid in hearts and not in notrump. The contract will make with five spade tricks, four hearts, two diamonds, one club and one club ruff.

It is time to discuss the specifics of certain bids after opener has jump rebid 2 NT.

A. 3♣ — The Wolff Adjunct

The subsequent auction depends on the initial response:

473

1. A 1♡ or 1♠ response

Responder uses The Wolff Adjunct for these purposes:

a) To check for a 5-3 fit in a major
b) To show a singleton in one of the unbid suits. When short in the other major, the shape is always 4-4-4-1
c) To show a slam try in the other minor, i.e., not opener's minor
d) To sign off at or below three of his major

The sequences look like this:

1♣ or 1♢	— 1♡
2 NT	— 3♣
3♢	— Pass (1)
	— 3♡ (1)
	— 3 NT (2)
	— 4♣ (3)
	— 4♢ (4)
	— 4♡ (5)

1♣ or 1♢	— 1♠
2 NT	— 3♣
3♢	— Pass (1)
	— 3♡ (1)
	— 3♠ (1)
	— 3 NT (2)
	— 4♣ (3)
	— 4♢ (4)
	— 4♡ (5)

1♣ or 1♢	— 1♡
2 NT	— 3♣
3♡	— Pass (1)
	— 3 NT (5)
	— 4♣ (3)
	— 4♢ (4)
	— 4♡ (6)

1♣ or 1♢	— 1♠
2 NT	— 3♣
3♠	— Pass (1)
	— 3 NT (5)
	— 4♣ (3)
	— 4♢ (4)
	— 4♠ (6)

(1) Signoff
(2) Signoff. Responder was looking for a 5-3 fit.
(3) Slam try in the other minor, i.e., the minor other than opener's original minor
(4) Singleton in the other minor. A fit in opener's minor is guaranteed.
(5) 4-4-4-1; short in the other major; slam try
(6) Signoff. Responder has found his 5-3 fit.

Thus to show a 4-4-4-1 slam try with shortness in the other major, responder bids 4 ♡ if opener has rebid 3 ◊ or he bids 3 NT if opener has shown a three-card fit for responder's major. Responder's control showing bids start with four controls as the first step when he has shown a 4-4-4-1 pattern or with three controls, if he has shown a 5-4-4-0 pattern.

Examples:

1. Le Bridgeur, October, 1982.

Opener	Responder
♠ A 10 2	♠ 4
♡ K 6	♡ A 8 4 2
◊ A J 8 6 4	◊ K Q 5 3
♣ K Q 2	♣ A 7 6 3

1 ◊	1 ♡
2 NT	3 ♣ (1)
3 ◊	4 ♡ (2)
4 ♠ (3)	5 ♣ (4)
5 ♡ (5)	5 NT (6)
7 ◊ (7)	Pass

(1) Wolff Adjunct to start a slam try
(2) Showing exactly 1-4-4-4
(3) Controls?
(4) Second step = Five Controls. The singleton king of spades would not be counted as a Control.
(5) Spiral for the trump queen. Cannot be natural as opener has denied a heart fit by rebidding 2 NT instead of 3 ♡.
(6) Diamond queen but no heart queen
(7) I don't need it!

2.

Opener	Responder
♠ A Q x	♠ K J x x x
♡ A x x	♡ K x x x
◇ Q x x	◇ —
♣ K Q x x	♣ A x x x

1 ♣	1 ♠
2 NT	4 ◇ (1)
4 NT (2)	5 ◇ (3)
7 ♣ (4)	Pass

(1) 5-4-0-4
(2) Controls? 4 ♡ and 4 ♠ would be non-forcing
(3) Second step = Four Controls
(4) Thank you very much!

3.

Opener	Responder
♠ A K x	♠ Q x x x
♡ A x	♡ K Q x x x
◇ K J x x	◇ A x x x
♣ Q J x x	♣ —

1 ◇	1 ♡
2 NT	4 ◇ (1)
4 NT (2)	5 ♣ (3)
5 ♠ (4)	5 NT (5)
6 ◇ (6)	Pass

(1) 4-5-4-0; slam is possible
(2) Controls?
(3) First step = Three Controls
(4) Do you have the diamond queen?
(5) No
(6) You should have both major suit queens for your slam try

4.

Opener	Responder
♠ A Q x	♠ K x x x x
♡ Q x	♡ A K x
◇ A x x x	◇ x
♣ A J x x	♣ K Q x x

1 ◇	1 ♠
2 NT	3 ♣ (1)
3 ♠ (2)	4 ♣ (3)
4 ◇ (4)	4 ♡ (5)
4 NT (6)	5 ◇ (7)
5 ♡ (8)	5 ♠ (9)
6 ◇ (10)	6 NT (11)
7 ♣ (12)	Pass

(1) Wolff Adjunct
(2) Three-card spade support
(3) Two-suiter — spades and the other minor, i.e., clubs
(4) Relay, asking about distribution
(5) First step = 5-4
(6) Relay, asking about remainders. 4 ♠ would be non-forcing.
(7) Second step = Lower singleton. Therefore 5-3-1-4
(8) Key Cards?
(9) Three Key Cards
(10) Super-Relay — Omit the spade queen and spiral for kings
(11) Third step = Heart king and club queen but not the heart queen
(12) Might try 7 NT at matchpoints in a good field. Too bad I can't ask about the jack of spades.

5.

Opener	Responder
♠ A x x	♠ K x x x
♡ A J x	♡ x
◇ K x	◇ A Q x x
♣ A J x x x	♣ K Q x x

1 ♣	1 ♠
2 NT	3 ♣
3 ♠	3 NT (1)
4 ♣ (2)	4 ◇ (3)
4 ♡ (4)	4 NT (5)
5 ◇ (6)	5 ♠ (7)
7 ♣ (8)	Pass

(1) 4-4-4-1 slam try with a singleton in the unbid major
(2) Accepting clubs and asking for Controls
(3) First step = Four Controls
(4) Spiral for the trump queen
(5) Trump queen but not the spade queen
(6) Maybe the other queen?
(7) Yes, but not the trump jack
(8) No problem

2. A 1 ◇ response

Responder continues:

1 ♣	— 1 ◇	(1) To play
2 NT	— 3 ♣	(2) 1-3-5-4 or 1-2-6-4
3 ◇	— Pass (1)	(3) 3-1-5-4 or 2-1-6-4
	— 3 ♡ (2)	(4) 2-2-5-4; non-forcing
	— 3 ♠ (3)	
	— 3 NT (4)	

Some notes

1. With other shapes that include a club fit, responder should prefer a first round club raise — either an Inverted Raise, a

2 NT Maxi-Raise or a void-showing jump.

2. With 2-2-5-4 and a hand too good to risk a pass of 3 NT, responder bids 4♣ — CONFIT.

Example:

Opener	Responder
♠ K J x	♠ x x
♡ A Q x	♡ K x
◇ J x x	◇ K Q x x x
♣ A Q J x	♣ K x x x

Opener	Responder
1♣	1◇
2 NT	3♣
3◇	3 NT (1)
Pass	

(1) 2-2-5-4; slam try; non-forcing
(2) Soft values, poor fit, poor shape, wasted major suit values

B. 3◇ — Slam Try in Opener's Minor

This applies after a major suit response. Opener replies to show or deny a fit in the major and his slam suitability if he lacks a fit:

1♣ or 1◇ — 1♡		1♣ or 1◇ — 1♠	
2 NT	— 3◇	2 NT	— 3◇
3♡ (1)	—	3♡ (4)	—
3♠ (2)	—	3♠ (1)	—
3 NT (3)	—	3 NT (3)	—

(1) Three-card support
(2) Only two hearts; accepting the slam try in opener's minor
(3) No slam interest
(4) Only two spades; accepting the slam try in opener's minor

Further bids by responder follow the Romex relay path: describing distribution, Key Cards and followed by Spiral Cue-Bidding. There is one special type of sequence:

1♣ or 1◊ — 1♡	1♣ or 1◊ — 1♠
2 NT — 3◊	2 NT — 3◊
3♡ — 3 NT (1)	3♠ — 3 NT (1)

(1) Only a four-card major; five or more cards in opener's minor

Examples:

1. Olympiad. Canada vs. Italy, 1968.

Opener	Responder
♠ 10 8 7 6	♠ A
♡ A K 2	♡ J 9 8 5
◊ A 8 6	◊ K Q 3
♣ A K 8	♣ Q 10 6 5 3

1♣	1♡
2 NT (1)	3◊ (2)
3♡ (3)	3 NT (4)
4♣ (5)	4◊ (6)
4♡ (7)	4 NT (8)
5◊ (9)	5 NT (10)
6♣ (11)	Pass

(1) Opener decides to suppress his bad four-card spade suit with 4-3-3-3.
(2) Shows a fit for opener's clubs
(3) Three-card heart support
(4) Five clubs; only four hearts
(5) Your singleton?
(6) First step = High singleton — 1-4-3-5 or maybe 1-4-2-6
(7) Key Cards?
(8) One Key Card
(9) Spiral, please
(10) Trump queen, diamond king but no heart queen
(11) This excellent slam was missed by both teams

2. Tuttobridge, 1982.

Opener	Responder
♠ K Q 6	♠ A J 9 7 4
♡ 7 4 3 2	♡ A
◇ A K Q 8	◇ 10 9 6 5 2
♣ A 4	♣ 3 2

1 ◇	1 ♠
2 NT	3 ◇ (1)
3 ♠ (2)	4 ◇ (3)
4 ♡ (4)	5 ♣ (5)
5 ♡ (6)	5 ♠ (7)
7 ◇ (8)	Pass

(1) Slam try in opener's minor
(2) Three-card spade support
(3) Second step = High singleton (hearts); five or more spades and five diamonds. 3 NT would have shown only four spades. 4♣ would have shown five spades and four diamonds.
(4) Key Cards?
(5) Two Key Cards but no trump queen
(6) Fragment king?
(7) No
(8) A difficult contract to reach

C. Responder Rebids His Suit — The One-Suiter

When responder rebids his suit, he promises a one-suiter with at least a six-card suit. With 5-3-3-2, use CONFIT with slam interest, or the Wolff Adjunct with a five-card major and no slam interest. A 3 ◇ rebid after a 1 ◇ response also guarantees slam interest.

Responder can sign off after a relay. The first step shows no singleton.

```
1♣  — 1♡          (1)  No singleton
2 NT — 3♡          (2)  Spade singleton
3♠  — 3 NT (1)     (3)  Diamond singleton
    — 4♣ (2)       (4)  No slam interest
    — 4♢ (3)       (5)  Club singleton
    — 4♡ (4)
    — 4♠ (5)
```

Relays then ask for Key Cards and Spiral Scan.

Examples:

1.

Opener	Responder
♠ K Q J	♠ x
♡ A x x	♡ K x x
♢ K x x	♢ A Q J x x x
♣ K x x x	♣ Q x x

1♣	1♢
2 NT	3♢ (1)
3♡ (2)	3 NT (3)
Pass (4)	

(1) One-suited slam try with a six-card or longer diamond suit
(2) Relay, asking for distribution
(3) Second step = High singleton
(4) Too much duplication

2. Olympiad, 1964.

Opener	Responder
♠ K 7 6	♠ A Q
♡ A Q 3	♡ K J 10 9 6 4
◊ A 10 7	◊ 9 2
♣ A J 8 3	♣ Q 9 2

1 ♣	1 ♡
2 NT	3 ♡
3 ♠ (1)	3 NT (2)
4 ♣ (3)	4 ♠ (4)
4 NT (5)	5 ♣ (6)
5 ◊ (7)	5 ♡ (8)
6 ♡ (9)	Pass

(1) Slam try; relay asking about shape
(2) Slam is a possibility; I'm balanced
(3) Key Cards
(4) Two Key Cards; no trump queen
(5) Side kings?
(6) No spade king
(7) Continue
(8) No diamond king
(9) For your slam try you must have the club king or some queens

At the Olympiad, the pair that opened with a strong notrump missed the slam. The pair that used a suit opening bid, did not.

3.

    Opener
    ♠ K Q J
    ♡ Q J x x
    ◇ A K
    ♣ Q x x x

Responder A	*Responder B*
♠ A x x x x	♠ A x x x x x
♡ A K x x	♡ A K x
◇ J x x x	◇ J x x
♣ —	♣ x

1♣	— 1♠	1♣	— 1♠
2 NT	— 3♡ (1)	2 NT	— 3♠ (7)
3♠ (2)	— 4♡ (3)	4♣ (8)	— 5♣ (9)
4 NT (4)	— 5♣ (5)	5◇ (4)	— 5 NT (10)
7♡ (6)	— Pass	6♠ (11)	— Pass

(1) Five or more spades; four or more hearts
(2) Three spades; relay attempt
(3) Fourth step = Void in lower suit (clubs); treating this pattern as a two-suiter
(4) Key Cards?
(5) Three Key Cards — hearts and spades are both ''key'' suits
(6) Dandy!
(7) Six-card spade suit
(8) I'm interested in a spade slam
(9) Fourth step = Low singleton (clubs). 4♠ would have been a sign off.
(10) Two Key Cards but no trump queen
(11) The limit

D. 4♣ — CONFIT

Responder must bid 4♣ over 2 NT on any balanced hand with slam interest; 4-3-3-3, 4-4-3-2, 5-3-3-2 or 5-4-2-2. 4♣ asks opener to show his controls:

```
1 ♣ or 1 ◇ — 1 ◇ , 1 ♡ or 1 ♠
2 NT        — 4 ♣
4 ◇ (1)     —
4 ♡ (2)     —
4 ♠ (3)     —
4 NT (4)    —
5 ♣ (5)     —
```

(1) Five Controls — the expected number
(2) Six Controls
(3) Seven Controls
(4) Fewer than five Controls — signoff attempt
(5) Eight Controls — almost impossible

After learning the number of Controls, responder has two choices:

1. Attempt to sign off in 4 NT or any slam. Opener can correct the choice of trump suit with good reason.
2. Bid naturally in an attempt to find a trump suit and assess the quality of the fit.

Any below slam suit bid by responder is forcing. With no slam interest responder must signoff in 4 NT. It is still possible to stop short of slam if opener bids 4 NT or five of one of responder's suits.

Examples:

1.

Opener	Responder
♠ Q 6 2	♠ A K 10 5 3
♡ K 4 2	♡ A 5
◇ A 8 7	◇ 10 6 4
♣ A K J 2	♣ Q 7 6
1 ♣	1 ♠
2 NT (1)	4 ♣ (2)
4 ♡ (3)	4 ♠ (4)
5 ♠ (5)	6 ♠ (6)
Pass or 6 NT	

485

(1) Denies four spades
(2) Control ask; balanced hand
(3) Second step = Six Controls
(4) Controls are OK; five-card spade suit; no side suit.
(5) An in-between hand. Not enough to insist on slam, but cards are well enough placed to raise rather than signing off in 4 NT.
(6) Very close. The club queen is likely to be useful.

2.

Opener	Responder
♠ A K 10	♠ Q 7 4
♡ 7 4	♡ A K 8 3
◇ A Q 9	◇ 6 2
♣ K J 9 6 3	♣ A 10 5 4
1 ♣	1 ♡
2 NT (1)	4 ♣ (2)
4 ♡ (3)	5 ♣ (4)
6 ♣ (5)	Pass

(1) Denies four spades
(2) Control ask; balanced hand
(3) Second step = Six Controls
(4) I have a club fit and slam interest. With no slam interest, I would have bid 4 NT.
(5) Happy to accept with a fifth club and a doubleton in partner's suit.

3.

Opener	Responder
♠ K 10	♠ A Q J 6
♡ A K 4	♡ J 3 2
◇ K 8 6	◇ A 10 3
♣ A 10 9 6 2	♣ Q 7 3

1 ♣	1 ♠
2 NT	4 ♣
4 ♠ (1)	4 NT (2)
6 ♣ (3)	6 NT (4)
Pass	

(1) Seven Controls
(2) Non-forcing. Seven Controls can't be a discouraging reply. What he needs is tricks — a club suit and spade honors will also help.
(3) Five clubs; choice of slams
(4) No advantage to playing in clubs

E. 4 ◇ (after a 1 ◇ response) — Key Card Blackwood (diamonds is the key suit)

This specialized treatment is useful when responder fears that a disappointing Key Card response would get the bidding beyond 4 NT.

Example:

Opener	Responder
♠ A x x	♠ K x x
♡ K Q 10	♡ x
◇ K	◇ A Q J x x x x
♣ A Q x x x x	♣ K x

1 ♣	1 ◇
2 NT	4 ◇ (1)
4 ♡ (2)	6 ◇ (3)
6 NT (4)	Pass

(1) Key Card Blackwood with diamonds as the Key Card suit
(2) Zero or three Key Cards
(3) One Key Card is missing
(4) A reasonable shot at matchpoints

L'envoi

I have often wondered why bridge enjoys such an impressive popularity around the world. It occurred to me that its attraction may be partially explained by the similarity it bears to some basics in life: communication, cooperation, challenge and the quest for excellence are some of our most powerful motivating forces; all are present in our favorite game.

History has taught us about the fate of ideas and theories. Some vanish, other evolve and flourish. A few of you will have the privilege of witnessing these changes and looking at the game as it will be played in fifty years. Hopefully some of the concepts presented here will pass the acid test of time.

It is now your turn to undertake the road to excellence. The thought of having assisted you in your endeavour will be my reward.

Appendix A

HCP	Relative Frequency	Expected number of controls in balanced hands												
		0	1	2	3	4	5	6	7	8	9	10	11	12
3	1216	67	33											
4	1891	40	39	21										
5	2505	23	48	29										
6	3129	12	41	47										
7	3795	5	30	46	19									
8	4192	2	19	44	28	7								
9	4377	*	10	35	44	11								
10	4379	*	5	24	44	27								
11	4179	*	2	14	40	33	11							
12	3755		1	8	30	42	17	2						
13	3242		*	3	20	39	34	4						
14	2687		*	1	11	33	38	17						
15	2115		*	*	5	24	42	23	6					
16	1596			*	2	14	36	37	10	1				
17	1155			*	1	8	27	39	24	1				
18	799				*	3	18	39	30	10				
19	526				*	1	10	32	40	15	2			
20	333				*	*	3	22	38	31	4			
21	201					*	1	13	35	35	15			
22	115					*	*	6	35	43	20	7		
23	62.9						*	3	26	43	17	9	1	
24	32.6						*	1	17	38	31	9	4	
25	16.0							*	9	31	43	26	21	6
26	7.32							*	4	21	37	41	9	9
27	3.21							*	1	12	28	41	25	18
28	1.28								2	6	18	44	32	4
29	0.48								1	9	35	41	49	6

Index

THE BEST OF DEVYN PRESS
Newly Published Bridge Books

WINNING BRIDGE INTANGIBLES
by Mike Lawrence and Keith Hanson $2.95

This book shows you how to achieve the best results possible with the knowledge you already possess. A few of the topics covered are: how to be a good partner, how to avoid giving the opponents crucial information, how to develop the best attitude at the table, and the best way to form a partnership. Recommended for: beginner through advanced.

THE FLANNERY TWO-DIAMOND CONVENTION
by Bill Flannery $7.95

Finally, a complete book on the Flannery convention, written by its creator. This teaches you the secrets to success so you will never have a misunderstanding with your partner. Included are sections on the mechanics, defenses against Flannery, the correct opening lead against the opponents' auctions, 62 example hands with explanations, and much more. Recommended for: intermediate through expert.

BRIDGE: THE BIDDER'S GAME
by Dr. George Rosenkranz $12.95

Bidding for the 80's; the concepts top experts are using today to increase their slam, game, part score, and competitive accuracy. Included are: an introduction to relays and how they can be incorporated into your present system, trump-asking and control-asking bids, new methods of cue bidding, revisions of popular conventions such as Stayman and Splinter bids, a complete update of the Romex System, with hundreds of examples. Recommended for: advanced through expert.

HAVE I GOT A STORY FOR YOU
by Patty Eber and Mike Freeman $7.95

These are humorous stories on bridge, submitted by players across the country, from the local to national level. Hundreds contributed their favorite tales; these are the best from club games, tournaments, bars and hospitality rooms. This entertaining collection is a perfect gift and is recommended for: anyone who enjoys bridge.

THE ART OF LOGICAL BIDDING
by Andrew Gorski $4.95

If you're tired of memorizing bidding sequences and still getting mediocre results at the table, this book is for you. It presents a new system, based on the inherent logic of the game. Because of the natural approach it reduces the chances of partnership misunderstandings, so you'll feel confident of reaching the best contract. Recommended for: bright beginner through intermediate.

STANDARD PLAYS OF CARD COMBINATIONS FOR CONTRACT BRIDGE by Alan Truscott, Laura Jane Gordy, and Edward L. Gordy $5.95

Contains the 150 most important card combinations so that you can maximize your trick-taking potential. The one skill that all experts possess is the ability to handle the standard plays correctly; here is this crucial information at your fingertips. Included are plays to the opening lead, suit-handling and finesses, second hand play and third hand play. Perforated so you may remove the cards from the book if you wish. Recommended for: beginner through advanced.

THE BEST OF DEVYN PRESS

Bridge Conventions Complete
by Amalya Kearse
$17.95

An undated and expanded edition (over 800 pages) of the reference book no duplicate player can afford to be without. The reviews say it all:

"At last! A book with both use and appeal for expert or novice plus everybody in between. Every partnership will find material they will wish to add to their present system. Not only are all the conventions in use anywhere today clearly and aptly described, but Kearse criticizes various treatments regarding potential flaws and how they can be circumvented.

"Do yourself a favor and add this book to your shelf even if you don't enjoy most bridge books. This book is a treat as well as a classic."
—ACBL BULLETIN

"A must for duplicate fans, this is a comprehensive, well-written guide through the maze of systems and conventions. This should be particularly useful to those who don't want to be taken off guard by an unfamiliar convention, because previously it would have been necessary to amass several references to obtain all the information presented."
—BRIDGE WORLD MAGAZINE

Published January, 1984

Recommended for: all duplicate players

ISBN 0-910791-07-4 paperback

Test Your Play As Declarer, Volume 1
by Jeff Rubens and Paul Lukacs
$5.95

Any reader who studies this book carefully will certainly become much more adept at playing out a hand. There are 89 hands here, each emphasizing a particular point in declarer play. The solution to each problem explains how and why a declarer should handle his hands in a certain way. A reprint of the original.

Published December, 1983

Recommended for: intermediate through expert

ISBN 0-910791-12-0 paperback

Devyn Press Book of Partnership Understandings
by Mike Lawrence
$2.95

Stop bidding misunderstandings before they occur with this valuable guide. It covers all the significant points you should discuss with your partner, whether you are forming a new partnership or you have played together for years.

Published December, 1983

Recommended for: novice through expert

ISBN 0-910791-08-2 paperback

101 Bridge Maxims
by H. W. Kelsey
$7.95

The experience of a master player and writer condensed into 101 easy-to-understand adages. Each hand will help you remember these essential rules during the heat of battle.

Published December, 1983

Recommended for: bright beginner through advanced.

ISBN 0-910791-10-4 paperback

Play Bridge with Mike Lawrence
by Mike Lawrence
$9.95

Follow Mike through a 2-session matchpoint event at a regional tournament, and learn how to gather information from the auction, the play of the cards and the atmosphere at the table. When to go against the field, compete, make close doubles, and more.

Published December, 1983

Recommended for: bright beginner through expert.

ISBN 0-910791-09-0 paperback

Play These Hands With Me
by Terence Reese
$7.95

Studies 60 hands in minute detail. How to analyze your position and sum up information you have available, with a post-mortem reviewing main points.

Published December, 1983

Recommended for: intermediate through expert.

ISBN 0-910791-11-2 paperback

THE BEST OF DEVYN PRESS
Bridge Books

A collection of the world's premier bridge authors have produced, for your enjoyment, this wide and impressive selection of books.

MATCHPOINTS
by Kit Woolsey
$9.95

The long-awaited second book by the author of the classic *Partnership Defense*. *Matchpoints* examines all of the crucial aspects of duplicate bridge. It is surprising, with the wealth of excellent books on bidding and play, how neglected matchpoint strategy has been—Kit has filled that gap forever with the best book ever written on the subject. The chapters include: general concepts, constructive bidding, competitive bidding, defensive bidding and the play.
Published October, 1982
Recommended for: intermediate through expert.
ISBN 0-910791-00-7 paperback

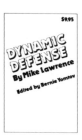

DYNAMIC DEFENSE
by Mike Lawrence
$9.95

One of the top authors of the '80's has produced a superior work in his latest effort. These unique hands offer you an over-the-shoulder look at how a World Champion reasons through the most difficult part of bridge. You will improve your technique as you sit at the table and attempt to find the winning sequence of plays. Each of the 65 problems is thoroughly explained and analyzed in the peerless Lawrence style.
Published October, 1982.
Recommended for: bright beginner through expert.
ISBN 0-910791-01-5 paperback

MODERN IDEAS IN BIDDING
by Dr. George Rosenkranz and Alan Truscott
$9.95

Mexico's top player combines with the bridge editor of the <u>New York Times</u> to produce a winner's guide to bidding theory. Constructive bidding, slams, pre-emptive bidding, competitive problems, overcalls and many other valuable concepts are covered in depth. Increase your accuracy with the proven methods which have won numerous National titles and have been adopted by a diverse group of champions.
Published October, 1982
Recommended for: intermediate through expert.
ISBN 0-910791-02-3 paperback

THE COMPLETE BOOK OF OPENING LEADS
by Easley Blackwood
$12.95

An impressive combination: the most famous name in bridge has compiled the most comprehensive book ever written on opening leads. Almost every situation imaginable is presented with a wealth of examples from world championship play. Learn to turn your wild guesses into intelligent thrusts at the enemy declarer by using all the available information. Chapters include when to lead long suits, dangerous opening leads, leads against slam contracts, doubling for a lead, when to lead partner's suit, and many others.
Published November, 1982.
Recommended for: beginner through advanced.
ISBN 0-910791-05-8 paperback

THE BEST OF DEVYN PRESS
Bridge Books

A collection of the world's premier bridge authors have produced, for your enjoyment, this wide and impressive selection of books.

TEST YOUR PLAY AS DECLARER, VOLUME 2
by Jeff Rubens and Paul Lukacs
$5.95

Two celebrated authors have collaborated on 100 challenging and instructive problems which are sure to sharpen your play. Each hand emphasizes a different principle in how declarer should handle his cards. These difficult exercises will enable you to profit from your errors and enjoy learning at the same time.
Published October, 1982.
Recommended for: intermediate through expert.
ISBN 0-910791-03-1 paperback

TABLE TALK
by Jude Goodwin
$5.95

This collection of cartoons is a joy to behold. What Snoopy did for dogs and Garfield did for cats, Sue and her gang does for bridge players. If you want a realistic, humorous view of the clubs and tournaments you attend, this will brighten your day. You'll meet the novices, experts, obnoxious know-it-alls, bridge addicts and other characters who inhabit that fascinating subculture known as the bridge world.
Recommended for: all bridge players.
ISBN 0-910891-04-X paperback

THE CHAMPIONSHIP BRIDGE SERIES

In-depth discussions of the mostly widely used conventions...how to play them, when to use them and how to defend against them. The solution for those costly partnership misunderstandings. Each of these pamphlets is written by one of the world's top experts. **Recommended for: beginner through advanced.** **95 ¢ each, Any 12 for $9.95, All 24 for $17.90**

VOLUME I [#1-12] PUBLISHED 1980

1. Popular Conventions by Randy Baron
2. The Blackwood Convention by Easley Blackwood
3. The Stayman Convention by Paul Soloway
4. Jacoby Transfer Bids by Oswald Jacoby
5. Negative Doubles by Alvin Roth
6. Weak Two Bids by Howard Schenken
7. Defense Against Strong Club Openings by Kathy Wei
8. Killing Their No Trump by Ron Andersen
9. Splinter Bids by Andrew Bernstein
10. Michaels' Cue Bid by Mike Passell
11. The Unusual No Trump by Alvin Roth
12. Opening Leads by Robert Ewen

VOLUME II [#13-24] PUBLISHED 1981

13. More Popular Conventions by Randy Baron
14. Major Suit Raises by Oswald Jacoby
15. Swiss Team Tactics by Carol & Tom Sanders
16. Match Point Tactics by Ron Andersen
17. Overcalls by Mike Lawrence
18. Balancing by Mike Lawrence
19. The Weak No Trump by Judi Radin
20. One No Trump Forcing by Alan Sontag
21. Flannery by William Flannery
22. Drury by Kerri Shuman
23. Doubles by Bobby Goldman
24. Opening Preempts by Bob Hamman

THE BEST OF DEVYN PRESS ♣

$4.95

The Devyn Press
Book of
BRIDGE
PUZZLES
By Alfred Sheinwold

Number 1

DEVYN PRESS BOOK OF BRIDGE PUZZLES #1, #2, and #3
by Alfred Sheinwold
$4.95 each

Each of the three books in this series is part of the most popular and entertaining collection of bridge problems ever written. They were originally titled "Pocket Books of Bridge Puzzles #1, #2, and #3." The 90 hands in each volume are practical and enjoyable—the kind that you attempt to solve every time you play. They also make perfect gifts for your friends, whether they are inexperienced novices or skilled masters.

Published January, 1981. Paperback

Recommended for: beginner through advanced.

TICKETS TO THE DEVIL
by Richard Powell $5.95

This is the most popular bridge novel ever written by the author of Woody Allen's "Bananas," "The Young Philadelphians," and Elvis Presley's "Follow That Dream."

Tickets has a cast of characters ranging from the Kings and Queens of tournament bridge down to the deuces. Among them are:

Ace McKinley, famous bridge columnist who needs a big win to restore his fading reputation.

Carole Clark, who lost a husband because she led a singleton king.

Bubba Worthington, young socialite who seeks the rank of Life Master to prove his virility.

The Dukes and the Ashcrafts, who have partnership troubles in bridge and in bed.

Tony Manuto, who plays for pay, and handles cards as if they were knives.

Powell shuffles these and many other players to deal out comedy, violence and drama in a perfect mixture.

TICKETS TO THE
DEVIL $5.95

A Novel by RICHARD POWELL
Introduction by RICHARD FREY

Published 1979. . . Paperback
Recommended for: all bridge players.

PARTNERSHIP DEFENSE
by Kit Woolsey
$8.95

Kit's first book is unanimously considered THE classic defensive text so that you can learn the secrets of the experts. It contains a detailed discussion of attitude, count, and suit-preference signals; leads; matchpoints; defensive conventions; protecting partner; with quizzes and a unique partnership test at the end.

$8.95

PARTNERSHIP
DEFENSE IN BRIDGE
BY
KIT
WOOLSEY

EDITED BY
BERNIE YOMTOV

Alan Truscott, Bridge Editor, New York Times: The best new book to appear in 1980 seems certain to be "Partnership Defense in Bridge."

The author has surveyed a complex and vital field that has been largely neglected in the literature of the game. The player of moderate experience is sure to benefit from the wealth of examples and problems dealing with signaling and other matters relating to cooperation in defense.

And experts who feel they have nothing more to learn neglect this book at their peril: The final test of 20 problems has been presented to some of the country's best partnerships, and non has approached a maximum score.

Bridge World Magazine: As a practical guide for tournament players, no defensive book compares with Kit Woolsey's "Part-

nership Defense in Bridge" which is by far the best book of its kind that we have seen. As a technical work it is superb, and any good player who does not read it will be making one of his biggest errors of bridge judgment.

The author's theme is partnership cooperation. He believes there are many more points to be won through careful play, backed by relatively complete understandings, than through spectacular coups or even through choices among sensible conventions. We agree. If you don't, you will very likely change your mind (or at least modify the strength of your opinion) after reading what Woolsey has to say.

Published 1980. . . Paperback
Recommended for: Intermediate through expert.

DO YOU KNOW YOUR PARTNER? by Andy Bernstein and Randy Baron $1.95 A fun-filled quiz to allow you to really get to know your partner. Some questions concern bridge, some don't — only you can answer and only your partner can score it. An inexpensive way to laugh yourself to a better partnership.

Published 1979   paperback
Recommended for: all bridge players.

DEVYN PRESS
151 Thierman Lane
Louisville, KY 40207
(502) 895-1354

OUTSIDE KY. CALL TOLL FREE
1-800-626-1598
FOR VISA / MASTER CARD
ORDERS ONLY

ORDER FORM

Number
Wanted

_____	DO YOU KNOW YOUR PARTNER?, Bernstein-Baron . . . . x $ 1.95	=	_____
_____	COMPLETE BOOK OF OPENING LEADS, Blackwood . . . . x 12.95	=	_____
_____	HAVE I GOT A STORY FOR YOU!, Eber and Freeman . . . . x 7.95	=	_____
_____	THE FLANNERY TWO DIAMOND CONVENTION, Flannery . . . . . x 7.95	=	_____
_____	TABLE TALK, Goodwin . . . . x 5.95	=	_____
_____	THE ART OF LOGICAL BIDDING, Gorski . . . . x 4.95	=	_____
_____	INDIVIDUAL CHAMPIONSHIP BRIDGE SERIES (Please specify) . x .95	=	_____
_____	BRIDGE CONVENTIONS COMPLETE, Kearse (Paperback) . . . . x 17.95	=	_____
_____	BRIDGE CONVENTIONS COMPLETE, Kearse (Hardcover) . . . . x 24.95	=	_____
_____	101 BRIDGE MAXIMS, Kelsey . . . . x 7.95	=	_____
_____	DYNAMIC DEFENSE, Lawrence . . . . x 9.95	=	_____
_____	PARTNERSHIP UNDERSTANDINGS, Lawrence . . . . x 2.95	=	_____
_____	PLAY BRIDGE WITH MIKE LAWRENCE, Lawrence . . . . x 9.95	=	_____
_____	WINNING BRIDGE INTANGIBLES, Lawrence and Hanson . . . . . . x 2.95	=	_____
_____	TICKETS TO THE DEVIL, Powell . . . . x 5.95	=	_____
_____	PLAY THESE HANDS WITH ME, Reese . . . . x 7.95	=	_____
_____	BRIDGE: THE BIDDER'S GAME, Rosenkranz . . . . x 12.95	=	_____
_____	MODERN IDEAS IN BIDDING, Rosenkranz-Truscott . . . . x 9.95	=	_____
_____	TEST YOUR PLAY AS DECLARER, VOL. 1, Rubens-Lukacs . . . . . . x 5.95	=	_____
_____	TEST YOUR PLAY AS DECLARER, VOL. 2, Rubens-Lukacs . . . . . . x 5.95	=	_____
_____	DEVYN PRESS BOOK OF BRIDGE PUZZLES #1, Sheinwold . . . . . . x 4.95	=	_____
_____	DEVYN PRESS BOOK OF BRIDGE PUZZLES #2, Sheinwold . . . . . . x 4.95	=	_____
_____	DEVYN PRESS BOOK OF BRIDGE PUZZLES, # 3, Sheinwold . . . . . . x 4.95	=	_____
_____	STANDARD PLAYS OF CARD COMBINATIONS FOR CONTRACT		
	BRIDGE, Truscott, Gordy and Gordy . . . . x 5.95	=	_____
_____	PARTNERSHIP DEFENSE, Woolsey . . . . x 8.95	=	_____
_____	MATCHPOINTS, Woolsey . . . . x 9.95	=	_____

QUANTITY DISCOUNT ON ABOVE ITEMS: 10% over $25, 20% over $50	We accept checks, money orders and VISA or MASTER CARD. For charge card orders, send your card number and expiration date.	SUBTOTAL ☐
		LESS QUANTITY DISCOUNT ☐
		TOTAL ☐

_____ THE CHAMPIONSHIP BRIDGE SERIES
    VOLUME I . . . . x $9.95 (No further discount) ☐

_____ THE CHAMPIONSHIP BRIDGE SERIES
    VOLUME II . . . . x 9.95 (No further discount) ☐

_____ ALL 24 OF THE CHAMPIONSHIP
    BRIDGE SERIES . . . . x 17.90 (No further discount) ☐

ADD $1.00 SHIPPING PER ORDER	TOTAL FOR BOOKS ☐ SHIPPING ALLOWANCE ☐ AMOUNT ENCLOSED ☐

NAME _____

ADDRESS _____

CITY _____ STATE _____ ZIP _____